Criminology: The Key Concepts is an authoritative and comprehensive study guide and reference resource that will take you through all the concepts, approaches, issues and institutions central to the study of crime in contemporary society.

Topics covered in this easy-to-use A–Z guide include:

- policing, sentencing and the justice system;
- types of crime, including corporate crime, cybercrime, sex and hate crimes;
- feminist, Marxist and cultural approaches to criminology;
- terrorism, state crime, war crimes and human rights;
- social issues such as antisocial behaviour, domestic violence and pornography;
- criminal psychology and deviance.

Fully cross-referenced, with extensive suggestions for further reading and in-depth study of the topics discussed, this is an essential reference guide for students of criminology at all levels.

Martin O'Brien is Reader in Criminology at the University of Central Lancashire. He is the author, with Sue Penna, of *Theorising Welfare: Enlightenment and Modern Society* (1998), and editor of *Integrating and Articulating Environments: A Challenge for Northern and Southern Europe* (2003).

Majid Yar is Senior Lecturer in Criminology and Director of the Centre for Criminological Research at Keele University. He has published widely in the areas of social and political theory, criminology, continental philosophy, cultural analysis and philosophy of social science, and is the author of *Cybercrime and Society* (2006).

ALSO AVAILABLE FROM ROUTLEDGE

Criminology: the basics
Sandra Walklate
978-0-415-33554-6

Available soon from Routledge

Fifty Key Thinkers in Criminology
Keith Hayward et al.
978-0-415-42911-5

CRIMINOLOGY

The Key Concepts

Martin O'Brien and Majid Yar

Routledge
Taylor & Francis Group

LONDON AND NEW YORK

First published 2008
by Routledge
2 Park Square, Milton Park, Abingdon, Oxon OX14 4RN

Simultaneously published in the USA and Canada
by Routledge
270 Madison Ave, New York, NY 10016

Routledge is an imprint of the Taylor & Francis Group, an informa business

© 2008 Martin O'Brien and Majid Yar

Typeset in Bembo by
Taylor & Francis Books
Printed and bound in Great Britain by
TJ International Ltd, Padstow, Corwall

British Library Cataloguing in Publication Data
A catalogue record for this book is available from the British Library

Library of Congress Cataloging in Publication Data
O'Brien, Martin, 1957–
Criminology : the key concepts / Martin
O'Brien and Majid Yar.
p. cm.
Includes bibliographical references.
1. Criminology. I. Yar, Majid. II. Title.
HV6025.O27 2008
364—dc22
2007050909

ISBN10: 0-415-42793-2 (hbk)
ISBN10: 0-415-42794-0 (pbk)
ISBN10: 0-203-89518-5 (ebk)

ISBN13: 978-0-415-42793-7 (hbk)
ISBN13: 978-0-415-42794-4 (pbk)
ISBN13: 978-0-203-89518-4 (ebk)

CONTENTS

LIST OF KEY CONCEPTS

Actuarial justice
Administrative criminology
Alienation
Antisocial behaviour
Biological criminology
Chicago School criminology
Class
Classical criminology
Community
Community crime prevention
  and community safety
Community sentences and
  community punishments
Constitutive criminology
Corporate crime
Crime and deviance
Crime data
Crime mapping
Criminal careers
Criminal justice system
Criminal psychology
Critical criminology
Cultural criminology
Cultural transmission
Cybercrime
Developmental criminology
Deviance amplification
Differential association
Discourse
Drug crime
Durkheimian criminology
Environmental crime

Environmental criminology
Family crime
Feminism and criminology
Gangs
Gender
Governance and governmentality
Green criminology
Hate crime
Hedonism
Hegemony
Homophobia
Human rights
Idealism
Identity
Ideology
Intellectual property crime
Justice
Labelling perspectives
Marxist criminology
Mass media
Moral panic
Net-widening
New media
Norms
Obscenity and pornography
Organised crime
Peace-making criminology
Policing and the police
Positivist criminology
Postmodernity/postmodernism
Prisons and imprisonment
Property crime

Punishment

Racism

Rational choice

Realism

Restorative justice

Risk

Routine activity theories

Sex crimes

Sexism

Social control

Social control perspectives

Social exclusion

Social harm

Socialisation

State, the

State crime

Street crime

Subcultural criminologies

Surveillance

Techniques of neutralisation

Terrorism

Underclass

Victimology

Violent crime

War crimes

White-collar crime

Youth crime

Zero tolerance

INTRODUCTION
The concepts of criminology

During a period of extensive change and expansion in British higher education the growth of university-level programmes in criminology has been a notable feature. From London to Lothian, Salford to Swansea and Birmingham to Belfast there is hardly a higher education institution that does not now offer a degree programme in criminology and criminal justice. For those interested in committing themselves to formal study in this area there exists a plethora of options. This picture was very different less than one generation ago. In the very recent past undergraduate degrees in criminology were confined to one or two universities, alongside a small handful of institutions offering crime-focused postgraduate degrees. The social scientific study of crime was dispersed across disciplines such as sociology, social policy, social work, psychology, and law. Students would be offered occasional modules on 'the sociology of crime', 'criminal justice policy', or 'social work with offenders' as part of degree programmes whose primary mission was to impart a wide-ranging, discipline-based education. Now, 'crime' has become the sole focus of dedicated degree programmes – rather than studying it in passing as part of some discipline or other, students can dedicate themselves to its study through the lenses of different disciplinary perspectives. The people who teach criminology nowadays are themselves representative of this variety – they come to the subject matter of 'crime' from disciplinary backgrounds that most commonly include sociology (as with the authors of this book), social policy, psychology, history, anthropology, economics, law and political science. Each has a different 'light' to shine upon crime and its associated problems, a distinctive way of looking, explaining and understanding. This is all to the good, as it exposes students to a wide variety of ways in which crime-related issues can be conceptualised, contextualised and analysed. For example, a psychologist will likely explain a particular kind of crime in a distinctive way, focusing upon the cognitive and/or developmental processes that might help account for an individual's actions. A sociologist, in contrast, will more likely examine the same phenomenon in the context of cultural norms and values, an individual's relationships with social groups, or the workings of power, exclusion and disadvantage in society at large. A historian may take yet another tack, seeking to understand what happens in the present by reference to the past, viewing the roots of current events and problems in light of long-term developments that might have begun decades or even centuries ago. These are, of course, simplifications but they point to the richness of criminology, the heady mix of debates and disputes, and the kaleidoscopic character of different viewpoints that focus on a single object of study. However, the aforementioned variety also represents one of the major challenges facing criminology students: the expectation that they come to grips with the concepts, methods and tools of different disciplinary perspectives. Equally, it tests those of us who teach criminology, as we are required to step outside of our own disciplinary 'comfort zone' and familiarise ourselves with insights and arguments originating elsewhere.

While students' appetite for criminology is currently all too evident, very few embark upon a degree-level programme of study with more than a vague understanding about what such study actually entails, beyond a general sense that 'crime' is interesting, important and worth knowing about. Indeed, some students starting their university career arrive with assumptions about what they are about to spend three or four years studying that may be unhelpful and, sometimes, inaccurate. These misapprehensions are no doubt shaped by everyday debates about crime. Students (like everyone else) are exposed to extensive media coverage about crime, which tends to deal predominantly with a small number and type of offences, such as murder, 'terrorism', and child sex abuse and abduction (we need only think about the coverage given to the Soham murders, the crimes of Dr Harold Shipman, or the disappearance of Madeleine McCann to get a sense of where news reporting tends to focus). Moreover, factual accounts are supplemented with a veritable deluge of crime-related fictions on television and in film. Shows such as *Spooks*, *Fatal Witness*, *Waking the Dead*, *The Bill*, *Cracker*, *Wire in the Blood*, *CSI* (Las Vegas, Miami and New York), *Criminal Minds*, *Without a Trace*, *24*, *The Sopranos*, *Bones*, and *Prison Break* all communicate assumptions about 'the crime problem' – what crimes are committed, who commits them, why they do so, and how they are 'brought to justice' and punished. While the entertainment value of such shows is not in dispute (criminologists, like everyone else, are avid fans), they have an unfortunate tendency to paint a misleading picture about the reality of crime in our society. Perhaps every lecturer in criminology has been approached at some time or another by an enthusiastic potential student who confesses a burning desire to learn how to profile serial killers, conduct a blood spatter analysis, or track down 'bad guys', only to be gently told that whilst these tasks are important they are only a very small part of what criminology is about and that there is a very long road to travel from initial expectation to final destination. In fact, criminology students quickly learn that identifying who the 'bad guys' are is not as simple or straightforward as the media tends to portray. For those who get beyond their initial disappointment, they can expect to learn about a world in which crime is more mundane, yet more complex and multifaceted, than they might ever have imagined.

What is criminology?

What then, exactly, does criminology deal with? This is not an easy question to answer for a number of reasons. First, as already noted, criminology involves a wide-ranging number of different viewpoints, and their proponents will often have enduring disagreements about exactly *what* the task of criminology is. Is it to explain why individuals choose to commit offences? Is it to understand the social conditions out of which crime problems emerge? Is it to examine what different societies at different times understand by the term 'crime' itself? Is it to demonstrate how common crimes reflect patterns of power and prejudice? Is it to uncover what it feels like to be a *victim* of crime? Is it to study how society responds to offenders, how it punishes them for their supposed transgressions? Is it to explain why, in a famous phrase, 'the rich get richer and the poor get prison'? Is it to find practical solutions to prevent crime from happening in the first place? Is it to find ways of rehabilitating offenders and so discourage them from repeating past offences? Is it to hold accountable those agencies (such as the police) charged with protecting us? Is it to ask why certain apparently harmful acts are not subject to criminal prohibition and sanctions, while other seemingly harmless actions feel the long arm of the law? The simple, yet daunting, answer is that criminology is about *all* of these things, and others beside.

Because of this great variety of questions, perspectives and interests, some have suggested that criminology is not an academic discipline at all. Unlike, say, economists, historians or psychologists, criminologists do not have a unique and unifying intellectual agenda, a unique and unifying way of asking questions about the world. What defines criminology is less its approach to its subject matter and more the subject matter itself, so that criminology is really a 'field of study' or, as Paul Rock (1986) famously opined, a 'rendezvous' subject where different disciplines encounter one another around the topic of 'crime'. As we shall see in a moment, however, this answer is not as straightforward as it might at first appear. In effect, criminology is a multidisciplinary framework whose focus is dominated by questions of crime and justice.

What is a concept?

In the most general terms a concept is simply an idea or notion about something in the world. So, for example, the word 'car' denotes an idea of wheels, engine, seats and fuel all combined to supply a means of mobility: in this sense the term 'car' does not distinguish between large or small, three-wheeled or four-wheeled, used for racing or used for transport, and so on. It simply invokes the general or commonly shared characteristics of things in the world that go by the name of 'car'. In the social sciences, including criminology, however, a concept is not (or should not be!) simply a vague idea about things-in-general. Instead, a concept has three dimensions: descriptive, analytical and theoretical.

A concept is 'descriptive' to the extent that it encompasses an entire class of phenomena: the concept of 'argument', for example, may be taken to include all examples of symbolic (e.g. verbal and written) disagreement or dispute and all examples of beliefs or opinions expressed in logical form. But, more importantly, the descriptive dimension of a concept is distinguished as much by what it excludes as what it includes. So an 'argument' is not a 'sermon' – we use the latter to refer to a spoken or written address (usually religious) involving exhortation or instruction. Similarly, an 'argument' does not refer to a physical conflict between persons involving sharp objects: even though there seems, on the surface, to be some clear dispute, such a conflict is more properly a 'fight' or an instance of 'combat'. The point is that concepts enable us to specify the subtle differences between things in the world by detailing those characteristics to which they do and do not refer. In everyday speech it matters little if concepts are used loosely – it is not uncommon to hear that two people 'traded verbal blows', for example, thus invoking the notion of a fight rather than an argument. But in criminology it is important to avoid this kind of slippage because of the second dimension of social science concepts: the analytical. A concept is 'analytical' to the extent that it enables us to measure something or to grasp the relationships between two or more things in the world. So, the concept of 'social mobility' enables researchers to measure changes in income, lifestyle and status across the life-course and/or across generations and reveal whether a society is characterised by upward mobility, downward mobility or rigid, unchanging divisions. Note that 'social mobility' refers not to income, lifestyle or status as such but to their *change*. In this sense the concept of social mobility is intrinsically *theoretical*, which is to say that it belongs to and makes sense only in terms of a series of other concepts that, together, comprise a logical framework. Social mobility, in fact, only makes sense in terms of a theory of social divisions, that is, broadly organised groups of differences in income, lifestyle and status. These divisions may themselves be understood in different ways: as differences of 'social class' (as in classic political economy approaches), as differences of 'socio-economic grouping' (as in the Registrar General's approach), or as 'status differentials' or differences in 'life-chances' (following Max Weber). A concept, then, is not just a vague notion about something in the world: it comprises a *description* of a class of phenomena that can be used to *analyse* their worldly relationships in a *theoretical* framework that seeks to explain those relationships.

In our experience, when students encounter concepts they rarely associate them with imagination. Yet, learning how to use concepts effectively − how to 'trade' in them − is the basis of imaginative understanding. Creatively articulating *what* are the key crime problems, *how* they can be measured or evaluated and *why* they are happening are the three crucial and interrelated tasks of criminological inquiry. Developing confidence in the use of criminological concepts offers the prospect not only of understanding crime and its control in the present, but of critically interrogating crime and its control: imagining a world that could be different to the present, problematic arrangement of things and, importantly, the steps that might be taken to get there.

What is crime?

Our discussion of the various dimensions of a concept may seem trivial, but its importance becomes clear when we consider what we mean by the concept of 'crime'. The subject matter of criminology (crime) is different from the subject matter of many other academic disciplines. For the purposes of illustration, let us consider biology. The subject of biology, what biologists examine (living organisms and the processes that sustain them) has an objective existence, and has done for billions of years. Through careful observation, experiment and analysis biologists can give us a better understanding of how life works (consider the impact of Darwin's work, and the way in which it helps us better grasp how species emerge and evolve over time). However, biological processes do not rely upon humans for their existence – they were happening before we arrived on the scene, and will continue to do so long after our species has joined the fossils. Crime, on the other hand, is a very different sort of creature. Crime does not exist outside of our definitions about it. It is we (as societies) who decide what counts as a 'crime'. One of the great insights afforded by history and anthropology is that 'crime' is an ever-shifting thing, and what is or is not a crime varies across societies and over time. What in the past may have been a crime in the eyes of a society's members might today be considered normal, unremarkable and perfectly acceptable. Consider, for example, homosexuality. In the past, in some societies at least, sexual activity between members of the same sex was met with widespread revulsion, condemnation, and subject to brutal punishments (one of our most beloved playwrights, Oscar Wilde, was famously convicted in 1895 of 'gross indecency' and sentenced to two years' hard labour). As late as 1974, the American Psychiatric Association's *Diagnostic and Statistical Manual of Mental Disorders* continued to define homosexuality as a 'mental disorder'. Moving forward to the present, both British and American societies have removed from homosexuality criminal sanctions and stigmatising official labels, and such relationships are increasingly accepted as part of the normal range of inter-personal behaviours. In contrast, it remains a 'crime' in other societal contexts – for example, in Iran it is a capital offence, and in 2005 two male teenagers were hanged for allegedly engaging in same-sex intercourse. Equally, a type of behaviour that in the past was considered entirely normal may be today classified as a crime and treated accordingly. For example, throughout a significant span of our modern history, violence committed by men against women and children within the home was legitimated as a 'right' of men to 'discipline' those who were subject to their unchallenged authority. The police, courts, lawmakers and community members took little interest in such abuses, and they did not fall within agreed conceptions of crime. But during the course of the twentieth century, sustained campaigning (most importantly by feminist and women's rights activists) succeeded in redefining such acts as violent harms that were properly subject to criminal laws and associated punishments. It is also possible, sometimes, to watch behaviours being slowly criminalised. For example, for centuries the practice of smoking tobacco (and other substances) was considered almost entirely a matter of personal preference. The worst that could be said was that, during the Victorian and Edwardian eras, it was considered uncouth for a person of refinement (especially a woman) to be seen smoking in the street. Now, in many Western nations, smoking is banned in public premises (including taxis and lorries), breaching the ban can result in a fine, and non-payment of fines can be brought before a criminal court. The consequence is the highly visible practice of smoking in the street! All of the above serves to illustrate the basic point that the subject matter of criminology is not a fixed constant, and the discipline's concerns must of necessity shift and change with wider movements of social sentiments and official laws.

The picture above is further complicated once we realise that crime is a deeply *contested* terrain. Definitions of crime and criminality are seldom a matter of detached and clinical judgement. Crime is inescapably a *moral* issue – any discussion will inevitably involve what we consider to be right and wrong, proper and improper, decent and indecent, harmful and benign. Different individuals and social groups may have very divergent views about what is (or *ought* to be) considered criminal, and they will inevitably come into conflict as they attempt to persuade others around to their own point of view. Moreover, academic criminologists are not exempt from these considerations, and there are very many lively debates about just which kinds of activities should be subjected to criminological attention. To take one current example, is human-induced climate change a 'crime'? After all, there is currently widespread acceptance that it destroys property and communities (through flooding or desertification, or extreme weather events, for example), results in thousands of deaths (through starvation, skin cancer and other personal threats to life) and indirectly generates threats to security (through civil strife over receding resources, for example). If human-induced climate change is not currently considered a crime, should we shift our viewpoint to make it one? Those who answer in the negative may point out that a global process emanating from the ongoing, normal activities of billions of people cannot be treated as in any way like interpersonal violence, or theft, or burglary, or rape. Those who wish to include human-induced climate change within our understandings of crime will point out the devastatingly harmful consequences it is having on our world, with the potential to cause massive suffering through famine, flood, and drought. Should not those who deliberately refuse to take responsibility for the consequences of their actions be forced to do so? If so, then *who* exactly is the 'criminal' here? Is it the oil companies? The manufacturers of 'gas guzzling' automobiles? The individual consumers who choose to buy a Sports Utility Vehicle (SUV) for inner-city driving, in spite of being informed regularly and loudly that they are contributing to a process that will produce great harm and suffering for future generations? In fact, as we have already noted, the effects of climate change are not some abstract, future risk: they are visible *now* in the retreating ice caps and advancing deserts, in destroyed communities and failed crops, in the mass migration and civil strife that accompanies increased pressure on water resources and fertile land. In considering such questions, we have come a long way from the conventional diet of crime issues served up by the media, yet such matters are inexorably coming to the forefront of criminological discussion. Thus, the systematic study of crime demands considerable mental flexibility and a capacity to step outside conventional and common-sense perceptions in order better to grasp the fullest possible range of relevant issues.

About the book

So far, we have endeavoured to provide readers with a flavour of the kinds of problems and issues that criminologists address. We have discussed the character of criminology as a field of study, the nature of social scientific concepts and the multifaceted and essentially contested meaning of the concept of crime. We have also noted that our understandings of crime are influenced by the media, that these understandings change over time and across cultures and that there are very many ways in which criminologists may study the complex phenomenon of crime. Our discussion of these issues and problems has not been arbitrary because all of these considerations were firmly in our minds when we set about writing the present book. We wanted to do justice to the complex, multidisciplinary, and above all uncertain and changeable character of criminology. Thus, in the pages that follow, readers will find a wide span of topics outlined and analysed – everything from sex crime to cybercrime, environmental harms to wartime abuses of human rights. Within the scope of such a book, it is of course impossible to give due attention to all (or even the majority) of matters that may properly have a claim to criminological attention. We have inevitably had to use our own judgement about what might be most relevant and useful for students who are starting out in their programme of undergraduate study. In forming such judgements, we have had the benefit of having taught criminology across five different university institutions over a number of years. We have tried, as best we can, to address those areas, concepts and theories that students typically have to come to grips with, and about which they most commonly come to their tutors in search of clarification. However, while these entries will, we trust, serve readers well, they should not be considered definitive, for two main reasons. First, due to constraints of space, we have inevitably had to compromise in many places when discussing quite extensive bodies of literature. Second, while we have endeavoured to be as even-handed as possible in our presentations of different viewpoints, our own (very different) understandings of the matters at hand will inevitably have shaped how we present and interpret them. It is for both of these reason that suggestions for further reading accompany most of the entries – they will not only provide a more detailed elaboration of any given matter, but just as importantly will reflect different viewpoints on it.

The entries of this book are presented alphabetically for ease of use and accessibility. However, it should be noted that entries vary considerably not only in length and detail, but also in their orientation. The longest entries generally introduce readers to key *theories* that feature prominently in the study of criminology. Theories are frameworks of ideas that attempt to explain crimes, to uncover their causes. Generally speaking, every criminological theory will attempt to answer questions such as 'why does crime occur?' or 'why do these individuals or groups commit crime?' As such, theories are the fundamental 'tools' for a criminological understanding of society. The perspectives discussed here offer a range of (often competing) answers to these questions, and readers of any given entry should always bear in mind that there are other ways in which the same things can be, and have been, explained. A second kind of entry deals with particular forms of crime. Thus the book includes entries on 'violent crime', 'white-collar crime', and the like. Each of these entries attempts to define what is meant by these terms, and overviews the criminological debate that has emerged around them. The book also elaborates upon some of the key issues, institutions and policies that figure in social and political responses to crime. Thus the reader will find entries about 'policing and the police', 'prisons and imprisonment', and 'community sentences and community punishments'. In these cases, the entries are mostly, but not only, *descriptive*: they are intended to provide readers with a basic grasp of the dimensions, processes and, sometimes, history of the main components that make up modern crime problems and criminal justice systems. Fourth, there are entries that unpack and explain concepts commonly used in criminological theory and research, for example 'racism', 'anomie', 'gender', or 'moral panic'. These entries are mostly *analytical* in that they are used by criminologists to measure or evaluate dimensions of crime, its control and its societal context. As we have remarked above, a clear understanding of concepts is critical for good criminological analysis. Taken together, the aim is to provide a clear and accessible point of engagement with criminology as it is taught and studied at university level. Finally, it should be noted that entries are extensively cross-referenced throughout the book. These redirections are meant to alert the reader when relevant matters are elaborated upon elsewhere, and to suggest other sections of the book whose content will further enrich the reader's understanding of a particular issue. We would hope that the book will serve as a kind of companion on students' journeys through their criminological education, a resource to which they can turn for clarification and instruction when they encounter new ideas, theories, concepts and issues for the first time.

Although the book is organised as a set of alphabetically organised articles and entries, it would make little sense to start at 'A' and read through to 'Z'. Rather, the reader can plunge in at any point where a matter of interest or relevance appears. From there s/he can follow the signpost of cross-referencing, following an ever-more elaborate trail of ideas, tracing a non-linear path through the book. In doing so, s/he will likely uncover a web or network of interconnected ideas and debates, concepts and practices, that converge and diverge in sometimes unexpected ways. The picture that emerges will be multi-faceted, full of sharp contrasts as well as homologies, and will lead off in many different directions. The reader should not find this surprising, as this is the nature of criminology itself.

Finally, we would want to endorse the view of the anthropologist Sally Slocum (1975: 49) who pointed out that the basis of any discipline (or even 'rendezvous' subject) is not the answers that it gives but the questions that it asks. This book is not a dictionary of definitive answers but a basic tool kit to help students on their personal journeys to discovering their own questions about crime and justice. To reiterate a point we made earlier, perhaps the key concept in criminology is imagination. If this little book helps you to develop the confidence to imagine crime and justice for yourself then our fundamental goal will have been achieved.

CRIMINOLOGY

The Key Concepts

ACTUARIAL JUSTICE

The concept of 'actuarial justice' was developed by Jonathan Simon (1988) and expanded on by Feeley and Simon (1992, 1994) in their work on the 'new penology'. Actuarialism refers to 'techniques that use statistics to represent the distribution of variables in a population' and consists in 'circuits of testing and questioning, comparing and ranking' (Simon, 1988: 771). The crux of the argument is that actuarialism represents a new form of criminal justice; one that has emerged alongside and is partner to a changed political culture underpinned by neo-liberal politics and a global concern with security. Unlike earlier criminologies, suggests Reiner (2006), actuarialism 'is not interested in the causes of offending other than as diagnostic indicators of risk'. The goal of actuarial criminal justice policy is not to 'cure' crime but to predict and manage it. Thus, the proposition that justice has become actuarial is based on an analysis of the extent to which criminal justice agencies (and criminologists) are now more concerned with calculating and reducing the **risk** of crime than with understanding its underlying causes or with questions of social reform and social rights – although the alleged newness of these strategies has been disputed by some (see Zedner, 2004). At the same time, the professional status of the criminal justice practitioner is said to have diminished since 'the locus of decision-making is shifted from judgments based on professional training and experience to judgments derived from the risk model' (Silver, 1998: 130). Here, it is the statistical model and its aggregate probability scores that determine criminal justice practice, rather than the experience, wisdom or local knowledge of the practitioner. There is undoubtedly an element of actuarialism in recent criminology and criminal justice – although quite how much is open to considerable debate. However, there are many other strands of criminology and criminal justice that are not dependent on statistical risk analyses, and it is unlikely that actuarialism could ever displace all of these diverse approaches to the study of crime.

See also: **administrative criminology; developmental criminology; risk**

Further reading: Feeley and Simon (1994)

ADMINISTRATIVE CRIMINOLOGY

'Administrative criminology' is a catch-all term covering a variety of theoretical perspectives and research enterprises. It is most closely associated with the Home Office Research Unit which, as Lodge (1974: 22) put it, always had the difficult task of maintaining 'scientific integrity while acting as a servant of the secretary of state'. The goal of administrative criminology is to supply useful information and practical guidelines to the criminal justice system to enable its agencies to manage and control crime. In a speech to Parliament on 13 March 1957 urging the establishment of the Research Unit, the home secretary, Rab Butler, claimed that the government needed to

> find out by systematic research much more than we know now about the results of the various methods of treatment which are available to the courts, and to place that knowledge at their disposal. We need also to put ourselves in a position to furnish the courts with the fullest possible information about the offenders before them so that in all proper cases they may be able to select the treatment appropriate to each individual on the basis of an expert diagnosis of his history and personality.

Such a goal may seem laudable from the point of view of government but the influence of the unit on the discipline of criminology more generally has generated serious unease ever since the unit's foundation. As can be seen from Rab Butler's plea for more information the research agenda was never intended to encompass crucial disciplinary questions about the *definition* of crime, nor about its politics, social causes or ideological effects. The kind of criminology the Home Office wanted was intended to help the criminal justice system to *administer* crime more efficiently and effectively – hence the label 'administrative criminology' (coined, incidentally, by Jock Young, 1986b).

The major contributions of administrative criminology have been in the areas of **environmental criminology**, situational crime prevention and the kind of cohort analyses undertaken by Farrington and co-workers on 'risk factors' and predictive criminology (see Farrington, 1996). In all of these instances the underlying assumption is of an individual offender who exercises rational choice when deciding whether or not to commit a crime. The offender weighs up the costs and benefits of criminal behaviour and engages in criminal activity where the likely rewards exceed the potential for punishment. The American criminologist James Q. Wilson sums up the view neatly when he asks his readers to:

> Imagine a young man walking down the street at night with nothing on his mind but a desire for good times and high living.

> Suddenly he sees a little old lady standing alone on a dark corner stuffing the proceeds of her recently cashed social security check into her purse. There is nobody else in view. If the boy steals the purse, he gets the money immediately. That is a powerful incentive, and it is available immediately and without doubt.
>
> (Wilson, 1983: 118)

It is clear, here, that the 'causes' of crime are the desires of the individual offender, the incentive offered by the criminal act and the immediate gratification attendant on its commission – 'he gets the money immediately' and 'without doubt'. There is no intention to address the much more difficult question of why some young men (and women) might be tempted to commit the crime whilst most would not. Neither does Wilson touch on the equally difficult question as to why the vast majority of such 'predatory' crimes are committed by poor people against poor people. Wilson's only response to these issues is to suggest that some people are less governed by 'internal restraints' on criminal behaviour than others and, thus, their crimes are a function of a lack of self-control.

Operating on the basis of these assumptions and justifications, the goal of administrative criminologies is either to manipulate the immediate environment to ensure that likely punishments outweigh potential rewards – by increasing visible police presence, installation of surveillance technologies, improving the security of property, and so on – or to initiate interventions in (actual or potential) offenders' lifestyles to curb their impulses to make deviant choices in the first place – such as introducing parenting classes or criminalising the parents of truants, early intervention with children who are 'failing' at school, and so on. In other words, these interventions are designed to increase the 'internal restraints' so that deviant choices become less rewarding in psychological, emotional and intellectual terms. Where critical and 'left' criminologists have focused attention on the wider society and the politics of crime control, administrative and 'right' criminologists have focused attention on the criminal opportunity and situational solutions to criminal behaviour.

Whilst it may appear reasonable to assert that criminal behaviour is a consequence of low self-control, the generality of crime and deviance in modern society implies that 'internal restraints on criminal behaviour' may be severely lacking on a grand scale. If this outlook is applied as a general theory of crime, then everything from motoring offences (including illegal parking), video and music 'piracy', flouting the smoking ban and littering to serial murder, gangsterism, wilful environmental degradation and wars on the basis of dodgy dossiers and manipulated intelligence information would have to be included. Of course, it might be that low self-control is a key factor in all of these criminal and quasi-criminal activities. However, the structure of incentives to their commission and the structure of opportunities for their realisation are so vastly different in each case that there is clearly something missing from the administrative equation. A 'young man walking down the street at night with nothing on his mind but a desire for good times and high living' has no incentive and no opportunity to invade a foreign country whilst an under-pressure politician has no incentive and (practically) no opportunity to steal an old woman's social security cheque! Similarly, it is surely a gross misrepresentation to explain the torture of so-called enemy combatants at Abu Ghraib prison – in direct contravention of the Geneva Convention on the treatment of prisoners of war – during the Iraq war as a consequence of the low self-control of the armed services personnel who carried it out. The techniques they used and the systematic brutality inflicted on the prisoners were developed consciously and with purpose, over a long period of time, by military and civilian intelligence agencies for the precise purpose of carrying out successful interrogation of enemy combatants and, in too many cases, civilians.

Where administrative criminology scores highly is in terms of implementing effective and immediate responses to the 'normal' crimes of the poor – including robbery, burglary, vehicle theft and damage, assault, and so on. Clarke (1997), for example, includes a diverse array of case studies to demonstrate the effectiveness of situational crime prevention covering the above categories as well as benefit fraud, retail fraud and drug markets. Moreover, the tightly defined character of these case studies means that they can be evaluated in concrete terms to discover 'what works' most effectively in any given situation. Of course, as with any focused research enterprise in crime control, much less attention has been directed at the failures of situational measures and the problems, rather than the benefits of their implementation. It would be foolish, even churlish, to deny the benefits of small-scale, practical measures to reduce crime and provide greater protection against mundane robberies, thefts, burglaries and other street crimes. Yet many criminologists are concerned that funds and energies are being directed towards repetitive research studies of such crimes at the expense of much larger – and potentially more harmful – crimes of the rich and powerful, of states and corporations, and that the ideology of administrative criminology has come to dominate over the critical development of criminology as an independent discipline. Perhaps, given the origins of adminis-trative criminology in the tension between 'scientific integrity' and the demands of government, it is understandable that larger social, political and philosophical questions are put to one side in the pursuit of practical and demonstrably useful responses to the daily grind of managing the criminal justice system. Although it is perhaps less understandable why Rab Butler's initial call for increased knowledge about 'methods of treatment' has been displaced in favour of increased knowledge about methods of administration.

See also: **rational choice; social control**

Further reading: Clarke (1997); Wilson (1983)

ALIENATION

'Alienation' is a concept developed most famously by Karl Marx (see Marx, 1964b) to describe the estrangement of workers from their labour and from each other within the capitalist labour process. In Marx's use the term has (at least) four meanings. First, alienation refers to the estrangement of the worker from the products of her or his own labour: whilst the workers produce objects through their own skill and effort, the object belongs to the capitalist. Second, it refers to estrangement from the work process as a whole: in industrial capitalism the worker has no role in determining how objects will be produced; s/he is simply another machine-like component in the overall production process. Third, it refers to estrangement from 'species being' or from the worker's own human potential to creatively and adaptively satisfy his or her own needs. Finally, it refers to estrangement from other workers: each worker-component is forced to specialise in a single task and to work individually in the larger production machine rather than collectively on commonly agreed tasks. More recently, 'alienation' has been plucked from its Marxist roots and is often used simply to refer to general feelings of isolation, meaninglessness or powerlessness in the face of 'the system'. Although these uses would have been rejected by Marx for all but polemical purposes, they nonetheless share the connotation of a loss of control and/or self-expression generated by industrial capitalism.

See also: **critical criminology; Marxist criminology**

ANTISOCIAL BEHAVIOUR

The term 'antisocial behaviour' is a very recent addition to the stock of criminological concepts. It was hardly used at all before the 1990s, but reference to it increased exponentially in the wake of the Crime and Disorder Act (1998). Here it refers to behaviour that causes *or is likely to cause* harassment, alarm or distress to persons not of the same household as the perpetrator. As can be seen by the 'is likely to' clause, the notion of antisocial behaviour covers a very wide spectrum of behaviours. Examples of such behaviours include graffiti-writing, abusive language or verbal intimidation, vandalism, littering, begging, assault, drunken behaviour in public and much, much more. Indeed, the Home Office definition includes the catch-all term 'yobbish behaviour' as well as 'misuse of fireworks' and 'dumping rubbish and abandoning cars'. In fact, it might be said that the notion of antisocial behaviour refers to behaviour that someone does not like or considers to be unpleasant, and signals a sense of social break-down caused, most particularly, by rowdy or uncontrolled young people.

A wide range of instruments is available to try and tackle antisocial behaviour, including warning letters, penalty notices, parenting orders, Individual Support Orders, injunctions and proceedings against tenants. Perhaps the two best known instruments are Acceptable Behaviour Contracts (ABCs) and Antisocial Behaviour Orders (ASBOs). ABCs are written agreements between perpetrators of antisocial behaviour, the Local Authority, Youth Inclusion Support Panel and police or landlords. They are voluntary agreements lasting for six months. Intended primarily for young people, they can also be used with adults. Antisocial Behaviour Orders are legally binding court orders that prohibit individuals from engaging in specific kinds of behaviour or from associating with specific groups. Whilst the order is a civil injunction and does not lead to a criminal record, any breach of the order's conditions can lead to criminal proceedings in a court of law. A worrying aspect of this is that ASBOs do not require the same evidential rigour as other criminal sanctions and can be applied almost entirely on the basis of hearsay evidence. Thus, breach of an ASBO can lead to a criminal record even though the order's initial application did not require the same test of evidential adequacy normally required in criminal proceedings.

Criminological interest in antisocial behaviour has focused largely on neurodevelopmental causes, social pressures and gender differences (see Moffitt *et al.*, 2001) or on developmental risk-factors (see Farrington and Coid, 2007). Neurodevelopmental causes refer to specific neurological anomalies that lead to abnormal behaviour amongst a very small section of the population, predominantly affecting males. The risk-factor approach refers to 'social' problems such as family breakdown or 'poor parenting', school failure and/or truancy, the influence of peer groups and problems associated with fractured or 'dysfunctional' communities. Some criminologists have attempted to depict antisocial behaviour from the point of view of its young perpetrators and to use that depiction to generate a critique of New Labour youth justice policy generally (see Squires and Stephen, 2005). Others have attempted to chart some of the political and social forces underpinning the rise of policy concern with antisocial behaviour in the UK and to situate these forces in the context of American and European developments (see Burney, 2005). Others again have taken specific forms of such behaviour and charted their apparent rise in the context of declining social bonds, fractured communities, the rise of consumerism and the dominance of a neo-liberal political ideology in late twentieth- early twenty-first-century society (see Winlow and Hall, 2006). Whatever focus is taken it is clear that with such an enormous investment of economic, political and academic resources the phenomenon of antisocial behaviour will continue to form a key dimension of criminal justice policy and research for the foreseeable future.

See also: **street crime; youth crime**

Further reading: Burney (2005); Muncie (2004)

BIOLOGICAL CRIMINOLOGY

The attempt to locate the origins of offending in individuals' biological make-up dates back to at least the early nineteenth century. Even before this, it was commonplace to make inferences about persons' moral character and likely guilt from their physical appearance. However, the first attempts to place biological understandings of crime on a scientific footing emerged around 1800 with the development of *phrenology* by the physician Franz Joseph Gall (1758–1828). The basic idea propounded by Gall was that different human character traits were localised in distinct areas of the brain. Where particular areas of the brain were over-developed (such as those responsible for aggression and destructiveness) or under-developed (such as those responsible for nurturing and honesty) criminal behaviour was thought likely to result. Gall further claimed that phrenologists could accurately infer such dangerous imbalances by carefully examining the contours of the human skull – where certain 'faculties' or traits in the brain were over-developed this would result in bulges manifesting themselves in the cranium. Therefore, a mapping of the brain's traits by examining the shape of the skull could allow scientists to determine the underlying character of any given individual, as well as enabling them to draw general conclusions as to which cranial features were markers of criminal and violent tendencies. Gall's ideas were developed and popularised by his student John Spurzheim (1776–1832), who was instrumental in the spread of phrenology to England and the United States. Following in the steps of Gall and Spurzheim, further works were produced by Charles Combe (1788–1858) in England and Charles Caldwell (1772–1853) in the USA. However, phrenology failed to secure the support of the wider medical and academic community, and by the 1840s its influence was ·on the wane.

The next major attempt to link biology with criminality emerged in the work of the Italian physician Cesare Lombroso (1835–1909) in the latter part of the nineteenth century. Lombroso, the 'father of criminal anthropology', sought to develop a positivist science of the criminal. He was greatly influenced by the evolutionary theory of Charles Darwin, in particular the claim that *homo sapiens* had evolved from earlier, more 'primitive' forms of primate. From this idea, he deduced that there was a distinct 'criminal type' who was in fact a 'throwback' to an earlier stage of human evolution, and thus devoid of the higher moral faculties and sensibilities associated with modern man. This evolutionary backwardness he termed *atavism*. The atavist, for Lombroso, was clearly identifiable through certain physiological traits that were indicators of his primitive constitution. He examined hundreds of convicted felons, and from this compiled a catalogue of atavistic 'stigmata', including smaller brains, large and protruding ears, fleshy lips, a receding chin, and excessive wrinkling of the skin. Lombroso also combined his evolutionary theory with discourses about different 'races' and their supposed characters. Such ideas were widespread in an era of European colonialism and imperialism, and it was commonplace to posit a 'hierarchy of races', with white Westerners at the apex, and Africans, Orientals and other subjugated 'races' occupying lower positions. Combining such notions with his theory of atavism, Lombroso identified certain 'races' as inherently disposed towards criminality as they represented a lower position in the evolutionary order. For example, he claimed that the higher crime rates recorded for southern Italians as compared to northerners was the outcome of the southerners' innate primitivism, something he felt to be clearly indicated in their typically swarthy and stocky appearance.

Almost immediately upon the publication of Lombroso's *The Criminal Man* (1876; see Lombroso, 2006), his theory came under sustained attack, and is today considered thoroughly discredited. First, and most obviously, it was apparent that by no means all offenders in fact had identifiable atavistic traits. This presented a problem for Lombroso, and over time he posited an ever-greater array of criminal sub-types whose behaviour could not be attributed to atavism in any obvious way (these included the alcoholic criminal, the insane criminal, the 'pseudo' or accidental criminal, 'criminaloids' who are influenced by environmental factors, and 'habitual' criminals whose offending resulted from poor education and weak parenting). Eventually, Lombroso claimed that only a third of convicted criminals in fact belonged to the atavistic type. Despite these difficulties, Lombroso persisted in the hope that criminal behaviour could ultimately be traced to its supposed biological roots in some fashion. The limitations of Lombroso's biological criminology were more readily conceded by his student and protégé Enrico Ferri (1856–1929), who set biological causes alongside other social and environmental factors. A second criticism levelled at Lombroso was that he ignored the ways in which socio-economic factors might be implicated in the genesis of crime. Thus, for example, in attributing southern Italy's higher crime rates to biological atavism, he overlooked a more obvious explanation, namely that while the north was economically advanced and prosperous, the southern part of Italy was mired in economic stagnation and widespread poverty. Lombroso's critics also pointed out serious methodological problems with his empirical studies of convicts, such as his selection of non-criminal populations with which to compare offenders, and his unsound use of statistical methods.

Despite the widespread rejection of Lombroso's work, his attempt to link inner dispositions to biological and physiological characteristics established a pattern that was later adopted by other criminological researchers. For example, in the 1930s the American anthropologist Ernest Hooton studied more than 14,000 US prisoners to determine the links between physiology and crime. He concluded that it was 'the biologically inferior ... who are responsible for the majority of crimes committed'. Like Lombroso, he claimed to have identified distinctive physical markers of criminality, including straight hair, folded skin and sloping foreheads. In another physiological theory of the same period, William Sheldon proposed that there were three distinctive 'body types', the *endomorphic, ectomorphic* and *mesomorphic,* each of which could be linked to different temperaments. The endomorphic body tended to be rounded, fat and small boned, and was associated with a relaxed, comfort-oriented personality. The ectomorphic body was lean, bony and small, and was accompanied by an introverted and shy temperament. The mesomorphic body, Sheldon claimed, was broad, muscular and strong, and was associated with an assertive and aggressive personality. By studying delinquent boys, and comparing them to non-delinquents, Sheldon concluded that the delinquents were much more likely to be mesomorphs, and that this distinctive body type accounted for their aggressive, confrontational and ulti- mately criminal behaviour.

As biological and medical sciences developed over the twen- tieth century, theories of genetic heredity and its influence were taken up by biological criminologists. Since the work of Richard Dugdale in the late nineteenth century, numerous studies have examined the **criminal careers** within particular families, in order to establish how criminality may be passed from parents to chil- dren. However, such studies are dismissed easily as they cannot distinguish between the influence of biological inheritance on the one hand, and the social and cultural influence of family environ- ment on the other. Therefore, one of the most popular strategies followed by biological criminologists has been to engage in studies of adopted children. Adoptees will inherit their birth parents' genetic material, but will have been raised in different family environ- ments away from their birth parents. If the children of criminal parents show a greater propensity for offending, despite not having been raised by those criminal parents, this can be taken as evidence for a biologically inherited disposition towards criminality. In one of the best known studies of this kind, by Mednick *et al.* (1984), it was claimed that children given up for adoption were significantly more likely to offend if one or both of their original biological parents were convicted offenders. Such studies are often taken as proof positive that there is a scientifically validated link between biology and crime. However, many methodological problems have been noted, including (1) the variable and rather loose definitions of 'crime' and 'criminality' used in judging both parents and children; (2) the amount of time the children may have spent being raised by their biological parents *before* being surrendered for adoption, which may well have shaped their character in important ways; and (3) the family environment of their adoptive parents, which may also shape the children's dispositions where it comes to offending. In short, the near impossibility of separating biological from social influences on behaviour means that such studies remain inconclusive.

Another form of study that has been favoured by biological criminologists over recent decades is that based upon the *XYY chromosome* theory. Humans possess 46 chromosomes arranged in 23 pairs. The 23rd pair determines the sex of individuals. A 'normal' male will have one X chromosome (from the mother) and one Y chromosome (from the father). Hence such males will be XY. Biological females will be XX, with both sex-determining chromosomes coming from the mother. However, in a small percentage of cases, chromosomal anomalies will occur. Criminological attention has focused upon those males with XYY sex chromosomes, i.e. an extra Y chromosome contributed by the father. The XYY inheritance has been linked to criminality. Jacobs *et al.* (1965), studying a population of maximum-security prisoners in Scotland, found that 3.5 per cent of the men had the XYY chromosome, as compared to only 0.1 per cent of the general male population. It has been suggested that the XYY chromosome stimulates the production of the sex hormone testosterone, whose excessive presence is linked to emotional volatility and violence. However, such studies have again been criticised as they use small population samples and so may not be statistically reliable. Moreover, even if the XYY chromosome does contribute to offending in some cases, this cannot help explain the offending of the vast majority of men in custody (96.5 per cent in Jacobs' study) who do not have the XYY marker.

Other recent biologically based arguments include those pointing to factors such as early childhood brain injury and hormonal imbalances as potential causes or triggers of crime. Borrowing from recent work in evolutionary psychology, authors such as Thornhill and Palmer (2000) have also controversially argued that there is in fact a genetically inherited basis for rape and 'sexual coercion' amongst males, insofar as maximising the opportunities for sexual reproduction is 'hardwired' so as to ensure the long-term reproduction of the species. Their argument has proven highly controversial, not least because they appear to be removing questions of power and sexism from the consideration of sexual violence, and providing an 'excuse' that rape is an outcome of (male) human nature. Equally provocative has been the argument of Herrnstein and Murray's book *The Bell Curve* (1994), which proposes that criminality is linked to genetically inherited low IQ. Moreover, they go on to claim that certain minority groups within the US population, such as African-Americans and Latinos, are on average less intelligent than whites, thereby making a connection between 'race', intelligence and criminality. Such arguments have on the whole been poorly received by criminologists, many of whom point out the major methodological flaws in these studies, and suggest that they tell us more about the political and cultural prejudices of the authors than about the realities of offending. Nevertheless, these and similar works continue to be widely read and discussed, not least perhaps because they appear to offer a simple answer to what in fact is a very complex and challenging problem, that of explaining lawbreaking behaviour.

See also: **feminism and criminology; positivist criminology**

Further reading: Curran and Renzetti (2001); Herrnstein and Murray (1994); Lombroso (2006); Rafter (1997); Savitz *et al.* (1977)

CHICAGO SCHOOL CRIMINOLOGY

In the early decades of the twentieth century the department of sociology at the University of Chicago emerged as an important centre for the sociological study of crime and deviance. Key figures such as Robert E. Park, Ernest Burgess, Louis Wirth, Clifford Shaw and Henry McKay pioneered a distinctive theoretical and practical approach for understanding the causes of crime. The University of Chicago was founded in 1892 in a city experiencing a dramatic growth and transformation. In 1840, Chicago (at the time known as Fort Dearborn) was a small trading outpost comprising barely a few thousand individuals, yet by the turn of the new century it had become a sprawling industrial metropolis. The city became home to millions, its population swelled by successive waves of immigration from impoverished regions of Europe and internal migration of African-Americans fleeing the misery and prejudice of the Deep South. It was this whirlwind of change that inspired Park and others to seek an understanding of how and why the many social problems of the city emerged and how they might be ameliorated. Park, a journalist who was appointed as Professor of Sociology at the university in 1914, played a decisive role in shaping the school's outlook. It was Park who proposed that the growth and population distribution of urban areas could be likened to the organisation of naturally occurring ecological systems. The city, he suggested, mirrored the development of plant life in that both were characterised by relationships of inter-dependence, symbiosis, and competition over scarce resources. Humans, like plants, embedded themselves in particular areas where it was possible for them to access the resources they needed, formed relationships of mutual dependence, and found themselves periodically threatened and displaced by others who arrived in their ecological niche. Just as the concentration, aggregation and dispersion of plant life could be understood by looking at their physical environment, so human community formation, location and movement could be analysed in terms of the social and material surroundings that they occupied. This basic proposition from Park set the ground for what subsequently became known as the *urban ecology* approach to sociology and criminology.

Park suggested that human populations inevitably became con-centrated into what he termed *natural areas*, and the lives of indivi-duals and groups were profoundly influenced by the social and material features of those areas. This idea was taken up by Ernest W. Burgess, who developed a geographical model of Chicago showing the different areas or *zones* comprising it. His model featured five *concentric zones* arranged in radiating circles like the rings of a tree. Zone I was identified as the *Central Business District*; Zone II was the *Zone of Transition*; Zone III comprised *Workingmen's Housing*; Zone IV was the *Residential Zone* and Zone V the *Commuter Zone*. The Zone of Transition, nestled around the industrial heart of the city, was the poorest and most run-down, and the zones radiating out around it were progressively more prosperous. It was the Zone of Transition that provided the focus for the school's studies, as it was here that the highest rates of crime, delinquency and other social problems were to be found. The Chicagoans explained this preponderance of problems by looking to the distinctive social, material and cultural features of the zone itself. Given its proximity to the central district of factories, this zone featured an unpleasant and polluted environment. It con-tained a large concentration of dilapidated tenement housing, over-crowded and unhygienic. However, given the low rents charged in this least desirable area, it became the first port of call for the newly arrived immigrants, who could afford to live nowhere else. As they established themselves over time, earning a degree of financial stability, residents would move outwards to the more prosperous zones. The space they vacated would be taken in turn by new immigrants. This pattern of residential occupation and mobility (what Park called *invasion-dominance-succession*) was critically important for the Chicagoans. The distinctive features of this environment (poverty, over-crowding, a diverse immigrant population, and constant movement) had a decisive impact on the social and cultural life of the area. The Chicagoans adopted a broadly **Durkheimian** perspective, seeing shared cultural **norms** as essential for controlling individuals' behaviour and suppressing the impulse to deviance. However, the Zone of Transition crucially lacked a strong, coherent set of norms and guidelines for its residents. This situation arose, first, from the extremes of ethnic and cultural diversity amongst its population – it was home to people from a bewildering array of origins, spanning different ethnicities, languages, religions and traditions, and so lacked common reference points. Second, the instability of the population (with a constant stream of movement out of the area, and replacement by new arrivals) created a heightened sense of anonymity and provided no real occasion for enduring social ties to develop. Third, there was a chronic weakness of key institutions that could play a role in creating and sustaining shared norms (such as churches and schools) due to a fundamental lack of resources. The combination of these factors meant that there appeared in this zone an under-regulation of behaviour, an absence of clear-cut and shared rules governing acceptable and unacceptable behaviour – a situation that the Chicagoans called *social disorganisation*. It was this disorganisation that accounted for the disproportionately high levels of crime and deviance in this area when compared to other parts of the city. Thus, for example, Shaw and McKay (1942) used the disorganisation concept to explain the distinctive spatial pattern in the referral records of Chicago's juvenile court system, which showed that delinquency rates were significantly higher in Zone II and remained so even over long periods of time.

The Chicago School's ecological approach was a highly original and daring perspective on the causes of crime and deviance. At the time, it was commonplace to either locate the causes of offending within individuals, or to see particular ethnic groups as inherently criminal. In contrast, the Chicagoans proposed that there was nothing about particular individuals or groups per se that led them to offend, but that such behaviour was the outcome of the environment in which they lived. Rather than blaming individuals or scapegoating minority groups such as immigrants, their perspective suggested that it was only through tackling the impoverishment and disorder of urban environments that crime reduction could be effectively achieved. This belief was manifest in the school's ongoing involvement in practical initiatives for social improvement, such as the Chicago Area Project that they established, and which aimed to strengthen key social institutions in deprived areas so as to restore the community's capacity to regulate behaviour. The Chicagoans' theory of social disorganisation, and the ameliorative measures it recommended, have inspired numerous criminological studies over many decades, and led to the development of various geographical and environmental perspectives.

A further dimension of the Chicago School's distinctive contribution can be found in their development of new methods for sociological research. Refusing to rely solely upon formal, statistical data they pioneered a kind of *appreciative sociology* that used *participant observation* and *interview* methods to understand individuals' lives 'from the inside', as they themselves experienced it. Such methods were used to great effect in a range of studies, including Shaw's *The Jack Roller: A Delinquent Boy's Own Story* (1930) and Cressey's *The Taxi-Dance Hall* (1932). These works in their turn have inspired sociologists and criminologists to use *ethnographic* investigation to closely examine a wide range of social phenomena and rule-breaking activity, including street gangs, drug dealing and drug taking, joy riding and graffiti art.

Despite its wide-ranging influence, the Chicago School's work has not been immune from criticism. First, it has been suggested that Park, Burgess and others fall prey to the so-called *ecological fallacy*, namely the erroneous belief that individual behaviour is solely or largely determined by their environment. The over-emphasis on environmental influence certainly creates difficulties for the Chicagoans' understanding of crime and deviance, since it is clear from their own research that by no means all people living in a socially disorganised area turn to crime, and conversely that people living in non-disorganised areas also engage in offending. Second, it may be suggested that their characterisation of the inner city as socially disorganised reflects the researchers' middle-class prejudices – just because working-class life in such areas does not fit with the notions of order used by middle-class academics, this does not necessarily mean that they are without order and organisation. Rather, it may be more accurately suggested that they are *differently* organised, making use of alternative rules, codes and **norms** of conduct that make sense to the members of the community themselves. A third criticism concerns the persistent **gender** blindness in the school's work. The Chicagoans' studies focused almost exclusively upon male offenders, and offered little or no insight into how women may experience or respond to the pressures of life in impoverished urban settings. These and other criticisms notwithstanding, the school's work continues to be widely read, discussed and utilised by criminologists today.

See also: **crime data; cultural criminology; differential association; Durkheimian criminology; environmental criminology; subcultural criminologies**

Further reading: Bulmer (1984); Park *et al.* (1967); Shaw (1930); Shaw and McKay (1942)

CLASS

Class (or alternatively *social class*) is a much-used concept in criminology and other social sciences. All uses of the term refer to the ways in which individuals and groups in a society are organised into *hierarchies*. Hence the analysis of society in terms of class is essentially the study of *social stratification*.

Different theoretical perspectives identify various grounds upon which class membership is held to rest. Marxism, for example, views society as basically divided between two social classes, the *bourgeoisie* and the *proletariat*. The two classes are differentiated on economic grounds, with the *bourgeoisie* owning and controlling the economic *means of production*, and the non-property-owning *proletariat* being compelled to sell their labour in exchange for wages. Max Weber (1864–1920) suggested that in addition to property ownership (or lack thereof) class position is also determined by differences in social *status* and political power. For Weber, individuals' class position will exercise a determining influence over their life chances, including their ability to access goods and find other satisfactions. In contemporary social science individuals' class is typically identified using a range of social, economic and other indicators, including earnings, educational attainment and type of employment (e.g. manual work, non-manual work, professional occupation).

Criminology's interest in social class has stemmed in significant part from the social patterns of offending that are apparent in crime statistics. It is widely claimed that there is a close relationship between class hierarchies and offending behaviour, such that criminal behaviour is disproportionately concentrated amongst those from the lower social class groups. This social concentration of crime has been explained in a wide variety of ways. Robert Merton, for example, suggested that it is the lack of access to legitimate life chances that encourages individuals to turn to crime in order to 'get ahead'. Many other criminologists have likewise proposed a causal link between **social exclusion** and crime, so that those most excluded from participation in social, economic and cultural life are most liable to offend. From a right-wing perspective, the likes of Charles Murray have argued that the lower social classes (or **underclass**) have a criminal culture that encourages crime and deviance. In contrast, **Marxist** and **critical** criminologists point to the ways in which the everyday activities of the socially disadvantaged are subject to legal regulation and intensive policing at the behest of more powerful and dominant social groups. In this way, the high level of recorded crime amongst the poor and marginalised reflects the biases of the state and criminal justice system, which almost invariably work in the interests of the privileged. Thus while criminologists may agree that there is an important relationship between crime and class, there is continued disagreement about just what this relationship is and how it might best be understood.

See also: **critical criminology; ideology; Marxist criminology; social exclusion; state, the; underclass**

Further reading: Giddens and Held (1982); Reiman (2003); Wright (2005)

CLASSICAL CRIMINOLOGY

The term 'classical criminology' is somewhat misleading, in that so-called 'classicists' were in fact writing well before the foundation of criminology as an organised discipline in the late nineteenth century. Rather, classicism refers to a number of late eighteenth- and early nineteenth-century thinkers who offered common reflections on crime, law and **punishment**, and whose ideas were subsequently appropriated by criminology. Their ideas continue to influence criminology to the present day.

In order to understand what classicists argued, and why, it is necessary to examine the social, political and intellectual context of their time. The eighteenth century saw the rise to prominence of Enlightenment thought across Europe. Enlightenment thinkers placed emphasis upon the need to organise society through the exercise of human rationality, the primacy of scientific insights as sources of reliable knowledge, and the human and political rights of the individual citizen. When looking at the organisation of law, criminal justice and punishment, they saw that its realities fell far short of such ideals. Consequently, classicists criticised the administration of justice as they found it in the society of their time, and proposed practical reforms that would place law and punishment on a systematic, efficient and rational basis.

The earliest major thinker associated with classicism is Cesare Beccaria (1738–94). Beccaria, the son of an aristocratic Italian family, became involved in his twenties with a group calling themselves the 'academy of fists' who were committed to reforming the system of criminal justice. Beccaria's inquiries culminated with the publication of his most important work, *On Crimes and Punishments* (1764; see Beccaria, 1995). Beccaria was influenced by a number of modern philosophers, including Thomas Hobbes (1588–1679) and David Hume (1711–76). First, from Hobbes he took the idea that an ordered society must be established through a 'social contract' that bound its members together. Citizens agreed to give up some of their freedom to do as they pleased, and in exchange were protected from arbitrary impositions from others. Under such an arrangement, individuals agreed to respect the property and physical integrity of their fellow citizens, thereby ensuring that all were secure from the fear of theft and violence. For Beccaria, those who committed criminal acts stood in breach of this contract, and so punishment must inevitably follow. Only in this way could the contract, which worked in the ultimate interests of all, be maintained. Second, Beccaria took from Hobbes the view that human beings are basically 'hedonistic' in nature. They are driven by a search for pleasure and satisfaction and a corresponding desire to avoid pain and discomfort. Individuals will rationally assess possible courses of action, and will act in a way that they believe will maximise the satisfaction of their wants and desires. Bringing these two points together, Beccaria believed that in order to be socially effective, criminal justice must be organised so as to make the punishment of crime *inevitable, consistent, proportionate* and *swift*. The inevitability of punishment would serve to convince potential offenders that the pain of punishment would always follow any criminal act, serving therefore as a deterrent. Equally important was the principle of consistency. This would ensure that the same kind and severity of punishment would always follow a particular crime. In this way, potential offenders would be made certain that they could not count upon arbitrary leniency from judges – it would be clear beforehand what kind of punishment would follow any particular offence. The principle of proportionality maintained that in order to be effective punishments must be of a severity that reflected the seriousness of the offence and the harm caused. Finally, the swiftness of punishment was held to be essential if it were to have a proper deterrent effect. This idea Beccaria based upon the philosopher David Hume's theory of the 'association of ideas'. Hume held that particular phenomena and experiences became linked together in the human mind because one followed closely upon another (for example, we associate fire with pain because upon burning ourselves pain immediately follows). Consequently, Beccaria felt that crime and punishment could only become firmly associated in the public mind if the latter followed the former as swiftly as possible. On the basis of these principles, he criticised the organisation of criminal justice in that it was typically characterised by inconsistency, arbitrariness, disproportionality and delay. Such a system could not use punishment efficiently to secure public order, and so would have to be radically reformed.

The second major figure identified with classicism is English moral and political philosopher Jeremy Bentham (1748–1832). Like Beccaria, Bentham emphasised a *utilitarian* understanding of human nature. Not only did he believe that individuals acted rationally so as to maximise their pleasure, but that a society which made it possible for its members to realise their desires was morally speaking a good one. Therefore, he held that the role of government was to ensure 'the greatest happiness of the greatest number' through public policies oriented to utility maximisation. Bentham's utilitarianism yielded a number of recommendations in the field of criminal justice. For example, he argued that punishment must be organised so as to always entail a little more pain than the pleasure the offender might hope to gain from the criminal act. The prospect of 'negative utility' (costs or pain outweighing the benefits or pleasure issuing from crime) would have a valuable deterrent effect. However, punishment should not be any more painful than absolutely required to perform its task of deterrence, otherwise it would unnecessarily increase the sum total of pain or unhappiness in society.

Classicist arguments have exercised considerable influence over the organisation of criminal justice, most apparent in the institutionalisation of principles of consistency and proportionality in sentencing, along with the deterrence function assigned to the sanctions set down in criminal law (examples of the latter would include mandatory minimum sentences and 'three strikes' laws). Similarly, classicism has shaped the development of criminology, especially in recent decades where it has enjoyed a significant revival. For example, the vision of human actors as hedonistic, cost-benefit calculators has appeared as a key feature of theoretical perspectives such as **routine activity theories**, **rational choice** criminology, and **social control**. It has likewise been taken up in practical crime-control strategies such as situational crime prevention. Classicism has also inspired the development of neo-classical criminology. Neo-classicists, while adopting central features of classicism, have amended and developed the perspective, in order to accommodate a range of other factors that might shape individuals' decision to offend. For example, Roshier (1989) concedes that social inequalities, such as those associated with poverty, can sway individuals towards offending behaviour.

Despite its influence, classicism has been subjected to criticism from a range of alternative perspectives. Positivists have taken issue with the notion that individuals are able to exercise free choice where it comes to offending, suggesting instead that a range of external (social, economic) or internal (biological, psychological) factors propel individuals into criminal behaviour. Sociologists have objected to what they see as classicism's individualistic bias, arguing that it neglects the ways that social interactions and relationships shape people's understandings of crime and criminality and their consequent behaviour. Most recently, cultural criminologists have challenged the notion that criminal conduct is the outcome of rational calculation, maintaining that powerful emotional forces in fact shape offending. However, despite such reservations, classicism continues to exert a powerful sway in contemporary criminology, and through this upon criminal justice and crime-control strategies.

See also: **administrative criminology; cultural criminology; hedonism; positivist criminology; punishment; rational choice; routine activity theories; social control**

Further reading: Beccaria (1995); Roshier (1989)

COMMUNITY

A term that is very widely used across the social sciences (not to mention in public and political discussion) yet is often ill defined or defined in widely varying ways. At its most fundamental the concept denotes a social group united by some feature or other held in common. One of the most frequent uses of the term refers to a collection of individuals united by a common place of residence; hence the frequently heard references to 'the local community'. A second sense of community is oriented around inherited features or shared origins that characterise a number of individuals, e.g. 'the black community', 'the Asian community', and so on. A third way in which community is mobilised is to identify those who have some shared views, beliefs or social practices, e.g. 'the Muslim community', 'the legal community', 'the gay community'.

There is a long-standing criminological interest in community and a tradition of theory and research that connects the weakening of community bonds with the likelihood of involvement in crime. Thus community is seen as an important agency of **socialisation** and **social control**. It has also been suggested that communities need to be more effectively involved in crime-control initiatives (for example through community policing and **community crime prevention**) and in the delivery of punishment and rehabilitation (in the shape of **community sentences and community punishments**).

See also: **community crime prevention and community safety; community sentences and community punishments; Durkheimian criminology; punishment; restorative justice; social control; socialisation**

Further reading: Bauman (2001); Crow (2002); Delanty (2003)

COMMUNITY CRIME PREVENTION AND COMMUNITY SAFETY

Community crime prevention and community safety refer to strategies for crime control that actively seek to involve a wide range of local actors in partnership with the police and other **state** agencies. Emerging in the UK in the 1990s, it was seen as a solution to rising crime levels, and especially the concentration of crime in certain (usually urban and impoverished) localities where formal policing interventions had seemingly failed to deter crime. In addition, there was a palpable sense during the 1980s that relations had almost irretrievably broken down between the police and socially marginalised (often ethnic minority) communities, where the police were widely seen as a source of harassment and conflict rather than as servants of the people. Community-oriented initiatives aimed to re-engage local residents, and to mobilise them in order to help reduce the levels of crime and incivility in their neighbourhoods. Under such initiatives communities are encouraged to help identify potential or actual sources of trouble, to liaise with police and local authorities, and they may also engage in self-policing through citizen organisations such as Neighbourhood Watch. Situational crime-prevention measures, such as CCTV monitoring, are also mobilised to increase deterrence and reduce fear of crime.

Despite the great political capital made of such community-oriented activities, they have been subject to a great deal of criminological criticism. First, it has been suggested that despite rhetoric of community engagement, most of the practical measures instituted are introduced from the outside and imposed upon communities. Second, the overwhelming focus of community strategies is upon relatively low-level street crimes and 'nuisance' behaviour, neglecting other kinds of less visible offences in the process. Third, it can be argued that such strategies constitute a form of *net widening* in which ever-tighter controls are instituted over a range of social behaviours that are now classified as uncivil and antisocial. Fourth, the emphasis upon community crime control can be criticised for failing to attend to the underlying social and economic problems in which the roots of crime may be located.

See also: **community; community sentences and community punishments; policing and the police; surveillance**

Further reading: Crawford (1998); Hughes and Edwards (2002)

COMMUNITY SENTENCES AND COMMUNITY PUNISHMENTS

There is a range of punishments to which the courts sentence offenders, and that do not entail custodial detention (imprisonment). Such punishments can take a variety of forms, including: financial reparations (such as payment of compensation to the victim); unpaid work in the community; mandatory rehabilitation programmes (such as treatment for drug and alcohol addiction); and incapacitation and monitoring (for example the imposition of curfews and electronic tagging).

Recent decades have seen a significant expansion in the use of such sentences and the variety of forms in which they are available. One of the major reasons behind this development has been a growing scepticism about the effectiveness of imprisonment in either deterring or rehabilitating offenders. Critics of imprisonment have pointed out that reoffending rates for those released from custody remain high, and that increasing prison populations have gone hand-in-hand with rising levels of crime. Moreover, community sentences have financial advantages in that they are considerably less expensive to administer than imprisonment. However, the use of community punishments remains publicly and politically controversial, with a widespread perception that they are a 'soft option' that does not entail adequate hardship for convicted offenders, alongside concerns that allowing offenders to remain at large will increase the threat they present to the public.

See also: **prisons and imprisonment; punishment; restorative justice**

Further reading: Brownlee (1998); Worrall (1997)

CONSTITUTIVE CRIMINOLOGY

Constitutive criminology is an approach to theory and research associated almost exclusively with Dragan Milanovic and Stuart Henry (see Henry and Milanovic, 1996). It is an eclectic, multidisciplinary strand of postmodern theory that construes the world as a continually produced and reproduced mass of social constructs that are always unstable and 'at the edge', to use part of the title of Milanovic's (2002) book. The phrase 'constitutive criminology' was inspired by the title of a major work by the British sociologist Anthony Giddens (1984) (*The Constitution of Society*) in which he outlined his 'theory of structuration'. Here, Giddens proposes that social structures (such as **class** or **gender**) are not external fixed objects that act on people, independent of their will, to determine their behaviours and identities. Nor are they simply the willed product of people's actions and interactions. Instead, 'social structures are both constituted by human agency and yet at the same time are the very medium of this constitution' (Giddens, 1976: 121). Structuration theory, in brief, is an attempt to outline and explain the 'co-production' of person and society. The logical framework of structuration theory is highly complex and the complexity increases exponentially in its translation to constitutive criminology by the addition of chaos theory, catastrophe theory, poststructuralism and psychoanalysis, amongst other theoretical and philosophical systems.

Underlying constitutive criminology's theoretical complexity is a desire to join the debate about what the proper object of criminology should be. The (supposed) traditional view is that criminology researches and analyses lawbreaking activity and the system of criminal justice that exists to manage, control and/or remedy that activity. However, such an outlook bypasses questions about why some activities are lawful and others are not, why the same activity is lawful in one context but unlawful in another, whose interests are served by dominant definitions of what is and is not lawful, and whether dominant definitions encompass adequately the greatest threats to personal safety and social stability. These questions have underpinned an influential strand of criminology for many decades and many different responses have been made to them – from the 'new criminology' of the 1970s (see Taylor et al., 1973) through the abolitionist movement of the 1980s (see Bianchi and van Swaaningen, 1986) to the integrative criminology of the 1990s (which is itself closely allied to constitutive criminology, see Barak, 1998). The overall goal of these various theoretical standpoints was summed up neatly by Shearing (1989) as the effort to 'decriminalise criminology'. What is at stake in this strand of criminology is not simply how better to respond to lawbreaking behaviour but a whole new way of understanding the relationships between crime, law and society. In Dragan Milanovic's words:

> Visions of social justice can only come about through a balance between theorising and social action. Praxis will no longer do, but transpraxis – both a deconstruction of repressive powers and arrangements and a reconstruction of the new order is the call.
>
> (Henry et al., 1997)

In this regard, constitutive criminology is somewhat less about generating new social constructions of crime and rather more about using the figure of crime to generate new social constructions of reality. It should be no surprise, then, that constitutive criminology's contribution to this critical endeavour depends heavily on a reinterpretation of fundamental sociological and philosophical concepts and theories. Indeed, large parts of Henry and Milanovic's (1996) book are devoted to critiques of scientific rationality, notions of self and human subjectivity, philosophical investigations of power and knowledge, sociological definitions of social structure, accounts of causation, and so on. On the basis of these extensive reinterpretations Henry and Milanovic (1996: 7) propose a redefinition of crime as 'the harm resulting from humans investing energy in harm-producing relations of power' and go on to suggest that crimes are 'no less than people being disrespected'. Crime, in this definition, is one amongst many kinds of harm that denies or prevents people from becoming 'fully social beings'. In particular, they characterise crime in terms of two kinds of 'harm': harms of reduction and harms of repression. Harms of reduction are those that produce an immediate loss or injury for a victim – including such actions as assault, theft or damage. Harms of repression are those that reduce or restrict the future potential of a victim to develop his or her ability to make a difference to the world – including such actions as intimidation, oppression or exploitation. In these cases, Milanovic (2002: 253) adds, offenders 'are better conceptualised as "excessive investors", investing energy to make a difference on others without those others having the ability to make a difference on them'. On the other hand, victims are those who 'suffer the pain of being denied their own humanity, the power to make a difference' (Henry and Milanovic, 1996: 116).

In spite of expending enormous effort on these redefinitions of 'criminal' and 'victim' constitutive criminologists have no explicit interest in what causes people to become perpetrators or victims of crime. Rather, their interests lie in the many ways that crime is discursively constructed because, at a societal level, 'crime' has many more meanings, and many more dimensions, than the relationship between an offender, a victim and a law. Crime means a lot more in contemporary society than an act of lawbreaking: it is a widespread and popular form of entertainment (as television listings and book sales demonstrate); it is a major source of news and current affairs; it provides widespread employment for academics of many stripes as well as officers of the criminal justice system and related agencies. Contemporary society invests a colossal amount of time, energy and resources in crime in many different forms. Since the reality of crime is visible in all of these different social sites, then, it is argued, the task or object of criminology lies less in supplying rational and effective ways of responding to lawbreaking activities and more in enabling the expansion of new understandings/meanings of and new societal relationships with crime and justice. To achieve these aims, constitutive criminologists propose to develop 'replacement discourses' – 'alternative visions' that invoke 'alternative realities' that may ultimately coalesce into emergent 'new discursive orders' (Henry and Milanovic, 1996: 186, 209). Such replacement discourses are intended to subvert mainstream, dominant conceptions of law, crime and social order and give voice to the perspectives of the marginalised and disenfranchised groups who are so often the targets of criminal justice activities – the poor and/or minority ethnic groups, for example.

Constitutive criminologists see themselves as belonging to the tradition of **critical criminology** insofar as they claim to establish crime as simply one element in a totality of structural and cultural relations. Like Marxist and other radical criminologists, Henry, Milanovic and colleagues aim to deconstruct crime and exhibit the ways that ideas about, relationships with, representations of and policies towards crime are intimately connected with much larger social currents in contemporary society. Also like earlier radical outlooks, constitutive criminology offers the prospect of redefining the discipline of criminology itself. Instead of seeing criminology as an adjunct of government – a body of useful knowledge that can be applied to crime-management as and when necessary – constitutive criminology puts the very definition of 'useful knowledge' to the test by asking 'useful for whom or what; useful in what way and according to whose standards?' Yet, even whilst reiterating these critical issues the approach begs a series of further questions. For example, there is undoubtedly some merit in deconstructing the concept of crime and investigating its tangled relationships with larger social forces. But it is far from clear how the concept of 'harm' that replaces it is to escape the same fate. If we ask 'who defines crime?' or 'whose interests are served by definitions of crime?' or 'why are some activities deemed criminal in some times and places but not others?' we must surely ask the same questions about the concept of harm. Who is to define what constitutes 'harm' on any given occasion – the person who perceives that they have been harmed? How are competing claims to be settled if two – or two hundred or two thousand, and so on – persons each claim they were harmed by the other(s)? Why are some activities considered harmful in some times and some places but not others – such as smoking tobacco, for example? There is no suggestion here that a notion of harm is not itself useful. Indeed, other criminologists (see Hillyard *et al.*, 2004) also use the term 'harm' as a means of broadening criminology's field of vision. The issue is how the concept of harm as developed by Henry and colleagues can avoid constitutive criminology's critique of the concept of crime, since it merely substitutes one set of definitions revolving around law with another set of definitions revolving around disrespect.

A further set of questions can be posed about the value of the project as a whole, rather than about the merit of its individual concepts. It is true that much criminology ignores important questions about global-scale threats to personal safety, property and public order – including questions about climate change and environmental degradation, oppression based on ethnicity or gender, for example, the nefarious and downright dangerous threats posed by military, security and intelligence services, the 'crime' of poverty in a world gorged on plenty, and so on. But do we really need to weld together chaos and catastrophe theory, French psychoanalysis, non-linear dynamics, (so-called) postmodernism and a host of other distinct and competing theories and philosophies in order to grasp the importance of these issues or develop plausible explanations for their origins and continued salience? Many radical as well as mainstream criminologists have been asking similar questions for a very long time without enveloping them in the dense and often contradictory terminology that inevitably ensues when such a wide range of different perspectives are congealed together. Milanovic may be right when he says that

> Neither the transcendental subject (Cogito, ergo sum) nor the 'death of the subject' is worthy of celebration. The decidability of the sign and subjectivity finds itself within the coordinates of historical struggles.
>
> (Henry *et al.*, 1997)

The important question is whether being right about this (in philosophical, epistemological and meta-theoretical terms) enhances criminology's grasp of the reality of crime – or harm. It is here, at this 'meta-theoretical' level, that debates around constitutive criminology are likely to continue. It is certain that the applied study of crime and deviance is advanced by close engagement with important philosophical, sociological and psychological theories; but it is uncertain whether constitutive criminology provides a constructive means of dealing with their inherently contradictory political consequences.

See also: **critical criminology; discourse; peace-making criminology; restorative justice; social harm**

Further reading: Barak (1998); Henry and Milanovic (1996)

CORPORATE CRIME

Corporate crime refers to those offences, punishable variously by criminal, civil or administrative law, that are committed by legitimate business organisations as part of their ongoing activities.

Critical criminologists (such as E. A. Ross and Willem Bonger) first drew attention to such offences in the early twentieth century. Later, Edwin Sutherland examined corporate crimes as part of his study of **white-collar crime**. However, more recent scholarship has drawn an important distinction between *occupational crimes* (those committed by individuals in the course of their legitimate employment) and *organisational crimes* (those committed by business organisations in the course of their legitimate economic activities) (Slapper and Tombs, 1999).

Analysts of corporate crime have detailed both the wide variety of corporate offending and the extent of the harms that accrue from them. These include:

1 Financial crimes, such as fraud and tax evasion. The former includes offences such as the 'misselling' of pensions, mortgages and other financial services, illegal dealing in or manipulation of stocks and shares, the deliberate over-charging of customers for goods and services, and price-fixing. Taken together, such offences run into many billions of dollars of losses for their victims, and in the worst cases can cause massive financial harm to many thousands of people who may variously be left destitute (as in the case of the UK pension frauds of the 1980s and 1990s) or jobless (as in the case of the collapse of Enron in the USA following its exposure for false accounting). Studies in the USA have estimated that corporate tax evasion costs the state hundreds of billions of dollars in lost tax revenues every year. Such activity inevitably deprives the state of crucial financial resources that could be spent on public services such as healthcare, education, policing, housing and suchlike, and increases the tax burden borne by the least well off.

2 Violence, abuse and physical harm. Analysts of corporate crime have exposed the massive extent of harms to individuals caused by businesses, including death, illness and serious injury. These can result, first, from employment of workers in unsafe conditions, resulting in fatalities, injuries and long-term illness and disease. Abuse of employees also takes the form of exploitation of labour under inhumane conditions, as with the use of child labour in contravention of laws governing human rights. Physical harms also impact upon wider communities through the emission of pollutants, which contaminate rivers and land, and poison the water and soil upon which people depend for their existence. Gross industrial negligence can have catastrophic consequences, as exemplified by the gas leak that occurred at the Union Carbide pesticides plant in

Bhopal, India, in 1984. Thousands in the surrounding residential communities were killed by the leak, many thousands of others were blinded and maimed by the gases, and the ongoing effects of the incident have been held responsible for high rates of cancers and birth defects. Corporations have also been implicated in violence through their support (financial and otherwise) for oppressive political regimes in countries where they do business. In Nigeria, Shell has been accused of directly funding military excursions by Nigerian forces against local communities who have resisted the company's drilling activities, excursions that resulted in dozens of fatalities. In the most explicit cases, corporations directly profit from death and injury to others, as with the growing market for 'private military companies' who are contracted by states to undertake military activities on their behalf. In the case of private contractors employed by the US government in Iraq, this has resulted in allegations of torture against civilians in detention at the hands of private security forces.

Critical criminologists have identified a number of recent social, political and economic changes that have, if anything, increased the scope and scale of corporate crime. First, they note the move towards privatisation by right-wing governments in many Western countries during the 1980s and 1990s. By handing the provision of ever-more goods and services into private hands, this has increased the range of opportunities for offending by business organisations. Second, criminologists have noted the impact of the globalisation process, which has resulted in greater corporate involvement in developing countries where they can benefit from lower standards of workplace and environmental regulation in their search for greater profits. Third, they have noted the growth of powerful transnational corporations who are able to use their financial and political power to minimise state control and evade punishment for offences.

An ongoing issue in the discussion of corporate crime is its marginalisation both within criminology and within criminal justice and law enforcement. Despite the fact that corporate crime is estimated to cause financial and material harms on a much greater scale than so-called 'street crimes', it receives comparatively little attention. Indeed, many of the harms caused by corporate business activities are not subject to formal criminal sanctions, but are treated under various forms of civil and administrative law. This not only means that offenders are liable to less serious sanctions if found guilty (for example fines rather than custodial sentences for business executives) but also serves to symbolically locate corporate offences outside the sphere of what are considered 'real' or 'serious' crimes. Moreover, where criminal sanctions *do* exist, their enforcement is sporadic at best, and criminal justice agencies devote only a small fraction of their resources to the detection and prosecution of such crimes as compared to low-level offences committed by individuals. Market liberals welcome under-regulation by the state, viewing the market as the proper environment for placing appropriate but not excessive constraints upon business activities, seeing state regulation as a form of interference that will place undesirable burdens upon corporations, thereby reducing profitability. However, from a critical perspective, this neglect is seen as a consequence of the power exercised by economic interests over legislation and regulation, and the close ties between business and the state in capitalist societies. In this way, corporate power ensures systematic under-regulation and the state's preference for self-regulation by business rather than the use of formal criminal sanctions. Criminology has largely followed the crime control agenda set by **the state**, and has tended to view the regulation of harmful corporate activity as falling outside the scope of the field's core concerns. Thus some sixty years after Edwin Sutherland's call for criminologists to examine the 'crimes of the powerful', corporate crime remains a relatively neglected topic within the discipline.

See also: **environmental crime; green criminology; Marxist criminology; social harm; state, the; state crime; white-collar crime**

Further reading: Slapper and Tombs (1999); Snider (2000); Sutherland (1947); Whyte (2003, 2004)

CRIME AND DEVIANCE

The terms crime and deviance are often used in tandem, or even interchangeably, in criminological discussion. However, they ought to be viewed as distinct, albeit interrelated, categories.

Crime, in its most straightforward sense, denotes those behaviours that are formally prohibited and punishable under criminal law. Such offences provide the subject matter of mainstream criminological investigation. However, criminologists may study activities that are not criminal as such (i.e. do not breach criminal law), but are instead subject to administrative law (regulations drawn up by government's administrative agencies). Criminologists deem such activities as relevant because they may cause serious harms to society and its members. Moreover, the fact that they are *not* criminalised is considered noteworthy in itself, as it invites us to examine why it is that some harmful behaviours are deemed crimes and not others. It is important to bear in mind that crime is a *social construct*, insofar as what counts as crime will depend upon the legal standing of an act at a particular time and place. As such, new crimes are constantly being created, and conversely behaviours that were at one time criminal may be decriminalised.

The term *deviance* in contrast denotes behaviours that breach *informal* social norms and rules, and hence are considered undesirable or objectionable. An act may be seen as deviant while being entirely legal (an example would be consensual sadomasochistic sex). Conversely, an act may be a crime, but not considered as deviant by the social majority (a good example would be speeding). Crime and deviance intersect in that societal perceptions about deviance may drive a process of criminalisation, as various actors call for the objectionable behaviour in question to be formally outlawed. On the other hand, behaviours may be eventually decriminalised as a result of a change in wider cultural understandings and sensibilities. In this way formal (legal) and informal (cultural) understandings of what is appropriate or inappropriate, normal or abnormal, desirable or undesirable, are clearly interconnected.

See also: **labelling perspectives; moral panic**

Further reading: Pfohl and Henry (1993); Sumner (1994)

CRIME DATA

A term used to denote the various sources of information about trends and patterns of crime. Crime data inform us about the levels of various kinds of offences, where and when they occur, and the social characteristics of both the offenders and victims. Crime data provide the basic material with which many criminologists work, for example in attempting to explain how and why certain crimes occur, why certain kinds of social actors are more or less likely to become involved in criminal behaviour, or why overall levels of crime may be rising or falling.

The most well-known and widely used form of crime data is derived from *official statistics*. These are measures of the scope, scale and nature of criminal offending compiled and published annually by the state and allied criminal justice agencies. The first such statistical compilations were produced in France in the early nineteenth century, with England and Wales following in the 1870s, and the USA in the 1930s. The statistics are derived from the incidents of crime recorded by the police. They are usually published having been sorted into different categories and types of offence, alongside a breakdown of the known offenders according to social characteristics such as age and gender. Official statistics show a consistent distribution of offences over time, with **property crimes** (such as theft and burglary) accounting for the great majority of crimes, as compared to a relatively smaller number of offences such as homicide and rape. The statistics also indicate a consistent profile for what amounts to a 'typical offender', who is likely to be a young male. Moreover, the publication of the statistics on a year-on-year basis indicates overall trends in crime levels, with most Western industrial countries exhibiting a large-scale increase in crime levels over the forty years after World War II. These statistics have directed the inquiries undertaken by criminologists to a great extent, with attention being focused on research questions such as: Why do young people offend? How might we prevent property crime? Why did crime increase so massively in the latter part of the twentieth century?

However, official criminal statistics have been subjected to criticism, and it has been argued that they do as much to hide or distort realities of crime as they do to reveal them. First, it must be noted that the official data represent only those offences *recorded* by police. Crimes may not be *reported* by victims in the first place for a wide variety of reasons (e.g. a lack of belief that there will be any satisfactory resolution, a distrust of the police, intimidation by the offender, or embarrassment and shame). Of those offences reported not all will be recorded by the police, depending upon the officers' judgement about the seriousness of the incident or the credibility of the witness or victim. More broadly, political and public concerns will shape patterns of policing, making it more or less likely that particular types of offences will be detected and recorded at any given time. It has also been argued that the official figures are partial in that they only record some types of offences and not others, thereby giving an incomplete or distorted impression of 'the crime problem'. For example, some criminologists question the focus upon relatively low-level property crimes while omitting white-collar and corporate offences from the data. In sum, it is now commonly acknowledged by criminologists that there is a massive 'dark figure' of undetected, unreported and unrecorded crime.

One way in which the problem of the dark figure has been tackled is through the development of *criminal victimisation surveys*. These may be conducted on a national or local scale, and typically involve a sample of households being interviewed about their experiences of crime over a given period. The aim of the surveys is to reveal more completely the nature and incidence of crime, including those offences that have otherwise gone unreported and unrecorded. From the 1970s onwards, victimisation surveys have played an important role in bringing criminological attention to a range of so-called 'hidden crimes', including rape and domestic violence. However, despite the gains made over official statistics, victimisation surveys are not without shortcomings. First, they depend upon individuals' or households' willingness to participate, and some social groups may be less likely than others to participate, thereby potentially undermining the survey's representativeness. Second, the accuracy of the survey depends upon the respondents' memories of past incidents, and individuals may forget instances of victimisation, inaccurately remember the nature and timing of the incidents or not even be aware that they have been the victims of a crime (for example if they are unaware that a particular kind of behaviour is legally prohibited). In short, what victims perceive as a crime (rather than perhaps a nuisance or just a part of everyday life) may be subject to significant variation.

An alternative method of statistical data collection is the *self-report survey*. Here, a sample of individuals is invited to anonymously reveal offences that they have themselves committed. This method aims to garner a more complete picture of offenders and their involvement in lawbreaking behaviour, including their significant social characteristics (such as age, gender, class and ethnic background). Yet again, however, such surveys are subject to some limitations. As with victimisation surveys, they are dependent upon the recall of the participants, and offenders may not accurately recall details or even the number of offences that have been committed in the case of prolific offenders. In addition, some individuals may be unwilling to participate or confess to a serious crime for fear of subsequent reprisals despite assurances about their anonymity. Finally, some respondents may be inclined to exaggerate their criminal 'achievements' as a form of self-assertion or expression of a deviant identity.

All of the above forms of crime data are *quantitative* in nature, comprising numerical counts of numbers and types of offences. An alternative research tradition within criminology favours the collection of *qualitative* data. Qualitative researchers are not so much interested in numerical measurement as in gaining detailed insights into offenders' and/or victims' own experiences of crime. Such data collection is intended to reveal how those involved understand their own actions and what meanings they attach to them. Qualitative data may be collected by a variety of methods. These include the use of open-ended *in-depth interviews* in which a researcher will seek to elicit from the respondent as complete a picture as possible not only of their offending but also of their wider life-experiences, feelings and beliefs. A second method is that of *participant observation*. Here, criminological researchers will spend an extended period of time immersed in the social world of their research subject, building up a relation of trust and sense of acceptance in the hope of coming to understand the offenders' conduct 'from the inside'.

Qualitative and quantitative data may be seen as alternatives but in reality much criminological research combines the two in an attempt to balance detailed understanding with broader and more general insights.

See also: **Chicago School criminology; cultural criminology; positivist criminology; realism**

Further reading: Coleman and Moynihan (1996); Maguire (2002)

CRIME MAPPING

Using sophisticated Geographical Information Systems it is possible for crime analysts to overlay numerous sources of data in multiple crime 'maps' – such as census and other demographic data, geographical data on the location of schools, businesses, and so on, and police data on neighbourhood crime rates. These maps can assist law-enforcement agencies to identify (primarily urban) crime trends, target resources where they are apparently most needed and allocate police officers. There is nothing new in the idea of producing crime maps – the effort to understand the geographical distribution of crime was a key element in the work of the **Chicago School** and was also an element in the emergence of nineteenth-century criminal statistics. Undoubtedly a valuable tool in criminal investigations and the management of police resources, crime mapping is nonetheless part of the rapidly developing association between policing practice and information and communication technologies. As such, it raises questions about the drift towards a 'surveillance society' in which any and all kinds of (personal and) social information becomes available to the criminal justice system, regardless of its actual utility in preventing crime or maintaining social order.

See also: **Chicago School criminology; environmental criminology; surveillance**

Further reading: Chainey and Ratcliffe (2005)

CRIMINAL CAREERS

The notion of a 'criminal career' was introduced into criminology by Sheldon and Eleanor Glueck (1930) in their book *500 Criminal Careers*, and by Clifford Shaw in his (1931) book *The Natural History of a Delinquent Career*. The Gluecks' research was a quantitative study of institutionalised young offenders, whilst Shaw used a series of case studies to describe the criminal histories of individuals. Neither Shaw nor the Gluecks define 'career' explicitly but it clearly references a sense of progression or development in the individual's criminal pursuits. Whilst the Gluecks and Shaw used the term loosely to depict the objective changes in the activities of their research subjects, Everett Hughes (1937) gave the term a subjective twist by defining 'career' as 'the moving perspective in which the person sees his life as a whole and interprets the meaning of his various attributes, actions, and the things which happen to him' (Hughes, 1937: 409–10). The key difference between the two senses of 'career' is that the objectivist approach is concerned entirely with changes in behaviour whilst the subjectivist approach concerns itself primarily with changes in **identity**. Although the term 'criminal career' is not commonly used in contemporary criminology (but see Piquero *et al.*, 2007), nonetheless both approaches have had important impacts on criminological research.

The subjectivist perspective was taken up by the interactionist sociologists of deviance – notably Edwin Lemert, Howard Becker and Erving Goffman. Lemert (1951), for example, in his distinction between 'primary' and 'secondary' deviance, proposed that the key to understanding progression in criminal (or 'deviant') behaviour was the societal reaction to it. 'Primary deviance' may be non-problematic from the individual's point of view, but once a person attracts the label 'criminal' or 'deviant' then their self-identity may undergo important changes. The individual may see themselves as 'outside' normal moral codes and increasingly identify, not with the 'normal', law–abiding majority but with a pathological, deviant minority. The importance of the idea of moral codes was underscored by Erving Goffman (1961) in his studies of the identity management of asylum inmates. Here, Goffman describes the 'moral career' of the mental patient in terms of the process by which inmates learned to take on the institution's definition of their identity as mentally ill individuals. Note, here, that Goffman is not saying that mental illness is entirely a matter of subjective definition. What he is saying is that, in the asylum, institutional definitions dominate over other kinds of definition: the institution requires inmates to behave in certain kinds of recognisably pathological ways in order to manage that behaviour effectively. In this sense, inmates may not learn to become mentally ill but they do learn to express their illness through the institution's dominant definitions. Goffman's subtle expansion of Lemert's early definition of secondary deviance became a crucial resource for a large number of qualitative studies of deviant careers – the most famous of which was the collection of essays in Howard Becker's (1963) *Outsiders*. Discussing the lives of drug–users, dance musicians and hustlers of various descriptions, Becker brought together key insights on 'moral careers' from Goffman with a focus on Lemert's category of 'secondary deviance'. Becker's goal was to 'analyze the genesis of deviant behaviour in terms of events which render sanctions ineffective' (1963: 61). In other words, he wanted to show how individuals *learn* to reject the 'normal' rules of the 'straight' society in favour of the 'deviant' rules of 'outsider' groups. What unites these approaches to the study of deviant careers is that they reject a focus on behaviour alone. The emphasis on rules, moral codes, societal (or institutional) reactions, labels, and so on, is intended to show that crime and deviance are bound up with social identities and social roles as well as with wider societal definitions of how deviants (be they mental patients or prison inmates) *should* behave. The deviant or criminal career is not simply a progression from one kind of behaviour to another but from one set of social identities and social roles to another: it has implications for a person's subjective sense of self as well as for their objective behaviour.

The objectivist perspective is most strongly associated with a series of statistical and cohort studies beginning, mainly in America, in the late 1970s and early 1980s (see Blumstein and Cohen, 1979). The research agenda included both retrospective studies (that is, work that looked back over the cohort data to extract common patterns) and prospective studies (that is, work that used the available data to develop probabilistic models of criminal behaviour) (see Blumstein *et al.*, 1986; Barnett *et al.*, 1987). The purpose of these studies was to examine whether criminal individuals and groups expressed common shifts in criminal activity ('crime frequencies') across the life course. In these early studies the notion of 'criminal career' was used only as a means of structuring the data – that is, it was used as a convenient label to represent changes in the patterns of an individual's criminal behaviour over time. It was not intended, as in the interactionist perspective, to expose the subtle interplay between individual behaviour, societal reaction and self-identity. Later research began to pay more attention to issues of onset (that is, ages at and circumstances under which individuals took up criminal activities) and desistance (that is, ages at and circumstances under which individuals ended their involvement in criminal activities) (see Farrall, 2000; Soothill *et al.*, 2004). Subsequently, this research has been supplemented by an interest in the length of criminal careers and whether there are differences in these lengths in different time periods (see Francis *et al.*, 2007). More importantly, these recent research efforts have been keen, in theory if not always in practice, to incorporate both qualitative and quantitative information about careers and to attempt an understanding of the career concept in terms of both objective and subjective elements.

The interest in desistance from crime has been taken up in several different ways – notably in **developmental criminology**. A novel, and striking, contribution to research into desistance was Julie Liebrich's (1993) qualitative study of the struggles and challenges facing a series of offenders attempting to give up their criminal lives. Liebrich's key point is that just as the onset and aggravation of offending behaviour can be conceptualised as processes so too can desistance from offending. For many offenders, giving up a criminal lifestyle is not a once-and-for-all event but a difficult series of steps and negotiations that can, at any time, be undermined by other life problems. Liebrich notes that criminologists should acknowledge that *going straight* – that is, making the difficult choices that enable individuals to move away from a criminal career – is just as important as *being straight* – that is, achieving a law-abiding, crime-free existence, and that criminologists should pay more attention to the process rather than concentrating simply on the event.

See also: **developmental criminology; labelling perspectives**

Further reading: Farrall (2000); Piquero *et al.* (2007)

CRIMINAL JUSTICE SYSTEM

The phrase 'criminal justice system' (CJS) refers to an array of institutions that are charged with controlling or otherwise responding to crime in society. In England and Wales the CJS comprises six agencies: the police, the criminal courts, the Crown Prosecution Service (CPS), the prison service, the probation service and the Youth Justice System. The police are charged with detecting crime and maintaining law and order. The criminal courts are mandated to try offences in law, establish innocence or guilt and, in the latter case, pass a sentence of appropriate punishment. The role of the Crown Prosecution Service is to decide whether there is sufficient evidence to bring a suspect to trial in a court of law and whether or not it is in the public interest to do so. The prison service is charged with protecting the public by holding those committed in a safe environment and, additionally, with helping to reduce crime by providing constructive regimes which address offending behaviour. The probation service monitors and supervises offenders who are sentenced to community punishments or whose sentence of imprisonment includes a period of statutory licence supervision in the community. Finally, the Youth Justice System aims to prevent offending and reoffending by children and young people under the age of eighteen either by the provision of programmes to address offending behaviour under the guidance of Youth Justice Teams (YOTs) or by placement in a secure institution – a secure training centre, a secure children's home or a Young Offenders Institution.

Whilst the six agencies are each mandated to address problems of crime, they are administered by different departments of government. The courts are the responsibility of the Department of Constitutional Affairs (formerly the Lord Chancellor's Office); the police service is the responsibility of the Home Office; prisons, probation and youth justice are the responsibility of the Ministry of Justice; the head of the Crown Prosecution Service, the director of public prosecutions, is appointed by the attorney general who is accountable to Parliament for the work of the CPS. Although the divisions of responsibility can create some inter-departmental rivalries, the system is set up so that one branch of government is accountable for the policing function, one for the prosecution function, one for the trial function, and one for the offender management function.

See also: **justice; policing and the police; prisons and imprisonment; punishment**

Further reading: Davies *et al.* (2005)

CRIMINAL PSYCHOLOGY

Criminal psychology is a broad label used to identify those perspectives that examine the individual's psychological make-up and mental processes in an attempt to explain offending behaviour.

Criminal psychology contains a wide range of competing and often contradictory perspectives. Some psychologists trace criminal tendencies back to biological and neurological processes, locating the origins of criminality in physiology. Psychoanalytic theories, in contrast, hold that the human psyche is made up of competing elements, and criminal behaviour can be seen as the manifestation of a failure to balance these elements. Following Freud, psychoanalytic criminologists see individuals as compelled by powerful sexual and destructive drives that need to be repressed, controlled and channelled by the mind. Failure to secure such control will result in aggression and an inability to exercise appropriate restraints over behaviour. Personality theories, as the name suggests, claim that individuals can be classified into distinct 'personality types', and that each type can be associated with a range of likely behaviours. It is suggested that, for example, some people may be psychopaths or sociopaths, unable to form attachments with others and unconstrained by feelings of guilt, responsibility or remorse. Through administering personality tests, psychologists hope to be able to identify those individuals whose personalities dispose them towards criminal and violent behaviour. In extreme cases psychologists may identify offenders as mentally ill or insane, suggesting that such persons have lost the ability to reason effectively or to understand the nature and consequences of their actions.

Psychological perspectives have been subject to numerous criticisms, particularly from those criminologists who favour more socially oriented explanations of crime. They argue that criminal psychology tends to extract individuals from the social context they inhabit, thereby ignoring the role that social relations and cultural understandings play in shaping human conduct. Psychology thereby downplays the complexity of meanings and motivations that inform behaviour, instead reducing an individual's actions to a simple array of inner determinants. More broadly, such theories tend to view criminality and deviance as objective and fixed categories, and in doing so ignore the ways in which our views of normal and abnormal behaviour are culturally dependent and variable. A frequently cited example is that of homosexuality, which was for many years deemed to be a mental illness or mental abnormality, thereby reflecting and reinforcing wider social prejudices through the application of stig-matising labels.

See also: **biological criminology; labelling perspectives; positivist criminology**

Further reading: Ainsworth (1999); Putwain and Sammons (2002)

CRITICAL CRIMINOLOGY

The central proposition of critical criminology is that understandings of crime are tied to social circumstances: what 'crime' is depends on the historical, political, cultural and economic conditions obtaining within society at a given point in time. Moreover, there is no neces-sary link between crime and social responses to it. Thus, 'street crime', for example, is invariably high on the agenda of the media, politicians and criminal justice agencies. Yet fraud – which generates significantly higher economic losses – is far less likely to become the object of popular political or media campaigns. The discrepancy between social responses to these crimes is a function of the political and economic forces that set the overall crime agenda.

The emergence of critical criminology as a distinctive approach to questions of crime and deviance can be traced back to July 1968, when a group of social scientists established the National Deviancy Conference (NDC) – sometimes known also as the 'York group'. The NDC became a loose association of sociologists, criminologists, social workers and others who sought to combine political activism and theoretical innovation in a 'new criminology' (Taylor *et al.*, 1973). The new criminology arose in response to both the positivist and 'correctionalist' bent of mainstream criminology and the anti-politics of labelling theory. The NDC embarked on the ambitious intellectual project of con-necting the creation of deviance to the social and political contours of post-war capitalism. In search of a fully 'social theory of deviance', rather than merely a just-so story of societal reaction, a generation of social scientists sought to shift the criminological lens away from the character and situation of the deviant and his/her behaviour and towards the social and historical patterns that produced 'deviance' as an object of state and social intervention. The task of critical crim-inology was to 'explain the continuance, the innovation or the abolition of legal and social norms in terms of the interests they support, the functions they serve to particular material arrangements or production in propertied societies' (Taylor *et al.*, 1975: 56).

In this regard, since its very inception, critical criminology has been 'resolutely sociological in orientation' (Carrington and Hogg, 2002: 5) – which is to say that its primary focus has been on the ways that grand societal problems of inequality, discrimination, exclusion, racism and sexism act as the root causes of crime. Jock Young (2007: 142) provides a neat illustration of this outlook. In the conventional way of looking at things, bad individual choices result in problematic behaviour which, in turn, creates challenges requiring societal responses. In the 'war on drugs', for example, 'drug use is seen to give rise to crime which creates problems for society'. Critical criminology, on the other hand, argues precisely the reverse of this position: that a 'problematical social order gives rise to crime and deleterious drug use'. Critical criminologists investigate the 'problematic' nature of society and through this investigation expose how unequal power relations result in the criminalising of poor and marginalised groups but not of wealthy and dominant groups.

Critical criminology's early constructions of the problem of crime revolved primarily around issues of class and the state and were underpinned by a Marxist interpretation of capitalist society. In this first phase much effort was put into a reinterpretation of the history of criminological thought (Taylor *et al.*, 1973). This reinterpretation was intended to reveal how the development of modern criminological theory's view of crime – its forms, motivations and effects – had been trapped in a 'conventional' account. This account had deflected attention 'away from a structural analysis of the forces conducive to crime and disorder' (ibid.: 263) and had failed to grasp 'crime as human action, as reaction to positions held in an antagonistic social structure, but also as action taken to resolve those antagonisms' (ibid.: 236). In this construction 'crime' is not the callous or greedy act of predatory individuals but a consequence of the contradictory circumstances in which (especially poor) people find themselves. At the same time as reinterpreting the history of criminological thought, several important research studies were undertaken by members of the NDC. These included the now famous analysis of 1960s youth cultures and the social reaction to them by Stan Cohen (1972), and Jock Young's (1971) study of the subcultures of drug-taking. Added to these were a series of lesser-known but no less important researches in the sociology of deviance – including the analysis of industrial sabotage by Laurie Taylor and Paul Walton (1971) and Ian Taylor's (1971) study of soccer hooliganism, together with studies of political protest and opposition and studies of the interactions between the media, policing and criminal justice (see Cohen and Young, 1973).

So whilst critical criminology comprised a thorough challenge to mainstream criminological theory, it also attempted to underscore that challenge through a range of detailed empirical studies of the connections between crime, law and the state. An immediate consequence of the commitment to empirically grounding critical criminological theory was that it undermined the very project of interpreting criminal laws in terms of 'the functions they serve to particular material arrangements or production in propertied societies' (see above). This, for two reasons. First, it became clear that 'material arrangements' could not be understood solely through the lens of class relations or the ownership of property in a classic Marxist sense. The inequalities of modern societies include systematic discrimination against women and minority ethnic groups, and institutionalised social exclusion of the poor and people with physical and mental disabilities. Yet the involvement of these different groups in criminal activities, and the response of the criminal justice system to that involvement, varies remarkably. Men are far more likely to be involved in crime than women, for example, yet women are more likely to be poor than men – so a criminal response to poverty is not equally shared amongst men and women. Nor, incidentally, is it equally shared across all ethnic groups. If crime is a 'reaction to positions held in an antagonistic social structure' how do we explain the myriad criminal and non-criminal character of such reactions? Second, even if there is some truth in 'materialist' explanations for crime it does not necessarily help those who are its most likely victims. The overwhelming majority of predatory crimes against persons and property are committed by poor people against poor people: their 'reaction' to an 'antagonistic social structure' involves the criminal victimisation of the structure's social victims.

The realisation that traditional Marxism was too blunt a tool to prise open the inherent complexities of crime and deviance caused something of a split in critical criminology. For some, such as John Lea and Jock Young (1984), criminologists needed to 'take crime seriously', by which they meant that the real experience of crime for its victims should be a central dimension of any criminology that purports to be 'critical'. In this plea for a victim-centred criminology, Lea and Young argue that criminology should be 'realistic' in its understanding of the impacts of crime – especially on poor and deprived neighbourhoods – and 'radical' in its proposals for addressing those impacts: hence the term left *realism* to depict this current in criminological theory. Left realist criminologists effectively abandoned Marxism as a source of inspiration and critical analysis and,

with it, the focus on the state, class antagonisms and property relations. In its place they developed a mid-range theory that sought to
explain crime in terms of the intersection between the offender, the
victim, the public and the agencies of social control.

However, a parallel theoretical current in critical criminology –
labelled left *idealism* – continued to view crime through the lens of
capitalist social divisions, arguing that taking crime seriously involves
close attention to the contradictions and anomalies of capitalist
society as a whole. In this outlook, criminal 'justice' is not a finished
project – a solid and immutable system whose defects are merely
technical glitches awaiting expert repair – but a social contrivance
that sustains, and is sustained by, vested political, economic and cultural
interests that can be challenged, subverted or overturned. The **criminal justice system**, far from being part of the solution, is a central
part of the problem of crime and crime control in capitalist society
because it is enmeshed in wider structures of power and domination.
In this view, according to Hall and Scraton (1981: 488–89), criminalisation is not simply a process of labelling this or that individual or
behaviour as deviant or immoral. It is, instead, a political logic
intended to mobilise 'popular approval and legitimacy behind the
state'. In other words, the targeting and heavy policing and punishment of 'problem populations' is one of the ways that the state
manages and contains the inequalities and oppressions of the capitalist
system. Rather than addressing the central economic and political
contradictions of capitalism, the state uses the criminal justice system
to regulate and control the victims of inequality – hence, prisons
overflow with poor people with limited life chances but not with
rich tax evaders, corporately negligent polluters, exploiters of
labourers in developing regions or business owners who flout health
and safety regulations, for example.

Critical criminology provides a valuable focus on broad sociological questions about the relationships between crime and the wider
society, but it does not provide a 'total theory' of crime, still less of
criminal justice. There remain questions: for example, about how far
critical criminology is simply sociology in disguise – dependent on
the whims of sociological theory for its insights rather than developing
specifically criminological analyses to explain crime and justice. In
this case, 'crime' simply becomes a lens through which to view other
social issues rather than a topic in its own right. Of course, it can be
countered that critical criminology is less a 'school' or 'perspective'
and more a testing and application of ideas, methods, and moral and
political commitments to the 'relationships between social and criminal

justice' (Carlen, 2002: 249): an extreme example of the nature of criminology itself as a 'rendezvous discipline' (Rock and Holdaway, 1997) where different perspectives, politics and paradigms collide. However, as Smart (1990: 77) pointed out, any intellectual project that fully located its core objects – rape, theft, fraud, violence, for example – in social processes per se would 'abandon criminology to sociology' and, further, 'it would involve abandoning the idea of a unified problem ["crime"] which requires a unified response'. With precisely this dilemma in mind, some early sceptics accused the sociology-dependent critical criminologists of behaving like 'glamorous partisans' eagerly dressing up their so-called 'radicalism' in 'scholastic metaphysics' (Walker, 1974: 47, 62) and refusing to engage practically with the real public and private circumstances of criminal activity. There is no doubt that, for three decades, critical criminology has been one of the most exciting and theoretically productive frameworks for the study of crime. It is also true that during that time it has transformed immensely into a multifaceted, reflective and, in some senses, contradictory enterprise as it has attempted to absorb more and different ways of using 'crime' as a vehicle for wider social criticism.

See also: **Marxist criminology**

Further reading: Carrington and Hogg (2002); Taylor *et al.* (1973)

CULTURAL CRIMINOLOGY

Cultural criminology is a label applied to a diverse range of criminological interests in the interaction between 'culture' and 'crime' in their broadest senses. The approach was developed by Jeff Ferrell and Clinton Sanders (1995) but can be traced back to much earlier sociological and criminological styles. Ferrell (1999) refers to the 'new criminology' of the 1970s (Taylor *et al.*, 1973) and the work of the Birmingham School of cultural studies (see Hall and Jefferson, 1993), in particular. Presdee (2000) refers to the same antecedents but adds Marxism and the sociologies of Durkheim, Parsons and Merton, whilst Hayward and Young (2004) further add social anthropology and the urban sociology of Jonathan Raban and Michel De Certeau. This wide range of intellectual precursors persuaded Ferrell (1999: 396) to suggest that cultural criminology is 'less a definitive paradigm than an emergent array of perspectives' concerned with representations, images and meanings of crime.

A further difficulty in defining cultural criminology lies in the fact that many criminologists investigate the relationships between dimensions of culture and crime but do not necessarily consider themselves to be 'cultural criminologists'. Nicole Rafter (2000) has investigated crime in Hollywood movies (as have the authors of this book – see Tzanelli et al., 2005); McLaughlin (2005) traced popular constructions of the English 'bobby' in post-war Britain; whilst Winlow and Hall (2006) unpicked the culture of violence in the night-time economy. All of these works take culture seriously in the investigation of crime and crime control, yet none of their authors would explicitly define themselves as cultural criminologists. Moreover, some criminological approaches that might be said to shed light on certain cultural characteristics of crime and crime control – such as **routine activity theories** and control theory – are explicitly rejected by cultural criminologists.

Thus, a concern with or commitment to the analysis of the relationships between culture and crime is not a sufficient definition of cultural criminology. The latter, in fact, belongs to no one tradition and is, in many ways, defined as much by what it is against as by what it is for. In particular, its practitioners are openly hostile to **administrative criminology**, situational crime prevention and **rational choice** theory. Presdee (2000: 276) accuses administrative criminology of being little other than a 'fact factory' doing nothing more than producing statistics that are 'demanded and devoured' by their 'political masters' in the Home Office Research Unit. Hayward and Young (2004: 262) imply that such criminology produces 'ill-developed theory, regression analysis usually followed by rather inconclusive results'. Hayward (2007: 234–35) claims that rational choice theory reduces crime to a 'two-inch formula' in order to cater for the demands of statistical analysis, and that situational crime prevention is guilty of 'hollowing out' the 'socio-cultural specificities' and 'existential motivations' of crime. In some respects, these hostilities and critiques of settled criminological schools and theories indicate that cultural criminology is more a political than analytical approach to understanding crime and crime control and, in fact, Ferrell et al. (2004: 296) claim that cultural criminology's assault on the 'boredom' of 'abstract empiricist' criminology derives from the 'politics of its theory and method' rather than its subject matter per se.

Perhaps the most famous (to date) example of cultural criminology is Jeff Ferrell's (1996) *Crimes of Style* – a detailed account of 'hip-hop' graffiti writing in Denver, Colorado. The account is based on Ferrell's own participation in and engagement with the graffiti writers' subculture during the early 1990s and, in particular, with members of a graffiti crew known as 'Syndicate'. It traces some of the cultural sources of the graffiti's hip-hop style, connections and distinctions between graffiti writing and mainstream and avant-garde art, the reactions of Denver City authorities and media to the graffiti, and concludes with a political analysis of graffiti as a form of subcultural resistance. The book portrays graffiti writing as a 'stylish counterpunch to the belly of authority' (ibid.: 195), an irreverent, insubordinate and playful dance of resistance to the drudgery of conformity and an escape from the 'conventional channels of authority and control' (ibid.: 173). The graffiti writers are represented not as vandals or anti-social nuisances but as creative stylists who risk legal sanction in order to express their artistic individuality. The meaning of graffiti writing, according to Ferrell, is less a desire to despoil the urban landscape or mark a territory with coloured signs and more a subcultural search for 'the adrenalin rush of illicit creativity', a challenge to and a celebration of the very illegality of the act of writing (ibid.: 148).

The reference to the 'adrenalin rush' of illicit activity exposes an important feature of cultural criminology, namely, an intense interest in the 'foreground' or experiential moment of crime. In this sense, cultural criminology is concerned with 'the situated meaning of criminal activity' (Fenwick, 2004: 385) or 'the interpretive frames, logics, images and senses through which and in which crime is apprehended and performed' (Kane, 2004: 303). The interest in 'situated meaning' and 'interpretive frames' can be traced to an important work by Jack Katz (1988) – *Seductions of Crime*. In this work Katz made a distinction between the 'moral emotions' (humiliation, arrogance, vengeance, righteousness, etc.) lurking in the foreground of crime and the 'material conditions' (notably gender, ethnicity and class) in the background of crime. Katz's point was that a criminology that seeks to understand 'normal' crimes – of violence, robbery, hustling, pimping, and so on – needs to pay careful attention to the emotional and moral rewards they provide for their perpetrators. These crimes are often not explicable in terms of their material rewards at all – domestic violence and domestic murder being particular cases in point. Instead, such crimes often arise in the context of deeper emotional and sensual needs, and it is only by grasping this deeper sensuality that variations in background factors can be explained: why do men commit more crime than women, why do some people in poverty turn to hustling and robbery but not others, why are there variations in ethnic participation in different kinds of crimes, for example? For Ferrell, this focus on the sensual foreground of crime turns criminology's attention away from columns of statistics purportedly showing the extent of the 'crime problem' and towards the 'immediate, incandescent integrations of risk, danger and skill that shape participation in deviant and criminal subcultures' (Ferrell, 1999: 404). Elsewhere, he writes that it serves to 'reclaim the criminological enterprise from a courthouse criminology of scientific rationalization and methodological objectification' (Ferrell et al., 2004: 297).

Stephen Lyng (1998) has added a further nuance to cultural criminology's interest in the foreground of crime by developing the concept of 'edgework' to describe voluntary risk-taking behaviour. Whilst not, initially at least, geared towards the interests of cultural criminology, the idea has been taken up rapidly as a means of linking criminal and deviant behaviour to risk-taking in more conventional spheres such as, in Lyng's case, sky-diving. 'Edgework' refers to the subjective experience of and engagement in activities that carry inherent personal risks: it is a form of 'purposive action grounded in the emotional and the visceral' and in the 'immediacy of excitement' of the risky event itself (Ferrell et al., 2001: 178). Whilst seemingly restricted to the subjective experience and meaning of risk-taking, Lyng and colleagues argue that such meanings and experiences are always related to a subcultural context: participants learn the meaning of their behaviour through interaction with others who are similarly engaged. Moreover, they develop distinctive linguistic and symbolic frameworks – particular codes, images and styles – through which to understand and communicate their experiences. Thus, the meaning of risk-taking is invariably embroiled in subcultural 'communities of mediated meaning and collective representation' (ibid.: 179). In this way, a social psychology of risky behaviour is related to the subcultural styles, symbols and values of the risk-taker's reference group which, in turn, both draw upon and challenge the wider culture in which they are situated.

From this brief discussion it can be seen that a central concern of cultural criminology is the extent to which deviant and/or criminal behaviour challenges, subverts or resists the values, symbols and codes of 'mainstream' culture. In fact, the concern to investigate deviant subcultures precisely in terms of the challenges and resistances they offer is the key dividing line between cultural criminology proper and those criminologies that take culture seriously but do not depict deviance in terms of challenge or resistance. It should be noted that the idea that deviant subcultures challenge mainstream culture does not necessarily imply that they do so consciously or directly. Although Ferrell, in particular, is dedicated to the detailed exploration of outsider groups – including graffiti writers, urban anarchists, dumpster-divers and trash-pickers – some cultural criminologists are more concerned to expose the wider social and cultural contexts in which these outsider groups operate. Of relevance here is work by Jock Young. Young's interest in cultural criminology is in how 'the intense emotions associated with much urban crime relates to significant and dramatic problems in the wider society' (Young, 2003: 391). In particular, for Young, these 'dramatic problems' consist of personal and economic insecurity, a combination of cultural inclusion and social exclusion, and the loss of familiar (class-based) identities through which to grasp the social world collectively. Whilst these problems cannot be taken as direct causes of crime in themselves they do, for Young, provide the perfect conditions in which criminal or 'transgressive' behaviour develops. In a culture which promises untold pleasures and freedoms for all via the mass media, the reality of economic marginalisation and social exclusion leads to widespread feelings of humiliation. In turn, it is the experience of humiliation that underpins much contemporary crime. Describing violent criminals and drug users, for example, Young (ibid.: 408) claims that these 'transgressors are driven by the energies of humiliation'.

Keith Hayward also attempts to link insecurity and exclusion to problems of crime, arguing that many forms of crime and deviance are psychological responses to the powerlessness and marginalisation experienced by the urban poor (see Hayward, 2004: 165, 197). Similarly, Hayward and Young (2004: 266), in moving the argument away from the individual towards the group, propose that 'it is through rule breaking that subcultural problems attempt solution'. In other words, forms of crime and deviance are the visible signals of deep-seated collective problems: criminals learn to 'break rules' in the context of specific subcultures which latter arise precisely as responses to the wider collective problems. In this way, Hayward and Young attempt to connect the (individual) feelings of powerlessness and exclusion to the (collective) subcultural styles, codes and values that feature so centrally in the work of Ferrell, Lyng and others.

There is no doubt that cultural criminology represents an exciting and politically charged arena of criminological research and theory. In some senses, it represents a branch of **critical criminology** in so far as it attempts to link the world of the deviant to the large-scale social, economic and political pressures faced by the urban poor in contemporary society. On the other hand, there remain some serious questions about the extent to which notions of 'subculture', 'subversion' or 'transgression' provide adequate reference points for explaining criminal and deviant behaviour.

First, there is the question of what is meant by 'culture' in cultural criminology. The question arises because it is common for cultural criminologists to operate with more than one concept of culture simultaneously. So, for example, Ferrell (1996) and Presdee (2000) use different meanings of culture depending on which groups of people they are describing. The '(sub)culture' of the deviant and criminal groups is described in terms of the creativity, skill and activities of their members – the 'minute-by-minute creation of our own realities', as Presdee puts it (Presdee, 2000: 21). So-called 'mainstream' culture, on the other hand, is described in terms of false ideas, vested interests and moral panics: the 'closure of language', subservience to a 'super-controlled consumer society' (ibid.: 136, 162) where ordinary (non-deviant) citizens behave like cultural sheep whose values, codes and styles are manipulated, distorted and directed by powerful groups (Ferrell, 1996: 134, 176). The obvious question that arises in this context is: how have the deviants (or the cultural criminologists, for that matter) managed to escape the suffocating power of mainstream culture either in order to challenge it (the deviants) or reflect critically upon it (the cultural criminologists)?

Second, and closely related, if the explanation for crime *is* to be found in subcultural responses to problems of exclusion, marginalisation, and so on, then how does cultural criminology explain the generality of crime? Corporate crimes, state crimes, environmental crimes, domestic abuse, video and audio piracy, motoring offences, bribery, fraud and forgery and an extensive list of everyday deviant behaviours cannot be explained solely in terms of subcultural contradictions or the experience of exclusion. Moreover, the very normality of contemporary society rests on criminal and otherwise harmful foundations: illegal logging and wildlife trading, people smuggling and trafficking, toxic-waste shipments and dumping, industrial espionage, land-theft, illegal fishing and hunting, exploitation of child labour, slavery, rape and sexual abuse and exploitation, and a host of other crimes and social harms, all continue apace as conditions for the supply of the raw materials and goods that developed nations take absolutely for granted. Thus, whilst cultural criminology vividly exposes some of the day-to-day realities of some deviant groups and the interactions between their deviance and wider social and cultural conditions, it struggles to provide a general theory of crime that could be applied to those wider social and cultural conditions.

Finally, as Colin Sumner (1994: 286) wittily noted about an earlier array of critical criminologies: is it always necessary to explain criminals and deviants in terms of external forces – exclusions, marginalisations, powerlessness, and so on? Should not criminology learn to 'recognize that some people become, for whatever reason, complete bastards'? Whatever the social, economic and cultural forces surrounding individuals and groups, it remains the case that some turn to (sometimes heinous) transgressions, some turn to (minor) illegal economies, and some get on with life trying to avoid causing harm to others, to be helpful and supportive to family, friends and community. How cultural criminology explains *this* wider context may determine its success, or otherwise, in explaining crime in contemporary society.

See also: **critical criminology; ideology; subcultural criminologies**

Further reading: Ferrell (1999); Ferrell *et al.* (2004); O'Brien (2005)

CULTURAL TRANSMISSION

Cultural transmission is a concept central to the criminological theories developed by **Chicago School** sociologists such as Shaw, McKay, and Sutherland. It denotes the inter-generational process through which norms and values supporting delinquent behaviour are reproduced. It was developed in response to the research finding that levels and patterns of delinquent behaviour remained remarkably constant across different Chicago neighbourhoods over long periods of time, despite significant changes in the social and ethnic characteristics of their inhabitants. Shaw and McKay argued that these patterns of delinquency were socially learned behaviours, and that older members of delinquent gangs played a key role in transmitting appropriate norms, values and skills to a younger generation of boys who would thus be brought into the world of rule-breaking behaviour.

See also: **Chicago School criminology; differential association**

Further reading: Shaw and McKay (1942)

CYBERCRIME

A major problem for the study of cybercrime is the absence of a consistent current definition, even amongst those law-enforcement agencies charged with tackling it. As Wall (2001: 2) notes, the term 'has no specific referent in law yet it is often used in political, criminal justice, media, public and academic discussions'. Rather than construing cybercrime as a single phenomenon, it is better to view the term as signalling a range of illicit activities whose common denominator is the central role played by networks of information and communication technologies (ICTs). Thomas and Loader (2000: 3) encapsulate this view in their definition of cybercrime as 'computer-mediated activities which are either illegal or considered illicit by certain parties and which can be conducted through global electronic networks'.

One common approach to classifying cybercrimes is through the relationship between the crime and the technology. In this classification a distinction can be made between 'computer-assisted crimes' and 'computer-focused crimes'. The first consists of those crimes that predate the internet but take on new forms in cyberspace – such as fraud, theft, money laundering, sexual harassment, pornography or hate speech. The second comprises crimes that emerged in conjunction with the internet and could not occur without it – such as hacking, viral attacks and website defacement. Whilst this is a useful general classification, it is somewhat limited for criminological purposes since it focuses on the technology rather than on the relationship between offenders and victims. A second way of classifying cybercrime is to subdivide it according to the object or target of offence. Thus, Wall (2001: 3–7) subdivides cybercrimes into four established legal categories:

- Cyber-trespass – crossing boundaries into other people's property and/or causing damage (e.g. hacking, viruses, defacement).
- Cyber-deceptions and thefts – stealing money or property (e.g. credit card fraud and intellectual property violations or 'piracy').
- Cyber-pornography – breaching laws on obscenity or decency.
- Cyberviolence – doing psychological harm to or inciting physical harm against others (e.g. hate speech, stalking).

In this system the first two categories comprise crimes against property, the third crimes against morality and the fourth crimes against the person.

An important part of the debate about cybercrime concerns precisely what is 'new' about it – especially in light of Wall's classification in terms of established legal categories. Of particular note in this debate is the question of whether cyberspace has generated new structures and contexts of social interaction that have changed the ways that offenders and victims encounter one another. Particular attention has been given to the ways that the internet transcends or collapses the constraints of space and time that limit interactions in the real world – by making possible near-instantaneous encounters between spatially distant actors. Such a transformation renders us vulnerable to an array of potential predators who can reach us almost instantaneously, untroubled by the barriers of physical distance. At the same time, the internet amplifies the range of victims that a potential offender can target. Cyberspace enables a single individual, with relatively low-level technological competence, to reach, interact and affect thousands of potential victims at the same time (the mass distribution of email scams and viruses being two clear examples). Moreover, the internet enables offenders more easily to mask their identities such that they can perpetrate their crimes anonymously – a feature that represents a significant challenge to those agencies charged with tracking them down.

A particular problem in grasping the global significance of cybercrime is the inherent difficulty of knowing how much of it there is. Whilst there are always general problems with accurately recording the extent of 'real world' crime, these problems are exacerbated when trying to measure cybercrime for several reasons. First, the relatively hidden nature of the internet may lead to crimes going unnoticed whilst lack of familiarity with the law may lead victims to be unaware that a given activity is illegal. Second, the limited allocation of criminal justice resources to cybercrime may result in the relevant authorities being unknown or unavailable for reporting purposes. Third, the global character of cybercrime may result in offenders and victims being located in different countries, with different laws, rendering police action difficult and time-consuming – a situation that can lead to the downgrading of internet crimes in favour of more manageable 'local' crimes. Moreover, some forms of cybercrime – such as the illegal downloading of video and audio material – have become so normalised amongst some population groups that they are all but ignored by the criminal justice system. Even acknowledging these difficulties in measuring cybercrime, it is clear that criminal activity via the internet is widespread and costly. Newman and Clarke (2003: 55) estimated that, worldwide, hacking alone cost business some $1.6 trillion in 2000; and the UK government estimates that the same crime costs British business £10 billion annually (Hinde, 2003: 90). Meanwhile, a credit card fraud is said to occur via the internet every 20 seconds (Everett, 2003: 1).

These various characteristics of cybercrime pose serious challenges both for criminal justice systems and for criminological explanations. Some of the difficulties for police and related agencies have already been discussed – including the spatial distances between offenders and victims, the different legal regimes that may operate in different geographical locations, and the relatively limited resources that are made available to combat cybercrimes. Added to these challenges is a shortage of expertise within the agencies themselves such that even when agencies are aware that such crimes are being perpetrated there may be a lack of technical competence to respond (Bequai, 1999: 17). Cybercrime also represents some challenges for criminology. In particular, many criminological theories have assumed, implicitly or explicitly, that crimes occur in places that have certain kinds of social, cultural and material characteristics that are conducive to offending behaviour. In such schools as **routine activity theories** and 'situational crime prevention', criminal justice efforts ought to be targeted at those features of those environments in order to discourage criminal behaviour. However, in cyberspace, it is difficult to classify environments on a continuum of 'more' and 'less' conducive to crime since the internet represents 'zero distance' between *all* environments. A further challenge emerges when considering that official statistics seem to show that crimes are overwhelmingly committed by those who are excluded, marginalised and of low social and market skills. However, cybercrimes require at least some measure of technological sophistication – as well as access to the resources to purchase, set up and operate a computer. Since those who are most socially marginalised have *least* access to these technologies and skills it may be that criminologists will need to revisit the use of concepts of exclusion and marginalisation in their explanations of offending behaviour.

See also: **identity; intellectual property crime; new media**

Further reading: Wall (2001); Yar (2006)

DEVELOPMENTAL CRIMINOLOGY

Developmental criminology, and its sister paradigm 'life-course criminology', are important, and relatively recent, strands of the criminological concern with criminal careers. Almost exclusively quantitative in focus, the approach specialises in cohort studies in order to map the deviant paths taken by individuals and groups over time. According to Le Blanc and Loeber (1998) the key insight of developmental criminology is that whilst engagement in deviant and criminal acts varies over time the propensity to deviance remains stable. What criminologists need to study, therefore, are the underlying or primary developmental processes of offending behaviour in order to make recommendations for appropriate interventions to prevent, or curtail it or facilitate its cessation. In this regard, developmental criminologists are interested in the processes of activation (the initiation of deviant activity), aggravation (the exacerbation of deviant behaviour) and desistance (the discontinuation of deviant behaviour).

This broad agenda means that criminologists working in this field take a view of criminal behaviour as being symptomatic of larger behavioural and attitudinal problems, arguing that the propensity to deviance is formed in childhood and persists throughout the individual's life. The antisocial child, remarks Farrington (2002: 658), 'tends to become the anti-social teenager and then the anti-social adult, just as the anti-social adult then tends to produce another anti-social child'. Thus, developmental/life-course criminology views crime as a series of trajectories followed by antisocial individuals 'from childhood to old age', as the subtitle of Sampson and Laub's (2005) edited collection puts it. In turn, this view of crime encourages the search for protective factors that might prevent the initial onset of antisocial tendencies or minimise their aggravation once they have been acquired.

Psychological research appears to demonstrate that infants who show irritability, heightened reactions to novel experiences and/or who are difficult to soothe (amongst other problematic characteristics) are more likely during childhood to have difficulty forming peer friendships, may engage in bullying or be bullied, may be destructive and/or have learning problems. In turn, these factors correlate positively in adolescence with smoking and drug-taking behaviour, violence, preference for delinquent peer groups, and other antisocial behaviours. Developmental criminologists add to these observations a range of intervening 'risk factors' that strongly correlate with the onset and exacerbation of criminal behaviour. These include factors associated with the family, neighbourhood, school and peer group. For example, individuals are more at **risk** of engaging in criminal and deviant behaviour if they come from 'broken' families, poor neighbourhoods and neighbourhoods with low levels of communal contact, if they attend low achieving and/or overcrowded schools and if they associate with delinquent peer groups (see Wikström *et al.*, 1995; Farrington and Loeber, 1999).

In addition to these factors, developmental criminologists are also interested in the impact of life-course transitions – such as leaving school or home, getting married or divorced, moving home or even receiving a conviction. Of particular interest is not the simple fact of these transitions but their duration and intensity for the individual. Obviously not everyone is persuaded to engage in or desist from criminal activities as a consequence of these transitions, so the goal for developmental criminology is to grasp their particular impact on individuals as well as their general impact across populations. Some life transitions (such as marriage and childbirth) generally appear to correlate with a diminution in criminal behaviour. Others, notably receiving a conviction, appear to correlate with an increase in such behaviour.

The general outlook of developmental criminology can be summed up as the view that crime is a self-perpetuating cycle. An individual's lack of resources and marketable skills means that legitimate opportunities are scarce whilst the desire to acquire material and status rewards remains. Add to this mix a dose of inadequate parenting and a fragmented community environment and both the material and moral inhibitors to criminal behaviour are in short supply. Hence, the proposed solutions tend to revolve around parental support and training, dedicated school programmes to provide low-achieving children with increased interpersonal and academic skills, and community partnership projects – not only to enable early identification of at-risk individuals but also to provide channels through which public services can reach those most in need of them (see Hawkins and Catalano, 1992).

Developmental criminology's highly pragmatic approach to the crimes of the poor seeks to derive policy recommendations from close investigation of the available data on crime and the life course. The approach is currently best suited to retrospective analysis – given an adult population there are strong correlations between those who have engaged in deviant and criminal behaviours and the various risk factors identified by developmental criminologists. Currently, however, it remains very difficult to predict the impact of those risk factors prospectively – given a new-born population developmental criminology's ability to predict which risk factors will impinge on which individuals and which of these in turn will engage in deviant and criminal behaviour is poor. This is not to detract from its achievements; for, clearly, the early intervention studies show that long-term benefits can be derived from focused family and school programmes based on the risk factors identified in retrospective analyses (see Farrington, 2002: 683–89). Yet the goals of providing better schools, better skills training, support for poor parents and fragmented communities, and so on, are shared by many criminologists for whom individual risk factors are not the primary criminological concern. Certainly, if developmental criminology is to become a general theory of crime it needs to consider a much broader range of issues than the mundane crimes of poor male youths. Since many corporate criminals display none of the risk factors identified in developmental criminology it must be asked whether these are actually of any relevance at all in explaining criminal behaviour in general. Moreover, there are many forms of behaviour that once were considered highly deviant or criminal (such as homosexuality or, historically, Catholicism in Protestant England) that could easily be explained in developmental criminology's terms yet which, today, are legal, openly practised and largely unnoticed. Contrariwise, there are behaviours that once were considered normal and in no need of explanation (such as smoking, for example) that are now frowned upon, criminalised in certain circumstances and associated with a range of 'antisocial' risk factors that characterise deviant and criminal lifestyles. In a world where the behavioural goalposts are constantly moving, today's antisocial risk factor may be tomorrow's transparent normality, and vice-versa.

See also: **criminal careers**

Further reading: Farrington (2002); Sampson and Laub (2005)

DEVIANCE AMPLIFICATION

A concept developed by the labelling theorist Leslie Wilkins. Wilkins used the concept to denote a social process in which an initial minor act of rule-breaking could result in a more entrenched and serious commitment to deviance through the application of stigmatising labels. Far from curtailing the behaviour that society deems undesirable, labelling might have the opposite effect as the labelled individuals react against their stigmatisation by further investing in the behaviour in question, which will lead to even more strenuous condemnation, and so on. The concept was subsequently used by criminologists such as Jock Young to explore how it was that relatively minor instances of criminal conduct (e.g. marijuana use) came to constitute a major social problem.

See also: **criminal careers; labelling perspectives**

Further reading: Wilkins (1964); Young (1971)

DIFFERENTIAL ASSOCIATION

A concept developed by **Chicago School** sociologist Edwin Sutherland. Building on the earlier work of Shaw and McKay, Sutherland examined the ways in which individuals' relationship to particular social groups or environments shaped their values and behaviour. However, while Shaw and McKay saw the social world of delinquents as *socially disorganised* (lacking coherent norms that could regulate behaviour) Sutherland disagreed. Instead he suggested that delinquency was the result of an individual's association with peers through whom the values and techniques of rule-breaking were learned and reinforced. The key difference between delinquent and non-delinquent youth was their different patterns of association with others; those who associated with delinquents were considerably more likely themselves to be drawn into unlawful and disruptive behaviour. Sutherland's perspective has enabled criminologists to examine the ways in which crime is supported as a normal and appropriate behaviour in the specific cultural contexts of particular groups. Although originally oriented to the analysis of juvenile delinquency, the concept has also been applied by Sutherland and others to examine other forms of offending, such as **white-collar crime**.

See also: **Chicago School criminology; cultural transmission; white-collar crime**

Further reading: Sutherland (1947)

DISCOURSE

In common usage 'discourse' refers to verbal expression or writing or a lengthy dissertation on a given topic – such as a 'discourse on free speech'. In linguistics and the social sciences, however, the term has several more specialised meanings. In linguistics, discourse refers to language structures above the level of the sentence – it is possible, for example, to analyse the opening and closing 'moves' in a conversation or to investigate how several sentences are used to make a 'promise' or a 'threat', and so on. Alternatively, discourse is also used to denote groups of statements that define the kind of speech or writing being analysed – such as 'legal' or 'medical' discourse, or 'racist' or 'ageist' discourse, and so on. In the social sciences and some critical literary approaches, discourse refers to the limits of permissible or acceptable speech: to the ways that language, and the meanings it conveys, are constrained by institutional and moral pressures. In Michel Foucault's approach discourses are methods for constituting knowledge as well as the relations of power that make knowledges legitimate or illegitimate. What these more specialised definitions have in common is the argument that discourses are not purely phenomena of language, they are intrinsically social and political: the right to speak and write, what it is permissible to say, whose speech and writing will be taken seriously, what counts as 'true' and 'false', and so on, are determined by social status and the authority of social institutions. In consequence, all speech and writing about the world is fundamentally political and the subject and vehicle of often hostile confrontation – classic examples being the conflict between religion and science over the character of the physical world (see Porter, 2000; for an indication of the continuing salience of this conflict see Dawkins, 2006) and the continuing struggle by feminists to ensure that women's speech and writing is taken seriously in criminology (see Naffine, 1997).

See also: **hegemony; ideology**

DRUG CRIME

In the popular imagination there is a direct association between drugs and crime – an association that is buttressed by the pronouncements of politicians as well as some academic researchers. The association is most often expressed through the view that drug use leads to crime because it lowers inhibitions, creates a need for users to obtain money to purchase drugs and distances them from the normal values and structures of the wider society. Goldstein (1985) summed up these associations in three categories: psycho-pharmacological, economic compulsive and systemic. The psycho-pharmacological category covers the impact of drugs on the brain; the economic compulsive category covers the ways that drug-dependence fuels acquisitive crime to feed a habit; the systemic category covers the ways that violent, corrupt and criminal organisations emerge to control the supply and distribution of drugs.

Those who favour strict controls over illegal drugs emphasise their psycho-pharmacological effects. It has been claimed that psychoactive drugs can affect metabolism, mood and cognition and through these effects lead to increased acquisitive and violent crime (see Amen *et al.*, 1997; Lavine, 1997). In this case, there is said to be a direct connection between the physical and psychological effect of drug use and the (criminal) behaviour of the drug user. Whilst it seems clear that illicit drug use is associated with crime it currently remains unclear precisely how a drug's psycho-pharmacological effects lead to specific criminal outcomes. The debate about drugs and violence tends to be concentrated around cocaine use, whilst the debate around drugs and acquisitive crime is most often conducted around heroin use. Meanwhile, the clearest link between drug use and violence has been established in relation to a legal and widespread drug – alcohol – rather than the illicit substances that have dominated the debate (see Rastrick *et al.*, 1999).

The most common argument about the link between drugs and crime has been to suggest that the cost of a drug habit compels the user to commit acquisitive crimes. According to the UK Home Office:

> The links between drug use and crime are clearly established. In fact, around three-quarters of crack and heroin users claim they commit crime to feed their habit.
>
> (Home Office, 2007b)

Meanwhile, the charity Drugscope (2004) notes that 'Examples of users needing £15,000 to £30,000 a year to fund drug habits have often been given' – a figure that adds up to an enormous amount of burglaries and thefts. This economic compulsive link – which is not without some substance – has been made on numerous occasions (see the claim in the parliamentary debate that 'the greatest cause of crime ... is drugs', in Commons Hansard Debates, 2004) and sometimes even more dramatically. A team of American psychologists (Deitch *et al.*, 2000) suggested that '60 per cent to 80 per cent of all crime is drug related'. These figures are highly dubious and are contested by other research. A Canadian team of researchers (Pernanen *et al.*, 2002) studied the links between drugs and crime amongst a population of prison inmates and found that only 10–15 per cent of their criminal behaviour was attributed to their drug use. But no matter which set of estimates is used there remains a difference between claiming a *correlation* between drug use and crime and proposing that drug use *causes* crime. Research has suggested that rather than drug use causing crime, criminal activity often predates drug use and that, in fact, by providing extra income in the first place it may be that acquisitive crime enables the offender to begin to engage in illicit drug use (Pudney, 2002).

At the systemic level it has been noted that there are connections between local drug markets and inner-city violence (Inciardi, 1999). Since such markets are illegal and highly competitive, those who would control supply and distribution tend to become involved in violence and to form cartels and conspiracies – which might also include 'legitimate' participants including police and security agencies as well as front companies. But these kinds of activities are more common at the higher levels of control and organisation where the profits to be made, and thus the stakes to be played for, are very high (see Chambliss, 1989). At the local level of the street dealer, profits are small, the market is very fragmented and there are multiple operators supplying different drug commodities (Hobbs, 1995). Violence still features in these contexts but not on the scale imagined by the popular press and some of these markets (such as those for cannabis and non-prescribed 'legal' drugs) are markedly less violent than others (such as the market for cocaine). However, there is no easy correlation between rates of drug use and rates of crime. Studies in America (Martin *et al.*, 2004) and in Europe (Van Kesteren *et al.*, 2000) found no link between overall levels of crime and overall levels of problematic drug use. Possibly the greatest harms generated by illegal drug markets are not in the consumer countries at all but in the producer countries – Afghanistan (heroin) or Colombia (cocaine), for example – where the 'war on drugs' is one more site of conflict in a much wider context of civil strife that sucks in criminals, politicians, armed forces, mercenaries, terrorist groups and innocent civilians alike.

Some have argued that it is not the illicit drugs themselves that cause the most problems but their prohibition. The most commonly cited example is the prohibition on cannabis use – a prohibition that has ensnared thousands upon thousands of young people in the nets of the criminal justice system, criminalising them for an activity that is widely seen as a recreational drug of choice. Not only has this made criminals of uncountable numbers of otherwise law-abiding citizens, it has also consumed vast criminal justice resources that might, some suggest, be better expended elsewhere (see Sharp *et al.*, 2001). On a wider scale, in spite of the UK Home Office's claims for the success of its Drug Interventions Programme, there is no independent evidence that drug-enforcement policies have had much impact on use. Consequently, legalisation, rather than prohibition, is proposed as a more effective solution (see Graham, 1991). There is, however, the possibility that legalising proscribed drugs might lead to more widespread use and bring yet more social problems in its wake (Inciardi and McBride, 1989).

As the debate about the link between drugs and crime rumbles on, possibly the most criminogenic drug available continues to enjoy popular support and its price has fallen remarkably across the past decade. Alcohol is cheap, legal and readily available, yet it is clearly associated with a huge range of social problems – including motoring fatalities and other accidents, violence and sexual offences as well as (apparently increasing) health problems, family breakdown and family violence. As in the case of prohibited drugs it is not entirely clear whether alcohol is itself a cause of crime rather than merely correlated with it, but its case does represent neatly the confused state of the debate about, and policies on, drug crime.

See also: **family crime; organised crime; terrorism; violent crime**

Further reading: Parker *et al.* (1998); Stevens *et al.* (2005)

DURKHEIMIAN CRIMINOLOGY

The French sociologist Emile Durkheim (1858–1917) is esteemed as one of the 'founding fathers' of the discipline. Over the course of his writings he offered many highly original sociological insights into the phenomena of crime, law and punishment, and these subsequently exerted a great influence over the development of criminology. To better understand his contribution to the analysis of crime and deviance, we will begin by outlining both the wider social context in which Durkheim was writing, and some basic elements of his sociological perspective.

The nineteenth century saw a period of rapid and turbulent change in France. The onset of modernisation brought with it a transition from a rural and agricultural society to one that was increasingly urban and industrial in character. The emergence of new class structures and divisions became manifest in bitter political conflicts, such as the 1848 Paris Commune, which saw the brutal suppression of socialist revolutionaries by the French authorities. The nation was further destabilised by its defeat in the Franco-Prussian War of the 1870s, which served to exacerbate further the financial and social hardships of the working class, such as the conscripted soldiers who returned to civilian life only to find unemployment and hardship. This potent cocktail of chaotic change and instability served to merely fuel the persecution of minority groups who were blamed by the nationalist and Catholic political right for France's ills. This problem was exemplified in the Dreyfus Affair (1894), in which a Jewish army officer was unjustly put on trial for treason, a case of anti-Semitism that became an international cause célèbre. Durkheim, a secularist and socialist, and himself of Jewish origin, was galvanised by such events, and they clearly informed his sociological project. The basic questions he sought to address consequently related to the problems of *social order* and *disorder* – how do societies achieve stability and harmony? How do they maintain such stability in times of rapid change? What negative consequences flow from the disruptions that change brings? And how could the demands of order and solidarity be reconciled with a respect for individual freedoms and rights in a forward-looking and fair society? It is in the course of answering these questions that Durkheim developed his insights into crime, law and punishment.

In his first major work, *The Division of Labour in Society* (1984), Durkheim argued that in order to maintain and reproduce themselves, all societies needed mechanisms that would create stability and maintain the social bond between their members. He went on to suggest that crucial for such stability was what he called the 'collective consciousness' of a society. By this term he meant the totality of shared beliefs, values and norms of behaviour that cemented individuals' commitment to the wider social group (*solidarity*) and which served to regulate their everyday conduct and exchanges with each other. He hypothesised that different social forms would have correspondingly different ways in which such regulation would take shape. He developed what is now a well-known and widely used distinction between what he called *mechanical solidarity* and *organic solidarity*. Mechanical solidarity was to be found in largely pre-modern and small-scale agricultural societies. In such societies, individuals were characterised by *similarity* – they all participated similarly in the system of production (tilling, planting, herding, and so on), and were part of largely self-sufficient small communities. Because of the close and immediate interdependence within such groups, beliefs emerged which stressed the importance of communal interests over and above those of individuals. Clearly defined norms of behaviour would be passed down across generations in the form of tradition, and clear moral directions would be prescribed by *religion*. Individuals would be closely regulated within the community, and deviations would be unwelcome and likely to incur severe sanctions. However, this balance was undermined by the transition to a mass, urban and industrial society. Individuals became increasingly to be characterised not by similarity but by *difference*, as each took on very specific roles within an increasingly differentiated *division of labour*. Intimacy and familiarity gave way to anonymity in the populous spaces of the city. In such a context, the old mechanisms of solidarity could no longer effectively perform the function of regulation, and consequently there emerged a problem of *anomie* or normlessness. Lacking binding conventions and guidelines for behaviour, there was a greater likelihood that individuals would engage in *deviant behaviour* (as explored in Durkheim's famous study of *Suicide* (1897, see Durkheim 1970)). However, Durkheim believed and hoped that eventually a new mode of social solidarity would emerge, one that corresponded to the values of individual rights and mutual tolerance. Until such time as this happened, society was vulnerable to an array of social problems associated with a deficit in moral regulation.

While Durkheim himself did not mobilise anomie to explain rising crime, the concept has been appropriated and adapted by subsequent criminologists and sociologists for just this purpose. The most influential use of Durkheim's concept is that developed by the American sociologist Robert K. Merton (1910–2003). In 'Social Structure and Anomie' (1938), Merton offered an original reinterpretation of the concept, and mobilised it to account for trends and patterns of crime in American society. For Durkheim, anomie comprised a deficit of moral regulation in the form of insufficiently strong and binding norms of behaviour. Merton, however, split the notion of normative regulation into two distinct parts. He proposed that all societies have, first, socially agreed norms that define the *goals* for which their members should properly strive. Thus in the United States of the 1930s, Merton pointed to the so-called 'American Dream' of wealth, material prosperity and status. Through this 'dream' American society defined its citizens' aims and ambitions, and thereby directed their strivings in a socially sanctioned direction. Second, Merton argued that in addition to the socially approved goals, all societies would stipulate approved and sanctioned *means* through which these goals could be legitimately achieved. To take the example again of Merton's America, the American Dream was to be achieved through individual hard work, self-improvement, education and entrepreneurship. Through the combination of these two elements, society was able to direct the behaviour of individuals in an ordered way. However, Merton argued that a situation could arise where there existed a disjunction between these two elements, especially where a society pressed its members to achieve certain goals while at the same time denying some of them the access to the approved means for doing so. This situation Merton understood as anomic, and he argued that it would lead individuals into a range of *adaptations* in order to cope with this contradictory situation. The most interesting of these adaptations, from a criminological point of view, was what Merton dubbed *innovation*. This occurred when individuals committed to pursuing socially approved goals found themselves blocked from accessing the approved means, which might lead them to adopt alternative, illegitimate means to realise their frustrated ambitions. To take again the example of the United States in the 1930s, the criminal behaviour of infamous gangsters such as Al Capone could be accounted for in this way – Capone was committed to achieving the dream of success, wealth and status, yet as a poor Italian immigrant was denied access to the means he would need to do so (such as education and the financial resources needed to access it). Consequently, Capone and others like him chose to pursue such ambitions by the only means available to them, namely crime, extortion and violence. Merton's interpretation of anomie thus pointed to the ways in which the dysfunctional normative regulation of society could directly inspire its members to resort to crime. This interpretation became very influential in studies of crime and deviance. For example, Albert Cohen in his study *Delinquent Boys* (1955) claimed that young working-class males turned to delinquent behaviour because they found themselves unable to achieve societal recognition on the terms defined for and by the prosperous middle classes – this situation he termed *status frustration*. Another more recent use of Merton's analysis is that found in the work of left **realist** criminologists such as Jock Young. Young (1999) claims that in contemporary consumerist society, with its cultural emphasis on material goods and lifestyle, the working classes feel themselves relatively deprived, not having the resources needed to acquire the goods that relentless media marketing tells them they 'must have' in order to be popular, attractive and satisfied. This in turn causes resentment and frustration, and a turn to criminal behaviour to satisfy the wants and desires created by consumer culture.

Durkheim was a renowned sociological *functionalist*, in that he believed social institutions existed and persisted not by chance but because they performed some valuable function in maintaining a society. This insight, alongside his views on the role of the collective consciousness in producing order, was central to his analysis of crime and punishment. He begins by noting that crime is in fact a normal feature of all societies, insofar as we find that all societies sanction certain types of behaviour and make them subject to denunciation and punishment. While the content may change (different societies at various times will consider widely varying actions as criminal), the existence of something called crime will be a constant feature everywhere. The existence of crime, he felt, was not only inescapable but actually useful and functional for society, provided it did not exceed a certain level. This he based upon an understanding of the relationship between crime and the collective consciousness. Crime, he argued, consists of acts that offend against the collectively held **norms** of a society. It is because these acts breach the most basic normative commitments of a social group that they elicit condemnation and a desire to punish the offender. When a crime is committed, it activates within society and its members a passion for **punishment**, a sense that something 'sacred' has been 'defiled'. The crime serves to remind society of the fundamental norms and values that it holds to (the collective consciousness) and the act of punishment helps to cement individuals into the moral order, thereby by helping to sustain social solidarity. In the event that crime were to disappear altogether from society, this would leave no occasion for moral outrage, and so deny society a valuable mechanism for uniting its members in accordance with shared values and sentiments. A second basis for judging crime as functional is that it helps to generate social change. In a society in which no one deviates, the norms of behaviour would never be challenged, and the society would never evolve or progress. Crimes sometimes serve to challenge the existing order, making it possible to change rules that are in fact unfair or unjust. A famous example given by Durkheim is that of the ancient Athenian philosopher Socrates, who was condemned to death for the 'crime' of corrupting the morals of Athens' youth by teaching them to exercise their reason and inquire critically about what society believed at that time to be true. By Athenian eyes, Socrates was a criminal, yet his determination to offend helped to promote the idea of free and rational inquiry which later inspired new and revolutionary understandings of the world and humans' place within it.

Some of the above insights have been incorporated into contemporary criminological theories. For Durkheim, human beings have potentially infinite desires, so shared normative prohibitions are crucial for constraining behaviour and limiting deviance. This idea is taken up by **social control** theorists who view the strength of individuals' commitment to societal norms as an essential force in insulating them from the temptation to deviate. Similarly, communitarian perspectives, such as John Braithwaite's *reintegrative shaming*, view collective moral disapproval as a powerful instrument for moral direction, and see communal denunciation and shaming of offenders as valuable in deterring them from further criminal activity. In sum, then, we see the many ways in which Durkheim's writings on crime and deviance continue to shape criminological thinking more than a century after they first appeared.

See also: **punishment; social control; subcultural criminologies**

Further reading: Durkheim (1970, 1984); Merton (1938)

ENVIRONMENTAL CRIME

The term 'environmental crime' is inherently confusing, since it refers to a very wide range of harms committed by individuals, groups, corporations and states. The (UK) Home Office, for example, notes that this kind of crime 'has a huge impact on our communities' but restricts its definition to forms of antisocial behaviour – notably, fly-tipping, littering, graffiti writing and vandalism. The (UK) Environment Agency's definition, on the other hand, includes pollution incidents, waste crimes, wildlife crimes and fishing offences. Hayman and Brack (2002), meanwhile, define *international* environmental crime as a form of 'enterprise crime' which 'involves the production and/or distribution of goods and services that are illegal by their classification' and produce an extensive list of offences including illegal logging, waste dumping and wildlife trading, biopiracy, trade in persistent organic pollutants and fuel smuggling. Others, such as Walters (2006: 41), seek to include the ways that corporations 'exercise and exploit law, international relations and power for political and economic gain' and even actively violate international conventions on environmental protection in pursuit of profitable ends. Nigel South (1998: 213) has pushed the definition even further, arguing that, in our wasteful over-exploitation of the earth's resources, 'the most serious crime that humanity is currently committing is against itself and future generations'. Here, the 'environmental criminal' is not an individual, group or corporation but all of humanity.

The intrinsic uncertainty around the meaning of 'environmental crime' has resulted in a complex – and equally wide-ranging – debate about the 'greening' of criminology (Lynch, 1990). That is, whether or not criminology has the conceptual and analytical tools to contribute to our understanding of environmental problems and solutions to them. Some, such as Lynch and Stretsky (2003), are optimistic about the potential of criminology's existing theories and methods for engaging with environmental problems. Others, such as Halsey (2004), are more sceptical about this potential, arguing that contemporary criminology has no adequate languages in which to theorise environmental entities – 'nature' and non-human 'species', for example – and that criminology (green or otherwise) is invariably anthropocentric (that is, it places humans at the centre of the universe). This debate is likely to continue for some time and shows no sign of clarifying what is unique or different about 'environmental crime' compared to other crimes. Moreover, 'green' criminologists are continuing to broaden their horizons even further by turning their attention to 'speciesism': the assumed human 'right' to exploit non-human animals for pleasure or profit (see Beirne and South, 2006; Sollund, 2008).

Notwithstanding the lively debate about criminology's green credentials, the increasing awareness of environmental problems has inevitably had an impact on criminological research. The impact can be divided into three sets of research issues. First, there is awareness of the environmentally destructive consequences of corporate malpractice. Second, there has been research into the ecological consequences of crime and criminal justice measures. Third, there is some interest in the criminogenic consequences of environmental change.

Early examples of criminological interest in environmental crimes include the Love Canal scandal and the Bhopal disaster. Love Canal is an area close to Niagara Falls in the USA. It takes its name from an old waterway that over several years was used by the Hooker chemical company as a dump site for its toxic wastes. The canal was covered over in the early 1950s and the land sold off to a developer. On the land were built a school and houses into which families moved with no knowledge of what lay beneath the ground. During the 1970s it became clear that the chemicals were seeping through the ground and contaminating the residents, although studies of their effects proved inconclusive. In 1978 a state of emergency was declared at the site and hundreds of families were evacuated. The incident prompted the establishment of the 'superfund' for environmental repair and led to an awareness that the vast bulk of America's toxic wastes were being disposed of without due care (see Szasz, 1994). Eventually, in 1995, the company responsible (whose name had changed to Occidental Petroleum) was sued for $129 million by the United States Environmental Protection Agency.

The Bhopal disaster refers to a massive explosion at the Union Carbide chemical plant in India in 1984. It is perhaps the worst industrial disaster of all time: as many as 20,000 people may have died and more than 100,000 people continue to suffer the after-effects of the explosion. The immediate cause of the explosion was the leakage of water into a holding tank containing methyl isocyanide. The mixture was highly volatile, raised the temperature inside the tank rapidly, and a build-up of toxic gas developed that sought release in the most tragic manner. However, the underlying causes of the accident were directly under the company's control. They included poor staff training, badly maintained equipment and plant, staff shortages, inadequate supervision, continuing underinvestment, and badly designed control systems in an extensive catalogue of glaring corporate failure. Moreover, the company had been warned that such a disaster could take place on several occasions and the plant had such a history of accidents that, it was claimed, the warning siren was turned off. In spite of the fact that tens of thousands of people were poisoned and that a very large area around Bhopal remains heavily contaminated with slow-release poisons, no senior member of the company has been convicted of any crime, although some employees at Union Carbide India continue to face legal proceedings.

Whether these incidents should be understood as uniquely 'environmental', rather than 'corporate', crimes is a matter of debate but they do indicate the extensive human and ecological consequences of corporate malfeasance. Following on from these particular examples, there has emerged an extensive literature on the environmental impacts of the legal, quasi-legal and illegal transport, trading and dumping of toxic wastes and the huge profits that can be derived from poisoning the environment (see Block and Scarpatti, 1985; Moyers, 1990).

More recent research has pointed to the impact of crime and criminal justice measures on the natural environment. Rosa Del Olmo (1998) examined the ecological impact of the cultivation of drug crops in Latin America *and* the impact of crop-eradication policies. She points out that the mass cultivation of coca in Colombia, for example, has destroyed thousands of hectares of rainforest; led to significant soil erosion; contaminated water resources with pesticides, fertilisers and chemicals used in the preparation of coca paste; and destroyed rare fauna and flora. Furthermore, the cultivation of poppy plants has led to the further 'deforestation of approximately 50,000 hectares of highland jungle in the Andes' (ibid.: 272). Efforts on the part of drug-enforcement bodies to eradicate the plantations are similarly environmentally degrading. Although there are several ways of destroying crops – including burning – the most common method is by aerial fumigation using a variety of herbicides. These herbicides include paraquat, glyphosphate (a chemical cousin of Agent Orange used for defoliation during the Vietnam War) and dichlorophenoxyacetate. Thousands of tons of these chemicals have been deposited on Latin American soil as part of the 'war on drugs' initiative led by the USA, and continue to contaminate vast areas of precious forest. Yet drug cultivation has actually *increased* since the eradication programme began, calling into question the value of poisoning Latin American soil in an apparently futile effort to interrupt drug production.

Finally, there has also been some research into the crime and justice consequences of environmental degradation, with special reference to the impact of resource scarcity that accompanies despoiled environments. John Crank (2003) argued that increasing resource shortages – especially water, fertile land and fuel – are already, directly and indirectly, generating strife within and between societies. Crank cites the example of water shortages in Oregon (USA) that are leading to conflicts between ranchers, farmers and indigenous groups. To this US example can be added conflicts around Sudan and the Horn of Africa – areas that have been particularly hard hit by climate change: as a whole Africa has warmed by around 0.7 degrees across the twentieth century whilst the Sahel has witnessed a 25 per cent decrease in annual rainfall in the last thirty years alone. Climate change also appears to be one of the causes of migration both within and between continents – a process that puts strain on the social and economic systems of the destination regions and can lead to further conflict.

As can be seen, recognition of environmental issues in criminology has led to some complex rethinking of the ecological consequences of crime and criminal justice activity and, conversely, the criminogenic consequences of ecological degradation.

See also: **corporate crime; green criminology; state crime**

Further reading: Pearce and Tombs (1998); South and Beirne (2006)

ENVIRONMENTAL CRIMINOLOGY

Environmental criminology is the study of the connections between space, place and crime and, in particular, is concerned with the *spatial patterning* of crime and the *spatial distribution* of criminality. These foci are rooted in the seemingly unambiguous fact that crime is not randomly distributed but is geographically concentrated in specific places – notably in particular urban areas – and that offenders are similarly concentrated in identifiable urban districts. Environmental criminology takes a positivist approach to the study of crime in that it seeks to use scientific methods to provide descriptive data on the incidence of crime and infer causal factors derived from those data.

Environmental criminology has a long history – the attempt to map crime rates and criminal residence originated in Europe in the nineteenth century under the influence of Adolphe Quételet in Belgium, Alexander von Oettingen in Germany and, to a lesser extent, Henry Mayhew and Charles Booth in England. In many cases these surveys were not directed primarily towards understanding crime or criminals per se, but were part of larger efforts to achieve social reforms and improve the living conditions of the poor. The most influential and by far the most famous precursor to contemporary environmental criminology was work conducted by the **Chicago School** of Sociology and, especially, the work of Clifford Shaw and Henry McKay (1942). Shaw and McKay used Ernest Burgess' 'zonal model' of city development when they investigated patterns of residence of juvenile offenders. What their research appeared to show was that the causes of crime lay not in individual factors but in environmental factors. They argued that juveniles did not commit crimes because they were inherently immoral or intellectually inferior to their law-abiding peers. Rather, the causes of their criminality were to be found in the structure and culture of the communities in which they resided. In particular, offenders tended to reside in 'socially disorganised' communities characterised by transient populations, competing moral frameworks and an underdeveloped and unstable culture. Such socially disorganised areas – labelled the 'zone in transition' in Burgess' model – tended to be much less affluent than other city zones, but it was not the factor of poverty itself that encouraged crime. Rather, it was the lack of established and durable shared values that underpinned the tendency to criminality characteristic of the socially disorganised community.

The 'social disorganisation' thesis remained the dominant paradigm for explaining environmental influences on crime for over a quarter of a century and was not seriously challenged until the 1970s. Drawing on earlier work by Terence Morris (1957), Baldwin and Bottoms (1976) showed that whilst Shaw and McKay's work had been important in establishing a link between crime and environment, their particular model did not explain the distribution of crime or criminals in cities generally. The geographical data for Croydon and Sheffield in the UK did not support the thesis that offender residence correlated neatly with the 'zone in transition'. Instead, Baldwin and Bottoms drew attention to the role of the housing market – they noted that variations in property values and property types correlated positively with variations in offender residence rates (that is, the rate of offenders per head of population). Moreover, there is a difference between offender residence rates and area offence rates (that is, the rate of offences in any given area). Studies have shown that there is remarkable geographical variation in the rates for different kinds of crimes in different areas of cities. Wikström (1991) looked at data on violence in public, vandalism, vehicle crime, burglary and domestic violence for the city of Stockholm and found that different types of offences were committed in different areas of the city. At the same time, further detailed studies have shown that even *within* high crime areas for any given offence there is yet more variation – some parts of 'high crime' areas have very low levels of crime (see Sherman, 1995). Whilst, to a certain extent only, it remains true that many crimes are committed close to where offenders live (that is, crimes are commonly limited in space) some locations are more, and some less, likely to be the scene of crimes (that is, crimes are encouraged or discouraged by characteristics of place).

Not surprisingly, these (and many more) detailed research findings have persuaded some criminologists to try and expose what it is about the different areas that encourage or discourage different kinds of criminal activity and to ask whether crime can be 'designed out' of the urban landscape (see Clarke and Mayhew, 1980). Two kinds of practical effort, in particular, have been developed in the effort to use features of space and place to deter criminal activity. In the first, there has been an increasing willingness to recruit the professional insights of architects and urban planners to the task of crime prevention, inspired, importantly, by Jane Jacobs' (1961) *The Death and Life of Great American Cities*. The book drew attention to the association between high crime rates and the soulless design of tower block architecture, the community fragmentation that it engendered, the mono-functional character of the ghetto landscape and the absence of opportunities for pedestrian use of the neighbourhood environment.

Later work by the architect Oscar Newman (1972) drew attention to the ways that urban housing design failed to provide 'defensible space' for residents and provided opportunities for offenders to commit crimes undetected. The insights offered by Jacobs, Newman and later scholars were systematised into strategies for crime prevention through environmental design by Tim Crowe (see Crowe, 2000). The strategies included recommendations for increasing a neighbourhood's capacity for self-surveillance – by ensuring that windows overlook access points, ensuring that alleys and other through-routes are well lit, and supplementing these and other measures with the use of CCTV where appropriate. Other recommendations include paying attention to area entry and exit points to reduce opportunities to escape detection, using natural features (such as thorny bushes under windows) to deter opportunistic entry, encouraging communal use of public spaces (by providing appropriate seating and other amenities) to increase residents' visible presence. The intention behind these measures is to make the commission of crime more difficult and its detection more likely by using the design of urban housing as a front-line defence against criminal behaviour.

The second kind of practical effort has revolved largely around situational prevention measures designed to 'harden' the target of crime or 'soften' the motivation to perpetrate it. Situational crime prevention shares environmental criminology's overall goal of reducing criminal opportunities, but deepens the project by paying attention to a much larger range of situations than neighbourhood design. Situational measures can be grouped loosely under four headings:

- increasing the effort required to commit crime (such as fitting steering locks to cars or security locks on doors);
- increasing the risks associated with committing crime (such as fitting electronic tags to shopstore goods or introducing neighbourhood watch schemes);
- reducing the rewards associated with committing crime (such as the removal of coin meters from houses to reduce the rewards of burglary);
- removing the excuses for committing crime (such as introducing alcohol-free zones to reduce drunkenness in public).

More recently, situational-crime-prevention scholars have turned their attention to systems and products (see Clarke and Newman, 2005) – putting some distance between environmental criminology's exclusive concern with space and place and simultaneously pointing to some of the challenges facing environmental criminology's overall mission.

These challenges are nowhere more visible than in the separation of space from place in criminal activity. With the explosion in electronic systems and services – in particular mobile telephony and the World Wide Web – there is a decreasing association between crime and the urban environment. Crimes can now be perpetrated across international borders, in different time zones, in circumstances where the offender and the victim are not co-present. Redesigning urban housing estates may help to create defensible *physical* spaces but does nothing to create defensible *virtual* spaces. Moreover, many crimes are not at all attached to particular places in the same way as burglary or vandalism. International drugs and people trafficking, the trade in endangered species, the illegal global trade in dangerous chemicals, the use of legitimate financial services to launder the proceeds of illegal activities, for example, certainly occur in space but designing a physical environment to reduce the opportunities for their commission is effectively and practically impossible. At the same time, it is not clear what contribution environmental criminology might make to the problem of corporate crime or extensive tax evasion or the wilful and widespread breaching of health and safety regulations, for example. When these issues are put forward it becomes clear that 'environmental criminology' is really a misnomer: what environmental criminology addresses, by and large, is local (urban) crime in which the wider social, political and natural environment is merely a context through which to interpret local events. There is also something of a puzzle in some of the core claims of environmental criminology, namely: if urban improvements in one area lead to a reduction in crime and at the same time do not displace that crime to another area then why, with some variation, have crime rates continued to rise across more than two decades of environmental and situational interventions? There is no doubt that some kinds of crime can be reduced in some areas as a consequence of environmental and situational improvements but there is no indication, yet, that the principles and practices of environmental criminology might be effective on a societal, let alone global, scale.

None of these criticisms undermines the value of environmental interventions aimed at reducing the opportunities for crime at the local level, but they do suggest that environmental criminology lacks a coherent theory of the connections between crime and the environment. Indeed, its practitioners might well agree that building a systematic theory of the environment–crime nexus is not high on their agenda. The practice of environmental criminology relies, to all intents and purposes, on opportunity theory and **routine activity theories**, and builds on these a series of insights into urban crime. But in doing so the approach focuses almost exclusively on the opportunities and routine activities of (local) offenders and victims. The routine activities of law-enforcement and related agencies, of 'moral entrepreneurs' or captains of industry, of politicians and circulation-desperate tabloid editors, do not enter the picture. Since the social environment of crime includes all of these, amongst other, crucial variables, there is perhaps a greater need for a general theory than environmental criminologists are currently willing to admit.

See also: **Chicago School criminology; positivist criminology; routine activity theories**

Further reading: Crowe (2000)

FAMILY CRIME

Family crime is a relatively new term used to denote a range of interpersonal offences that occur in the domestic context of the home and family. These can include domestic violence between spouses/partners; sexual, physical and emotional abuse of children; and violence, maltreatment and neglect of elders.

Historically, family crime has been largely ignored both within criminology and in the priorities of the criminal justice system, reflecting wider social sentiments about the 'sanctity' of the home and private life. It was not until the 1960s that the physical abuse of children became the object of sustained attention, followed by domestic violence in the 1970s, child sex abuse in the 1980s, and elder abuse in the 1990s. These changes were induced by a combination of activist agenda-setting (for example by the women's movement) and the revelation of the extent of hidden domestic crime by victimisation surveys. Walby and Allen (2004), for example, found there were an estimated 12.9 million incidents of non-sexual domestic violence against women, and 2.5 million incidents against men, in England and Wales over a 12-month period. Many such incidents involve *repeat victimisation*, with women each having been subject to an average of 20 assaults over the 12 months. In the area of child sexual abuse, some 4 per cent of under-16s in the UK are estimated to have been abused by a parent, carer or other relative. When we also factor in acts such as child and elder neglect, bullying and emotional harm, the family is revealed as a primary site of criminal victimisation, and far from the common vision of a safe haven from crime and danger. The increasing awareness of crimes within the home has been paralleled by the development of new laws, such as the criminalisation of rape within marriage and the tightening of definitions of bodily harm against children. Many police forces have also established specialist units dedicated to investigating family crime and supporting its victims.

See also: **crime data; sex crimes; violent crime**

Further reading: Mooney (2000); Payne (2005)

FEMINISM AND CRIMINOLOGY

According to official statistics, crimes are overwhelmingly committed by men. The predominance of men in criminal activity appears relatively stable over time and across space. For example, Heidensohn (2002: 494–96) notes that, in 1984, 16 per cent of known offenders in England and Wales were female. In 1999 the figure was just 17 per cent. In France, in the mid-1980s, a little under 19 per cent of known offenders were female, in Germany a little over 20 per cent and '[similar], or lower, shares can be found in the Netherlands and Scandinavia'; and there has been no great change in these ratios in the intervening period. Moreover, women are far less likely to commit predatory crimes of violence, burglary, or intimidation and far more likely to commit crimes involving handling stolen goods (which may well have been stolen by men). Around half of all women prisoners have been convicted of theft and handling charges; a high proportion of these women are considered vulnerable to self-harm and problems of mental illness. The peak age of offending for men lies between 17 and 18 years old, whilst for women the peak offending age is around 15 years old. The surprising consistency of these offending categories and the differences in male and female offending rates represents something of a conundrum for criminology: how do we explain gender differences in crime and criminal justice? Throughout the history of criminology there have appeared sporadic attempts to theorise the relationships between gender and crime, and these have taken several distinct forms.

Early positivist theories looked for the determining factors that caused a minority of women to abandon their normally 'passive' and 'subservient' roles and engage in criminal and/or salacious behaviour. Lombroso and Ferrero (1895) suggested a physiological basis for such behaviours, ascribing them to abnormal biological 'types'. As with men, women's deviance could be read or interpreted from the physiological characteristics they displayed. Thus, the detailed description of outward characteristics revealed maps of women's inner moral outlooks. In particular, deviant women were seen as being closer to men physiologically than they were to 'normal' women: they were said to have more body hair, a 'virile type of face' and a 'narrow or receding forehead', amongst other 'abnormalities'.

Whilst the particular attempt to relate physiology to deviant behaviour was soon discredited, the underlying idea that male and female criminality might be explained in biological terms has exerted a powerful force on the criminological imagination – partly because it invokes 'natural' differences between the sexes and dovetails with a range of related beliefs about men's and women's roles in society. Women, in these common-sense beliefs, are 'naturally' less aggressive, weaker, and more attuned to domestic and nurturing activities, whilst men are 'naturally' predatory, stronger, and more attuned to public and political engagement. Men's criminality, in these common-sense constructions, is really an extension of the more predatory and aggressive nature built into their biological make-up, whilst women's criminality is a deviation from their biological destiny.

Psychological theories took up the positivist challenge but moved the account in a rather different direction. In psychodynamic approaches, physiology remained significant but its importance was understood in terms of its impact on psychological drives and desires. Freud, for example, suggested that women's criminality – and its rarity compared to men's criminality – could be explained in terms of sexual neurosis. Criminal women were those who had failed to adjust, emotionally and cognitively, to the passive and receptive role determined for them by their lack of a penis. 'Normal' women seek approval and comfort from men, and this 'receptive' character simultaneously deters women from breaking (men's) criminal laws. 'Neurotic' women, whose desire to possess a penis overrides their natural submissiveness, seek to become more like men and it is this neurosis – the lack of adjustment to physiological and psychological reality – that explains women's criminality.

Sex-role theories link men's and women's involvement in crime to behaviours and characteristics that are partly rooted in biology but also deeply embedded in cultural traditions and social structures. In *The Unadjusted Girl*, W. I. Thomas (1923) suggested that women criminals were amoral seekers after excitement or new experience: they had failed to adjust to their passive, domestic roles and the 'cure' for female criminality lay in reforming the habits and values ingrained in the slum-dwelling classes. Thomas' views on women were actually ambiguous – he claimed that women's social inferiority was a consequence of male control of key institutions and, in particular, property. Nonetheless, for Thomas, women's criminality represents a failure of psychological adjustment to the dominant social norms and values surrounding gender.

The notion that traditions and social structures influence criminal behaviour was taken up by Adler (1975) and Simon (1975) to argue that as men's historical dominance diminished so women's criminality increased: in this case, women's liberation was seen as a cause of crime. Adler suggested that the women's movement of the late 1960s and early 1970s had been accompanied by 'dramatic' increases in women's involvement in criminal activities – including murder, robbery and corporate crime. Thus, the argument runs, the more women break into roles and environments once traditionally dominated by men, the more they adopt masculine values and behaviours and the more they are incorporated into the deviant, corrupt and criminal normality that is masculine society.

Each of these approaches – including that of Adler – takes male roles, values, behaviours and lifestyles as the norm and seeks to account for the ways that women deviate from this norm. In this sense, none of them can be construed as being explicitly 'feminist' even though the focus of their attention is women's criminality. Instead, each represents a traditional criminological response to the question of gender and crime: what is being explained is women's relationships to the 'normal' *masculine* world rather than critiquing that world from a *feminist* point of view.

Whilst there have been periodic efforts to construct feminist analyses of crime since the 1960s (cf. Heidensohn, 2002; Bertrand, 1969) no systematic effort was applied to the problem until the mid-1970s, and it took several more years before issues around gender and sexuality were addressed with any seriousness in criminology as a whole. For example, in 1973 Stan Cohen and Jock Young edited a book on how 'the mass media respond to deviant behaviour and social problems'. Of the book's twenty-six chapters there was not one on gender and crime. The revised edition of the same book, published in 1981, included two chapters (out of thirty) relating to women. In between these points in time neither the self-avowedly *Critical Criminology* (ten chapters) (Taylor *et al.*, 1975) nor the thoroughly conservative *Crime, Criminology and Public Policy* (twenty-nine chapters) (Hood, 1974) made any attempt to explain gender differences in criminal behaviour or proffer even the most cursory feminist explanation for crime and deviance. This absence is all the more notable given that each text, from opposite ends of the political spectrum, was intended as a definitive survey of criminology's contribution to key problems of crime and crime control. Women, and women's accounts of crime, were either absent altogether or included only as passive victims or adjuncts of dominant (masculine) constructions of criminology's central problems. Indeed, in 1977, Carol Smart challenged criminology to become 'more than the study of men and crime' – a challenge so poorly met that by 1990 Smart urged feminists to abandon criminology altogether (Smart, 1977: 185; Smart, 1990).

However, to speak of 'feminism', in the singular, is a mistake since there are many different feminisms: liberal feminists seek to create equality of opportunity between men and women by reforming civil institutions; Marxist feminists view the central problem as one of class inequality rooted in the capitalist mode of production; radical feminists propose that a patriarchal system upholding men's power pervades all social institutions and relationships and that the problem is not capitalism but men. Added to these are 'socialist feminism', 'postmodern feminism', and 'Black feminism', amongst others – each of which construes the gender–deviance connection differently. Although these feminisms differ from one another in important ways there are, nonetheless, common emphases. These are:

- the systematic exploration and representation of *women's experiences* of crime, deviance and criminal justice institutions both historically and in the present;
- the commitment to providing a distinctive *women's voice* in explanations of crime and deviance which does not simply complement dominant masculine criminologies but challenges the absence of a concept of gender in their assumptions and theories;
- the overarching determination to make *women visible* in theories and analyses of social life – including crime and deviance;
- the wider political obligation to *confront sexism* (both overt and covert) in the academy and in the world at large and to expose the impacts of sexist norms, behaviours and structures on women's lives.

Feminist scholars and activists have been remarkably successful in changing societal attitudes to some deeply troubling phenomena. These include confronting head-on domestic violence and family abuse, rape and sexual assault, as well as drawing attention to the iniquities of women's imprisonment and their differential treatment in the criminal justice system (see Kersten, 1996). The consequence of these distinctive emphases has resulted in more than new answers to old questions about the different rates of men's and women's involvement in crime and criminal justice. Feminism has been instrumental in redefining criminology's core concerns – although it remains the case that the redefinition is still not 'mainstreamed' in criminological inquiry.

Some issues that have been highlighted by feminist scholarship include the greater approbation that is applied to women who deviate from their ascribed roles of dutiful and 'good' daughter, wife and mother, the levels of masculine violence against women, and the continuing domination of both criminology and the **criminal justice system** (CJS) by men.

In the first case classic examples of popular vilification of women criminals include the treatment of Myra Hindley and Maxine Carr. Hindley was convicted of the murder of two children in 1966 in what came to be known as the 'Moors murders'. Although no direct evidence of her involvement in the killings was ever produced, Hindley remained in jail for thirty-seven years until her death and, unlike her co-accused Ian Brady, remained an icon of evil in the popular press. Maxine Carr was the girlfriend of Ian Huntley – the school caretaker who murdered two 10-year-old girls in Soham in 2002. Carr had nothing at all to do with the deaths of the girls but foolishly provided an alibi for Huntley. In spite of the fact that she was hundreds of miles away from the murder scene she was branded as 'evil' by the *Sun* newspaper, as 'poised and deadly' and a 'mistress of dissimulation' by the *Daily Mail*. Indeed, so powerful an icon did Hindley become in popular consciousness that Carr was labelled 'Myra Mark 2' by inmates of Holloway prison. On her release, Carr had to be given a new identity in order to protect her from media-fuelled public retribution.

In both of these cases the opprobrium heaped on the women can be understood in terms of the perception that they are 'doubly deviant' (Lloyd, 1995). Not only have they broken the law but they are also seen as having deviated from their 'natural' womanly roles – of carer, nurturer, child-rearer, mother – and it is this double deviation that accounts for criminal women's greater popular vilification compared to criminal men. In this regard, popular – and academic – views of criminal women often focus less on their crim-inality per se and more on their departure from common-sense ideas about womanhood.

Whilst questions about women's femininity have often featured centrally in explanations of their criminal behaviour, the same is less true for men's masculinity although a number of feminists have noted that masculinity is a crucial concept in explaining men's violence across all levels of social structure. That it took a very long time for violence against women to be taken seriously by the CJS – and by criminology – is not in dispute. Rodmell (1981) observed that serious and widespread offences against women – including rape and sexual abuse, domestic violence and assault – were to all intents and pur-poses ignored by criminology and were a very low priority of the CJS. These observations were repeated by Hanmer (1990) and Walklate (1995), and whilst it is true that violence against women and sexual exploitation have come to feature more centrally in recent criminal justice measures the effectiveness of these measures is ques-tionable. For example, only around one in twenty prosecutions for rape results in a conviction, and this number takes no account of those cases that are not pursued through the courts (see Kelly et al., 2005). The high levels of male violence generally, and against women in particular, have led some to suggest that a key factor in men's violent and otherwise criminal activities is their masculinity (see Hanmer, 1990; Whitehead, 2005). Messerschmidt (1993) and Cavender (1999) argue that men's violence represents an effort to have their masculinity recognised by others and this search for recognition is more prevalent among males who lack socially vali-dated means for realising their self-worth – educational qualifications, steady and reliable income, achievements in the community, and so on. Where such routes to recognition are closed off, violence and predation become alternative methods of demonstrating 'masculine' status.

It is also true that both criminology and the CJS remain male-dominated industries. There have been some significant changes across the last four decades but women are still under-represented in the decision-making grades of the key agencies of the CJS. In 2002 only 18 per cent of police officers were women; and whilst 49 per cent of lay magistrates were women, only around 6 per cent of circuit judges, high court judges and lords justices were female. Women make up much higher proportions of 'front-line', community services – such as probation and victim-support services – but they account for much smaller proportions of higher grades. In 2004, for example, only 31 out of 138 prison governing officers were female and only 5 out of 43 chief constables (Home Office, 2002; Fawcett Society, 2004). Similarly, there has been an increase in the number of women studying, researching and publishing in criminology, yet the discipline as a whole has tended to operate a division of labour around questions of gender. Naffine (1997: 2) noted that gender had become ghettoised in criminology: 'the standard case is the study of men as non-gendered subjects and the speciality is the study of women as gendered beings'. In other words, in spite of the few exceptions noted above, 'gender' in criminology tends to mean 'women' and the struggle to ensure that gender is taken seriously across the discipline continues (see Wykes and Welsh, 2007).

See also: **critical criminology; gender; identity; sex crimes**

Further reading: Naffine (1997); Walklate (1995)

GANGS

Gangs have featured as a significant object of criminological analysis, especially within **subcultural** perspectives on youth offending. The Chicago School sociologist Frederic Thrasher developed the first systematic analysis of gangs. Thrasher viewed gangs as structured and coherent social units, with internal rules and codes of behaviour as well as well-defined hierarchies and social roles. Like other Chicagoans, he placed the origins of gangs in the context of *socially disorganised* inner-city life. Subcultural criminologists have viewed gangs as performing significant social functions, such as enabling their otherwise socially marginalised members to establish identity, recognition and self-esteem, as well as providing a basis for material survival through engagement in criminal enterprise. While the study of gangs has traditionally focused on urban working-class contexts, it is only relatively recently that the dimensions of 'race' and ethnicity have been addressed. Similarly, the traditional focus upon delinquent males has now been supplemented by a growing literature of female participation in gang life, so-called 'girl gangs'.

See also: **cultural transmission; differential association; subcultural criminologies**

Further reading: Huff (1990); Thrasher (1927)

GENDER

In common social scientific usage the term 'gender' refers to the qualities and characteristics (real or imagined) associated with persons on the basis of their sex. Whereas as sexual distinctions (male/female) are based upon biological and physiological features, gender traits are cultural constructions mapped onto those physical features. Thus gender will comprise the various ways in which societies, groups and individuals imagine masculinity and femininity, often in stereotypical ways, e.g. 'men are tough', 'women are emotional', and so on. Constructions of gender tend to *naturalise* such understandings, such that they are presented as the natural and inevitable consequences of biology, rather than being viewed as culturally contingent and changeable.

Historically speaking, patriarchal (male–dominated) societies have drawn clear gender distinctions that almost invariably present males as superior to females. In Western societies characteristics associated with 'maleness' have included rationality, physical strength, emotional self-control, dynamism and aggression, while 'femininity' has been deemed to entail emotionality, irrationality, physical weakness, nurturing and passivity. These supposed traits have been used to enforce and justify male authority and to restrict women's role and participation in the public arenas of politics, economics, science and the arts. It was only with the emergence of feminism in the twentieth century that such gender stereotypes were brought into question.

Through most of its existence the discipline of criminology has drawn upon wider gender stereotypes in its explanations of crime and deviance. Thus for example **biological criminologists** such as Lombroso viewed female offenders as 'abnormal', since they were supposedly acting against their 'natural' instincts as carers and nurturers. Similarly, male offending has been understood as an expression of men's supposedly inbuilt aggressive urges. For example, biologists such as Thornhill and Palmer (2000) have argued that rape is the result of reproductive imperatives 'programmed' into men at the genetic level through evolution. The persistence of such views demonstrates the continued hold that discriminatory constructions of gender have over criminology.

However, recent decades have seen a significant impact of feminist analysis upon the discipline. Feminist criminologists have challenged the discipline's reliance upon gender stereotypes, and explored the ways in which they lead to discrimination against women within the criminal justice system. Critical criminologists have also examined the complex relationship between *masculinity* and crime. Far from suggesting a natural basis for male offending, criminologists such as Messerschmidt (1993) have argued that dominant constructions of masculinity (what it means in our culture to be seen as a 'real man') contribute to men's engagement in often violent crime.

See also: **biological criminology; feminism and criminology; identity; sexism**

Further reading: Dobash *et al*. (1995); Messerschmidt (1993)

GOVERNANCE AND GOVERNMENTALITY

Governance is a term used to signal that power in modern societies is exercised in very many different ways and by very many different institutions. Where 'government' has been used to refer almost exclusively to the powers of the state and the elected or unelected body that directs it, governance and governmentality are used to refer to the interlocking networks of economic, social, political and cultural power through which contemporary societies are administered, regulated and directed. The terms are used to signal a blurring of the distinction between the powers exercised by states and the powers exercised by non-state institutions. In Rhodes' (1997: 57) terms, governance refers to 'interorganisational networks made up of governmental and social actors', all of whom are mutually dependent on each other. Governance is also used to signal that power is exercised through the very social problems that 'government' is intended to resolve. Of particular relevance here is Simon's (1997) thesis that, in important respects, American society is being 'governed through crime' in that crime has become an increasingly crucial means of distributing public resources, designing public spaces, determining who will be included and who excluded from key social institutions – of education, consumption and welfare benefits, for example. As crime and security come to occupy larger and larger fractions of the political agenda, so more and more political decisions about residential and commercial zoning and surveillance systems, for example, are justified on the grounds of the need to respond to the threat of crime, disorder and, more recently, terrorism. Where 'governance' has tended to refer to the process of exercising power across many and varied sites in contemporary society, 'governmentality' has tended to refer to the assemblage of discourses and institutions whose collaboration continuously renders specific social problems (such as 'crime') as objects of governance.

See also: **discourse; risk; state, the**

Further reading: Simon (1997)

GREEN CRIMINOLOGY

Green criminology is a very new addition to the discipline of criminology as a whole – less than two decades old and only really becoming a current in criminological thought in the last ten years. Although there were many studies of the relationships between **corporate crime**, **organised crime** and environmental degradation before this time (see Mueller, 1979; Szasz, 1986), the 'greening' of criminology took off alongside the greening of other disciplines in the social sciences – sociology, psychology and social anthropology – under the impact of a changed public agenda and, in the United Kingdom, a large programme of research funding provided through the Economic and Social Research Council from 1992 to 2002. Prior to this decade-long, dedicated research initiative, criminological *theory* paid scant attention to natural environmental matters – nowhere more clearly demonstrated than in the fact that the sub-branch of **environmental criminology** was used to refer not to climate change, species extinction and habitat destruction but to local urban crime problems. In fact, no edition of what is virtually the bible of British undergraduate criminology – *The Oxford Handbook of Criminology* – has ever contained a chapter on green criminology and the latest (fourth) edition subsumes these issues under the topics 'globalisation', 'risk', 'corporate crime', and so on. Similarly, Davies *et al.*'s (2005) otherwise comprehensive introduction to the criminal justice system makes no mention of 'green' or 'environmental' matters at all.

The dearth of serious criminological attention to the natural environment cannot be explained by a lack of awareness of the mounting problems of human-induced environmental change. Amongst many other landmark publications, Rachel Carson's (1962) *Silent Spring* had alerted the industrial world to the perils of unregulated toxic releases, whilst the Nobel laureate Denis Gabor and colleagues (1978) had virtually accused modern society of wilful criminal negligence in its consumption-addicted destruction of nature. The dearth of attention has much more to do with the political agendas under which criminology has been operating in the post-war period and, in the UK, the founding of the Home Office Research Unit in 1957. With the exceptions of some of the more critical criminologies, that agenda has tended to be driven by government requirements to manage street crime (and the public's perception of it) rather than to connect matters of environmental degradation to the operations of the criminal justice system. Environmental problems were seen as the province of other expert disciplines – in the natural sciences primarily, with some potentially useful contributions from economics. The first recognised use of the term 'green' in criminology was Michael Lynch's (1990) short essay in *The Critical Criminologist*, although it was several years before Lynch's idea was incorporated into mainstream scholarship. Important to this incorporation was a special issue of the journal *Theoretical Criminology* (1998) entitled 'For a Green Criminology?' This special issue contained essays on food production, masculinities, human and animal rights, drug cultivation and ecofeminism. Whilst some elements of these topics had been making slow but steady inroads into the margins of criminological theory, this was the first time that criminology's core academic audience was engaged directly in terms of their interconnections.

Naturally, in such a new branch of criminology the impact of 'green' principles and ideas is, as yet, far from clear but three strands of theoretical engagement can already be discerned. In the first, environmental incidents are viewed through traditional criminological perspectives. Here, 'environmental crimes' are defined in the same terms as crimes against persons and property, and the criminological challenge is to devise control systems that can effectively enforce existing laws and punish offenders. Most often the debate centres on the behaviour of corporations and firms and how to ensure their compliance with existing requirements. Currently, the sanctions available to national and international enforcement bodies tend to be inadequate for their purpose. Where sanctions are imposed they tend to be after the event – that is, after the dumping of toxins, the destruction of habitats, the release of pollutants, and so on – and consist overwhelmingly in comparatively small financial penalties whose deterrent effect is dubious. Some criminologists suggest that a more effective strategy against corporate breaches of environmental laws may be to 'name and shame' (Braithwaite, 1989; Hawkins, 1990) the companies involved on the grounds that businesses are sensitive to attacks on their reputation. Others have proposed that corporate regulation needs to become 'ecocentric' – that is, it needs to start from the assumption that the natural environment has a 'right' *not* to be polluted or degraded. In this scenario, the onus would be on a company (or individual, potentially) to demonstrate that any discharge or activity was harmless rather than on a justice agency to discover who was at fault for a harmful emission (see Miller, 1995). This 'ecocentric approach' has been further developed by the critical sociologist Ted Benton, who advocates a universal system of human *and* non-human rights geared towards a project of transformation in social and political as well as ecological relationships (see Benton, 1998: 171; see also Beirne and South, 2007).

The second theoretical strand has been to view environmental incidents through the lens of struggles in and through **discourse** – that is, according to Lynch and Stretsky (2003: 218), 'green crimes, like other crimes, are social constructions influenced by social locations and power relations in society'. Here, 'environmental crimes' are not simply 'events' defined unproblematically by a disinterested law. Rather, the criminalising (or not) of environmental damage is a struggle between competing social forces. Like the confusing and contradictory regulations surrounding drug use – cannabis is a proscribed substance whilst alcohol is not – environmental laws and the definition of environmental crimes are the subject of conflict and contestation. Even what counts as being environmentally friendly and what as environmentally harmful is subject to endless disputation. Recently, there has been a great deal of public debate about whether flying by jet aircraft is a serious contributor to climate change, with Green groups lambasting the airlines and the airlines lambasting the Greens. Less than a decade ago the idea of planting a few trees to 'offset' some of an individual's or a company's 'carbon footprint' was extremely popular. Today, the impact of such schemes is seen as being more harmful than beneficial. In this circumstance, the challenge for criminology is to 'understand *which* behaviours become the focus of law and *why*' (ibid.: 228) and, it might be added, *where* and *under what conditions*, since some environmentally dangerous activities are legal in one place and illegal in another – the use of certain pesticides and animal feed additives being cases in point (see Shanahan and Trent, 2003).

Finally, some have suggested that criminology, currently, is ill equipped to address environmental crimes and that new disciplinary orientations are required if criminology is to rise to the challenge of environmental sustainability. Indeed, Mark Halsey goes so far as to argue 'against "green" criminology' on the grounds that the project is

flawed from the outset and deeply enmired in 'shortcomings associated with modernist thought' (Halsey, 2004: 834). The green
criminological project, Halsey suggests, suffers from problems of
'anthropocentrism' (it invariably begins and ends with a human-
centred view of ecological problems), 'biocentrism' (it is destined to
adopt the classifications, categorisations and assemblages of other scientific disciplines) and 'ecocentrism' (it invariably struggles to define
how 'rights' can apply to non-humans and stumbles over the problem
of how such rights might be enforced). What Halsey proposes to put
in the place of the green criminological project is far from clear but it
is certainly a kind of postmodern enterprise somewhat akin to the
constitutive criminology of Henry and Milanovic (1996). Here, the
challenge for criminology is to enable 'new modes of envisioning the
human/earth nexus' and a 'reconceptualisation of the relationship
between speed and damage' (Halsey, 2004: 849).

There is no doubt, as Walters (2006) has observed, that criminology's
encounter with environmental issues has pushed its disciplinary concerns towards questions of **human rights**, globalisation and **governance** and that these questions have helped to deepen criminology's
engagement with problems of corporate regulation, transnational
policing and the social and ecological damage that ensues from modern
systems of production and consumption. At the same time, the
'greening' of criminology has also put into question the discipline's
very object of study. The sheer complexity of environmental harms
means that criminology's traditional concern with crime per se is
simply not adequate to understanding or responding to those harms.
Many so-called environmentally damaging behaviours are not only
legal but also culturally valued: driving cars, travelling in aeroplanes,
over-fishing of valuable marine stocks, using chemicals to clean
houses and then flushing said chemicals down the drain – all of these
are normal, routine activities with severe environmental impacts. If
criminology is to concern itself with environmental harms, then its
practical orientation will have to change from how to address the problem of assault or burglary, for example, to how to address the problem
of driving or cleaning up! There is nothing intrinsically wrong with a
focus on the damage caused by normal, legal behaviour but there are
already disciplines – sociology, politics, environmental science, for
example – geared towards studying precisely those kinds of issues.

See also: **environmental crime; state crime**

Further reading: Beirne and South (2007)

HATE CRIME

Hate crime is a complex problem in modern society and its recent emergence as a criminal justice (and criminological) concern signals shifts in public perceptions about the impact of prejudice and discrimination on a range of social groups. The development of criminal sanctions against offences motivated by hatred is part of a suite of policies aimed at tackling discrimination on grounds of ethnicity, gender, sexuality, age, disability and religion. According to the UK Home Office (2007a):

> Hate crime is any criminal offence committed against a person or property that is motivated by an offender's hatred of someone because of their:
>
> - race, colour, ethnic origin, nationality or national origins
> - religion
> - gender or gender identity
> - sexual orientation
> - disability

Hate crimes may take the form of physical attacks on persons or property, threats or intimidation, verbal or written insults and abuse or bullying – they may involve the co-presence of a perpetrator and a victim (as in the case of physical assault) or these may be distributed in time and space (as in the case of hate speech on the internet). Note that it is not the hatred itself that is a crime – prosecutions cannot be brought simply on the grounds of hating some person or group. Rather, prosecutions are brought on the grounds that criminal offences are aggravated or motivated by, or are intended to provoke or incite, such hatred. These questions of motivation, aggravation, and so on, are the most difficult of all since they are not defined in law. Rather, a hate crime is defined as 'any incident, which constitutes a criminal offence, which is perceived by the victim or any other person as being motivated by prejudice or hate'. Thus, in line with developments in other areas of the criminal justice system (such as Antisocial Behaviour Orders) the key issue is how the behaviour is subjectively perceived, rather than what it objectively effects. In England and Wales, hate crimes began to make their way onto the statute books with the 1998 Crime and Disorder Act, which introduced several categories of racial and religious aggravation in criminal prosecutions. The Criminal Justice Act of 2003 added legal provisions relating to the prosecution of criminal offences motivated by hatred of a victim's sexual orientation. The 2006 Racial and Religious Hatred Act 'made it a criminal offence to use threatening words or behaviour with the intention of stirring up hatred against any group of people defined by their religious beliefs or lack of religious beliefs' (Home Office, 2007a). Across England and Wales in the year 2005–6 the police recorded 50,000 racially and religiously motivated crimes whilst the British Crime Survey estimated that around 260,000 such incidents took place.

The dominant image of hate crime is that of crime between strangers – that is, of perpetrators randomly selecting targets based simply on the fact that they represent some hated characteristic. Indeed, some criminologists propose the same view – that victims and perpetrators tend to be unknown to each other and that one of the defining characteristics of hate crimes is that perpetrator and victim are mutual strangers. Whilst much hate crime is indeed reported as being committed by strangers (see Lawrence, 1999; Clancy et al., 2001), the picture is not as simple as this. For a start, official figures suggest that perpetrator and victim often live in close proximity to each other and that the crimes themselves tend to occur relatively close to the victim's home. This suggests the possibility that it is more, rather than less, likely that the offender will be at least familiar, if not directly acquainted, with their chosen victim. Moreover, a growing body of criminological research (Bowling, 1993; Stanko, 2001; Ray and Smith, 2002) suggests that hate crime is a far more ordinary and mundane feature of the urban landscape than has been represented in much of the literature. When sexual, racial and homophobic assaults are considered overall it is, in fact, relatively common for perpetrator and victim to be known to each other. Often, the perpetrators tend to be family members or other intimates, neighbours, local youths or, in the case of some racist assaults against business premises, known customers (Mason, 2005). These observations have persuaded some criminologists to argue that such crimes should be considered not as discrete events but as dynamic social processes – particularly as racial and sexual victimisation tend to be repetitive, long-term and, in too many cases, systematic (Bowling, 1993: 239). The specific offence occurs in the context of ongoing relationships between intimate familiars (as in the case of domestic assault) or between locally acquainted individuals (as in the case of many racially motivated crimes). Yet, even here, the situation is not straightforward because there are significant variations in the experiences of different groups and variations in levels of familiarity between victims and offenders in different crime categories. Bowling points to important differences in the experiences of Afro-Caribbean and Asian victims, whilst Mason (2005: 840) reports that

> research has consistently found that lesbians are more likely to know the perpetrator than gay men; victims who live in a non-metropolitan area are more likely to know the perpetrator than those who live in the city; younger victims appear more likely to know the perpetrator than older victims; and those who suffer physical injury are more likely to know the perpetrator than those who do not.

To return to an earlier comment, a major problem in interpreting the research findings is deciding whether or not 'hate' is a motivating or aggravating factor in the commission of different offences. Given that the official definition of a 'hate crime' requires that it be *perceived* as being motivated by hatred, it is inherently difficult to stipulate when 'hate' is and is not the key to understanding any given incident. Clearly, not all criminal incidents involving persons of different ethnic backgrounds, sexual orientations, genders, and so on, should be described in the language of 'hate crime'. On the other hand, the routine and widespread character of racial, sexual and gender victimisation suggests that there is a background framework of prejudice that needs to be referred to in order to make sense of these crimes.

See also: **homophobia; sex crimes**

Further reading: Bowling (1999); Mason (2005)

HEDONISM

Hedonism refers to the view of human nature as fundamentally motivated by the search for pleasure and the avoidance of pain. Hedonism has traditionally featured in criminology through **rational choice** perspectives that view criminal behaviour as a result of individuals' calculated attempts to satisfy their desires. More recently **cultural criminology** has also sought to introduce hedonism as a central element in understanding offending by examining the pleasures and 'seductions' of crime and deviance.

See also: **classical criminology; cultural criminology; rational choice; routine activity theories**

Further reading: Cornish and Clarke (1986); Katz (1988)

HEGEMONY

The Italian Marxist Antonio Gramsci (1891–1937) developed the concept of 'hegemony' to describe the way that a social class achieves and sustains its dominance over other social classes. Hegemony refers not only to political control (via the organs of the state) and economic control (via the organisation of industry and commerce) but also to ideological and intellectual leadership. By the latter terms, Gramsci was referring to the ways that a dominant class persuades subordinate classes to accept its own moral outlooks and cultural constructions of the world. In this sense, Gramsci was concerned to argue that power in society could be exercised in the form of coercion (using repressive measures available to the state such as the army or the police) or in the form of persuasion (building consensus by forging alliances with useful social groups and using mass media of communication to persuade subordinates to accept the dominant world view). Note that in Gramsci's view both of these forms are always simultaneously present, to different degrees, but that states functioned most effectively when exercising power through leadership and consent rather than domination and coercion (see Strinati, 1995).

The general social scientific, and specific criminological, issue that arose out of Gramsci's work revolved around the means by which a ruling group manufactures the consent of subordinate groups: how does the dominant group persuade the dominated groups to share its world view? According to some, the figure or image of crime is a tried and tested strategy for securing the consent of the population for draconian, excessive or otherwise intrusive interventions into social life in the name of maintaining order and social stability. A striking example of this strategy was explored by Stuart Hall and colleagues (1978) who investigated how the media, the judiciary, the police and the government of the time produced a particular set of images, narratives and common-sense outlooks on the phenomenon of 'mugging'. However, whilst the predatory mugger was the overt and explicit target of these images and narratives a more important process was occurring simultaneously: the 'hegemonic' control of urban space and the manufacture of consent for more politicised and targeted policing (specifically focused on inner-city, working-class youth). Within the discipline of criminology itself it has been said that forms of administrative criminology have become 'hegemonic', displacing and sidelining critical criminological analyses in favour of government-sponsored risk-factor analysis and the endless production and interpretation of crime statistics.

See also: **critical criminology; ideology; Marxist criminology**

Further reading: Strinati (1995)

HOMOPHOBIA

Homophobia denotes an aversion to or hatred of homosexuality, and utterances, representations or actions that discriminate against an individual or individuals on the basis of their homosexuality. Recent criminological research has uncovered the extent of **hate crimes** motivated by homophobia. Homosexuals have traditionally been afforded little protection by the law, and it is only recently that discrimination on the grounds of sexual orientation has begun to be addressed by legislation. Moreover, the criminal justice system for many years played a key role in persecuting and criminalising homosexuality through the enforcement of laws that prohibited same-sex relationships.

See also: **hate crime; sex crimes**

Further reading: McGhee (2005)

HUMAN RIGHTS

The Universal Declaration of Human Rights was adopted by the General Assembly of the United Nations on 10 December 1948 (Resolution 217 A (III)). It proclaims that 'the inherent dignity and [...] equal and inalienable rights of all members of the human family is the foundation of freedom, justice and peace in the world'. The declaration consists of thirty articles, the most well known of which is the proclamation that everyone 'has the right to life, liberty and security of person'. Amongst other things, the declaration also seeks to bestow rights to own property, to marry, to freedom of thought and religion and of association and assembly. It also proclaims 'the right to work, to free choice of employment, to just and favourable conditions of work'. The declaration was adopted by the Council Members of Europe in 1950 in the European Convention on Human Rights. Three sets of institutions are charged with safeguarding its provisions. These are the Committee of Ministers of the Council of Europe (representing the member states themselves), the European Commission on Human Rights (established in 1954) and the European Court of Human Rights (established in 1959).

Whilst the United Nations Declaration, and the subsequent European Convention, inured member states to adopt the thirty articles, their basis in law remained unclear in the United Kingdom until the Human Rights Act (1998), which provides a legal framework for safeguarding sixteen of the original thirty fundamental rights and freedoms. These are:

- the right to life
- freedom from torture and degrading treatment
- freedom from slavery and forced labour
- the right to liberty
- the right to a fair trial
- the right not to be punished for something that was not a crime when you did it
- the right to respect for private and family life
- freedom of thought, conscience and religion
- freedom of expression
- freedom of assembly and association
- the right to marry or form a civil partnership and start a family
- the right not to be discriminated against in respect of these rights and freedoms
- the right to own property
- the right to an education
- the right to participate in free elections
- freedom from the death penalty

It does need to be noted that these rights and freedoms are not absolute in law. They may be curtailed or controlled by governments in times of emergency (such as during war) which means, as Hudson (2003a: 213) points out, that far from being 'fundamental' these rights and freedoms are in fact conditional and often subject to intense debate. An obvious example of the difficulty of ensuring these rights can be seen in the contradiction between the 'right' to privacy, on the one hand, and the extensive fact of surveillance and intrusion into private life, on the other.

Some argue that, in a time of cosmopolitan (even 'postmodern') societies, it is effectively impossible to guarantee fundamental rights and freedoms. The religious and secular values of different ethnic or cultural, religious or political groups mean that there will always be conflict over the meaning of terms: what is a 'fair trial' in one culture is not a 'fair trial' in another; what one culture considers 'degrading treatment' another considers normal; what one culture upholds as a 'free election' another castigates as political gerrymandering. Moreover, at the international level, these human rights and freedoms are all but impossible to enforce. The largest self-proclaimed democracy in the world (the United States of America) and the most rapidly growing economy (China) both continue to make use of the death penalty, have been harangued for the use of torture and degrading treatment, and serious questions have been raised over the freedom and fairness of their electoral processes. Additionally, in an age of global economic migration, it is clear that, human rights declarations or otherwise, millions of people around the world are subjected to forced labour in every sector from food production to the sex industries.

From a criminological point of view the debate about human rights reveals the inherent difficulty of ensuring fair, equal and just treatment for different social groups in a world defined by serious inequalities, discriminations and systematic abuses. As Schwendinger and Schwendinger (1970) pointed out, class, sexual and racial discrimination have been endemic to industrial democracies for centuries and, in spite of recent legislation on racial and sexual equality, women and minority groups are still the most likely to suffer poverty and oppression. Add to these gross social facts the impacts of ageism and disablism and it is clear that safeguarding human rights is more difficult in practice than in theory. Whilst few would seriously argue that human rights legislation, protocols and conventions are irrelevant, it is important that such rights and freedoms be seen not as an enforceable end-point to which recourse is made only when they have been curtailed, but as a starting point on which to build more effective guarantees of life, liberty and security.

Further reading: Hudson (2003a, 2003b)

IDEALISM

In philosophical terms, 'idealism' refers to the doctrine that humans cannot gain access to knowledge of the external world. The only things that we can know are the contents of our own consciousness. In fact, for an idealist, mental 'things' (ideas) are the only 'real' things about which we can know anything at all.

There is no school of 'criminological idealism' in the same way that there are clear adherents to 'criminological realism', although some perspectives in criminology (such as postmodernism and labelling theory) have been accused of harbouring idealist tendencies. Such accusations, largely, are levelled whenever criminologists focus attention on the concepts or labels through which crime is understood rather than on the material or personal impacts of criminal activities. The most famous – and controversial – use of the term 'idealism' occurred in Jock Young's essay 'Working Class Criminology', where he accused the critical criminologists of the late 1960s and early 1970s of a 'theory and practice of voyeurism' (Young, 1975: 69). In other words, he suggested, rather than engaging with the real circumstances and impacts of, and suffering caused by, crime, the critical criminologists marginalised or played down crime problems in favour of sweeping critiques of the state, capitalism or the criminal justice system as a whole. In fact, Young's essay did not do justice to the innovative and deeply committed research that was being carried out in criminology (see Cottee, 2002) and his accusation stands more as a reminder of the deep-seated divisions that beset criminological theory during the first wave of the discipline's post-war expansion than as an accurate depiction of a criminological idealism.

See also: **critical criminology; labelling perspectives; postmodernity/ postmodernism; realism**

Further reading: Cottee (2002); Young (1986b)

IDENTITY

A term widely used across the humanities and social sciences in a great variety of ways. At is most basic, identity denotes a particular person's or group's sameness and continuity over time and place, such that we are able to identify them. All persons will have an *individual identity* (e.g. 'I am John'). The formation and nature of individual identity has largely been the concern of disciplines such as psychology, psychoanalysis and philosophy. However, in addition to individual identity, persons will have a range of *social identities*, through which they will understand themselves as part of particular social groups, and in terms of which others will understand them. Thus for example we can speak of gender identity (e.g. 'Alex is a woman'); ethnic identity (e.g. 'he is Jewish'); national identity (e.g. 'we are Americans'); sexual identity (e.g. 'she is gay'); class identity (e.g. 'they are all working class'), and so on. Identities of this kind are not naturally occurring, but must be viewed as *social constructions* that attribute common characteristics to those who are associated with them. Criminology's interest in identity has been oriented in the main to the question of how and why *deviant identities* are produced and sustained, and how identifying persons in terms of such classification will shape their social, political and legal treatment. Thus for example we can note how historically those attributed with deviant sexual identities, such as homosexuals, have been persecuted and criminalised.

See also: **gender; hate crime; homophobia; labelling perspectives; racism; sexism**

Further reading: Hall and DuGay (1996)

IDEOLOGY

The term 'ideology' is used in two very different senses. In one sense it is used to refer to a system of thought or belief that is associated with an identifiable social group or political project. Thus, one often hears of 'green' ideology or a 'socialist' ideology, and so forth. In this usage the term 'ideology' is neutral and in its original meaning, according to Alvin Gouldner (1976), implies the rejection of tradition and authority as the arbiter of truth in favour of logic, evidence and rationality. Here, 'ideology' is simply the way that groups represent and/or symbolise their political and social visions. The second sense of the term 'ideology', however, is very different and implies false or incorrect thoughts or beliefs. Thus, one often hears of 'false' ideology and this pejorative sense is always implied in the phrase 'dominant ideology'. This second meaning, what John Thompson (1984) calls a 'critical conception' of ideology, is certainly dominant in contemporary social science (including criminology) but begs the question as to how anyone might escape its clutches in order to be critical about it in the first place. For some, notably Karl Marx, systems of belief derive from positions in the class structure – specifically the relation of a group to the ownership of the means of production. The proletariat 'own' nothing but their labour power and thus are able to see (correctly, according to Marx) that the source of all wealth is organised labour. All other groups, because they 'own' various different portions of the means of production and distribution, believe (falsely, according to Marx) that land, rent, labour in the abstract, technology, the market, and so on, are the basis of all wealth and thus their systems of belief are 'ideological' in the critical sense. For others, ideology is less a fully worked up system of belief and more a set of taken-for-granted assumptions about power and powerlessness, domination and subordination that are embedded in discourse. In other words, ideology is less a system of (false) beliefs and more a pernicious structuring property of language because 'it is within language that meaning is mobilised in the interests of particular individuals and groups' (Thompson, 1984: 73). The dilemma for any would-be criminologist is that, all too often, these rather different senses of 'ideology' are readily confused.

Further reading: Eagleton (1991); Gouldner (1976); Thompson (1984)

INTELLECTUAL PROPERTY CRIME

Ordinarily, understandings of property crime centre upon the illegal appropriation of material goods. However, recent decades have seen a massive growth in crimes involving a different form of property, what is known as intellectual property (IP). IP refers to property that takes the form of ideas, expressions, signs, symbols, designs, logos and similar 'intangible' forms. Rights of ownership of such property is established through a range of distinctive property rights such as copyright, trademarks, patents, industrial designs and trade secrets. IP rights confer upon the owner exclusive control over the use of ideas and expressions, and unauthorised use is increasingly subject to a range of sanctions under criminal law. IP crimes include the unauthorised copying and distribution of copyrighted materials (such as musical recordings, computer software and motion pictures), commonly referred to as 'piracy'; the use of brands, logos and symbols in counterfeit goods (such as fake 'designer' goods ranging from cosmetics and perfumes to clothing and personal accessories); and the unauthorised use of formulae, technical knowledge and production processes that are protected by patents.

IP crime is now estimated to cost property rights holders billions of dollars per annum. For example, the US government places losses to counterfeiting at $200–250 billion every year, and European and US economies are said to lose some 200,000 jobs per annum as a result of such illegal activities. The rapid increase in economic costs from IP violations can be attributed to a number of wider social, political and economic processes. First, recent years have seen the growth of the so-called information economy, one in which economic value is realised through the production of knowledge and information rather than the manufacture of material goods. As the profit potential of illegally exploiting information expands, so do the incentives for a variety of actors to involve themselves in IP crime. Second, the development of new technologies, such as computers and the internet, have created new opportunities for the illegal reproduction and distribution of information goods, something witnessed in the widespread phenomenon of music downloading. Third, the process of economic globalisation has entailed the dismantling of barriers and borders to the transnational flow of goods, enabling counterfeit goods to be more easily moved across the world to reach potentially lucrative markets.

Given the above developments, both individual states and international bodies (such as the World Trade Organisation) have responded by introducing and strengthening criminal penalties for IP violations. For example, both the USA and the UK now have criminal law provisions that provide for custodial sentences for those convicted of commercial counterfeiting. There has also been an increased level of policing and enforcement in relation to IP crimes. Not only have public agencies devoted greater resources to such efforts, private policing has also been undertaken by groups representing the interests of businesses in the music, software, fashion and other industries. As information and culture continue to constitute a greater source of economic profits, we can expect IP crime to rise further up the agendas of police and lawmakers in coming decades.

See also: **cybercrime; policing and the police; property crime**

Further reading: Paradise (1999); Tom *et al.* (1999); Vithlani (1998); Yar (2005)

JUSTICE

A term widely used in criminological debate, justice is a concept concerned with the proper distribution of rewards and punishments within a society. It is usual to distinguish between two forms of justice, *distributive* and *corrective*. Distributive justice (also referred to as *social justice*) is concerned with the appropriate distribution of social goods (for example money, property, education, healthcare and housing). Debates about distributive justice turn on questions about what individuals are entitled to expect from others by way of goods, and what obligations society as a whole has to provide for the wants and needs of its members. Deprivation of social goods through their unequal distribution is associated with patterns of **social exclusion**. Corrective justice, in contrast, is concerned with the proper distribution of punishments. It deals with questions of what kinds and degrees of punishment are appropriate responses to wrongdoing. The kinds of social arrangements that would be necessary to satisfy the demand for justice (be it distributive or corrective) are deeply contested, and play a central role in disputes over appropriate responses to crime.

See also: **punishment; restorative justice**

LABELLING PERSPECTIVES

Labelling perspectives emerged from the 1930s onwards as a critical reaction against the **positivist** orientation that had been dominant within criminology until that point. For the positivists, the criminal and/or deviant standing of an act was a self-evident fact – a crime is an act that breaches rules set down in criminal law, whereas deviance is behaviour that transgresses informal codes of socially acceptable behaviour. Therefore, what is or is not criminal can be objectively identified, and the task of the criminologist is to explain why it is that some individuals are drawn to act in this way. Labelling perspectives in contrast see crime and deviance as *social constructions* that emerge from processes of social interaction in specific historical and cultural contexts. As such, what is identified as criminal or deviant is a social accomplishment that will vary according to the subjective perceptions and meanings that are attached to particular persons and their conduct. Labelling theorists do not seek to explain why individuals or groups behave in a criminal manner, but instead elect to examine the social and interactional processes through which the label of criminality comes to be associated with certain phenomena.

One of the earliest formulations of a labelling approach was developed by Frank Tannenbaum (1938). Tannenbaum argues that *societal reactions* to behaviour play a crucial role in the creation of deviance. While many people may commit rule-breaking acts, the vast majority will pass without remark. However, in a minority of instances individuals and their behaviour will be identified and targeted by others, and treated according to a negative label. It is this selective process that will lead to certain persons becoming deviants in the eyes of society. This insight was further developed by Edwin Lemert (1951), who distinguished between what he called *primary deviance* and *secondary deviance*. Primary deviance comprises those acts that may breach rules about proper behaviour, but will not yet have been labelled as such. Individuals will engage in such conduct from time to time, but neither they nor others will view it as unusual or problematic. Secondary deviance emerges after a deviant label has been imposed upon the actor. As a consequence of labelling, society will treat the 'deviant' as different, and the individuals marked out in this way will begin to identify themselves in terms of the label that has been given them. This will lead them to behave in a manner that is consistent with the deviant label, thereby producing more of the behaviour that has been condemned. In this way, it is the process of making and applying rules about what is deviant that ends up inciting the very behaviour that is held to be undesirable. This process, following the work of Leslie Wilkins (1964), is often called **deviance amplification**.

A detailed labelling approach to criminology was developed by Howard Becker in his influential book *Outsiders* (1963). His basic proposition was that:

> *Social groups create deviance by making the rules whose infraction constitutes deviance,* and by applying those rules to particular people and labelling them as outsiders. From this point of view, deviance is not a quality of the act the person commits, but rather a consequence of the application by others of rules or sanctions to an 'offender'. The deviant is one to whom that label has been successfully applied; deviant behaviour is behaviour that people so label.

Using this understanding Becker points out that, first, what is or is not considered deviant will depend upon social and cultural context. An act may be considered unremarkable at one point in time, yet later be reconfigured as deviant, improper, or immoral. We can see an instance of this with the case of narcotics. In the nineteenth century the use of drugs such as cocaine and opium was commonplace and socially accepted (famous users included Sigmund Freud and Queen Victoria). However, over the course of the twentieth century, such drug use became labelled as deviant and those who engaged in it as dangerous outsiders, beyond the pale of 'normal' society. Conversely, acts that are considered deviant may become normalised over time, and come to fall within the bounds of social acceptability. A clear historical example is that of male homosexuality, which was once punishable by death or imprisonment, but is now increasingly viewed as unremarkable by many in Western countries. Second, Becker notes how *power* plays a key role in determining whose behaviours come to be successfully labelled as deviant. Those who are relatively powerless (such as the poor and minority ethnic groups) are more likely to be identified with deviance, and are least able to resist such labelling. The more powerful social groups in contrast will have greater ability to evade labelling and its consequences. They will also have a greater authority and influence when it comes to defining who and what is to be considered deviant. Such groups and persons comprise what Becker calls the *moral entrepreneurs*, those who engage in creating new rules and applying them so as to classify others as outsiders. In this way, construction of deviance inevitably reflects the structure of social relations and the interests of powerful groups within a society. By applying this insight we can understand how and why 'street crimes' have come to be so closely identified with 'the crime problem' in the public mind, while arguably more serious and socially harmful offences, such as corporate crimes, remain on the margins of the public and law-enforcement agenda.

Labelling theorists' insights into the social construction and amplification of deviance have been usefully applied to examine the emergence of a wide range of crime problems. For example, Cohen (1972) investigated the role of the **mass media** in creating new categories of deviant subjects and behaviours, a process that can create **moral panics** about threats to social order. Hall *et al.* (1978) explored the ways in which long-standing forms of conduct were identified as a new crime problem under the label of 'mugging', and a new deviant created in the shape of the 'black mugger'. Labelling theories have also played a significant role in shaping the recent emergence of **cultural criminology**. Jeff Ferrell (1996) has mobilised the labelling perspective to analyse how cultural practices such as graffiti art come to be criminalised by those in positions of social authority. More recently, Hayward and Yar (2006) have charted the rise of deviant labels applied to working-class youth, labels that identify them as 'antisocial' troublemakers, and serve to organise new strategies of policing and crime control.

Labelling perspectives, it has been argued, over-emphasise the influence of socially applied labels over individuals' subsequent behaviour. Critics suggest that labelling theorists tend to view actors as rather passive, simply accepting the labels others place upon them and adopting the behaviour associated with those negative classifications. However, writers such as Becker concede that labelling cannot be seen as a sole determinant of conduct, and that individuals have the capacity to reject and contest as well as accept and conform to deviant labels. What matters, they claim, is that labels will define society's expectation of those it deems deviant, and these will constrain individuals' ability to lead a 'normal' life. However, critics have also suggested that labelling theorists have been rather inconsistent in applying their understanding of deviance as a social construct. On the one hand they hold that behaviour only becomes deviant after it has been publicly labelled as such. Yet on the other hand, they deploy notions such as *primary deviance* and *secret deviance*, suggesting that acts can in fact be deviant prior to their public labelling. This being the case, the claim that deviance is purely a quality conferred by societal reactions appears to be contradicted by labelling theorists themselves. Such criticisms notwithstanding, labelling perspectives have made a vital contribution to the understanding of crime and deviance as the product of social processes, and continue to provide a valuable counterpoint to positivist criminology.

See also: **critical criminology; cultural criminology; moral panic; positivist criminology**

Further reading: Becker (1963); Cohen (1972); Ferrell (1996); Hall *et al.* (1978); Hayward and Yar (2006); Sumner (1994)

MARXIST CRIMINOLOGY

Marxist approaches to crime cannot be separated from wider concerns in Marxist theory with political economy and historical change. Marx and Engels made few references to criminological issues and certainly produced no 'theory' of crime. The latter effort was left to later interpreters – and the interpretive effort sometimes overshadowed the criminological explanations that were being offered. Indeed, some Marxists proclaimed that the effort to develop a 'Marxist criminology' was a doomed enterprise because Marxism was a philosophy and politics of the totality of historical relations. There could be no 'Marxist criminology' any more than there could be a 'Marxist sociology' or 'Marxist geography' since these independent disciplines represented the fragmentation of knowledge under capitalism into disconnected and competing areas of expertise. As such, they were antithetical to the Marxist project as a whole which, according to Hirst (1975), treated criminology as a bourgeois discipline that (inevitably) failed to grasp true circumstances of class conflict under capitalism.

We make these preliminary remarks because Marxist criminology, more so than any other strand of criminological theory, represents less of a school, paradigm or perspective and more of a *debate* about how sociological, political and economic analyses ought to be applied to real world problems of crime and crime control. These debates are both intense and unresolved – there is no definitive 'Marxist criminology' and there is a great deal of confusion over what such a criminology might look like. Part of the reason for the confusion is that a key task of Marxism is to explain not only the existence of crime but the existence and the form of the criminal law. Why does the law criminalise some things and not others? Why is the criminal law applied to some groups of persons (invariably the poor and marginalised) with much greater regularity than others (invariably the rich and powerful)? An easy, and frequent, response is to propose that the laws are made by the rich and powerful to serve the interests of the rich and powerful. Whilst Marx would, partially, have agreed with this claim it is not in itself a Marxist explanation. For Marx, the bourgeoisie (i.e. the rich and powerful law-makers) were as constrained in their actions as the proletariat (i.e. the poor and marginalised who were criminalised by the criminal law). The rich and powerful criminalised the poor and marginalised not because it served their personal interests (even if their interests were in fact so served). Rather, they enacted such laws because they served the interests of the capitalist system as a whole. Where Marx does discuss the capitalist logic of the criminal law it is usually in the most caustic and sarcastic prose. Thus, explaining why 'our friend [the capitalist] has a penal code of his own', he writes that it is because

> all wasteful consumption of raw material or instruments of labour is strictly forbidden, because what is so wasted, represents labour superfluously expended, labour that does not count in the product or enter into its value.
>
> (*Capital* I (Marx, 1954): 190–91)

Here, any effort or work on the part of the labourer that does not lead – directly or indirectly – to an increase in surplus value is, in effect, 'wasted labour' and a candidate for criminalisation. Elsewhere, Marx scornfully asks whether the criminal has any use under capitalism and responds that the criminal 'produces not only crimes but also criminal law, and with it the professor who gives lectures on criminal law'. Furthermore, the criminal produces 'the whole of the police and of criminal justice, constables, judges, hangmen, juries, etc., and all these different lines of business which form equally many categories of the social division of labour':

> Would locks ever have reached their present degree of excellence had there been no thieves? Would the making of bank-notes have reached its present perfection had there been no forgers? [...] Crime, through its constantly new methods of attack upon property, constantly calls into being new methods of defence, and so is as productive as strikes for the invention of machines.

In these provocative comments, Marx is observing that capitalism has no more interest in solving crime than it has in solving industrial unrest. Whilst individual capitalists may rue individual crimes and strikes, the system as a whole profits from them and they are, indeed, part of its dynamic pattern of change. There is undoubtedly an overall capitalist interest in *containing* crime in order to prevent the premature collapse of the system but, for Marx, capitalism and crime are mutually interdependent.

An early effort to generate a theory of crime on the basis of Marx's work was made by the Dutch criminologist Willem Bonger (1876–1940) in his justifiably renowned *Criminality and Economic Conditions* (1969; first published in 1916). In it, he claimed that capitalism encouraged greed, egoism and self-interest at the same time that it stunted the intellectual and moral development of the poorer classes. Put these two sets of conditions together, Bonger argued, and what ensued was a series of social conflicts over property, morality and responsibility. In this circumstance, *all* crimes – be they economic, sexual, political or pathological – are the result of a perverted social system that has demoralised the body politic, diminished the altruism of mutual care and support and opened the floodgates of unbridled egoism. Whilst Bonger's main emphasis is on crimes committed by the poor against the poor, he suggests that the system's perversion is also the cause of upper-class crimes as well as crimes committed by persons with 'psychic defects' since, in the latter case, such persons would have the greatest difficulty adapting to the social and economic environment of egoistic capitalism. Summing up his analysis, Bonger (1969: 168) claims that the principal causes of crime are 'first, the present [capitalist] structure of society, which brings about innumerable conflicts; second, the lack of civilisation and education among the poorer classes; and, third, alcoholism, which is in turn a consequence of the social environment'.

Following Bonger, a small number of social scientists continued the effort to develop Marxist approaches to crime and crime control. Thus, Rusche and Kircheimer (1939) accounted for changes in punishment practices in terms of the control of labour, arguing that the severity and intensity of punishment varied according to the availability of labour. When labour was scarce and the working class in a relatively powerful bargaining position, punishments tended to be more humane; when there was a surplus of labour and the bargaining power of the working class weakened then punishments became harsher. In this way, Rusche and Kircheimer sought to explain changes in penal law as a function of class conflict. Quinney (1977) interpreted crime in terms of the 'fiscal crisis of the state'. In Quinney's view, capitalism is responsible for steady increases in the crime rate and so, to sustain its legitimacy, the capitalist state must spend more of its resources on controlling crime. However, this expenditure undermines the state's ability to ensure the continued accumulation of capital so that crime itself is a threat to capitalism's continued expansion. Whereas Rusche and Kircheimer interpreted crime and the criminal law in terms of class conflict, Quinney interpreted these in terms of problems of capital accumulation. Quinney's political economy of crime and crime control was supplemented by William Chambliss (1975). In an essay entitled 'Toward a Political Economy of Crime', Chambliss argued that criminal acts are so defined because the definitions serve the interest of the ruling class; members of the ruling class are able to violate laws (virtually) without penalty whilst the working class are regularly punished; the widening gap between rich and poor necessitates an expansion of penal law (and, by extension, the criminal justice system) in order to force the working class into submission. Taking a further lead from Marx, Chambliss suggested that crime helps to reduce surplus labour by creating employment in the war against crime; that it diverts the lower classes' attention away from the iniquities of their own exploitation; and that it is wholly created by those whose interest it serves.

Marxist criminologies have been instrumental in sustaining the links between ideas about crime and ideas about the wider societies in which it occurs, but they are not without problems. Although Bonger, for example, drew on Marxism as a source of critical *inspiration* it is far from clear that his work presents a Marxist *expla-*

nation for crime. This is partly because Bonger expends little energy working out why some things are defined as criminal and others are not. As we have seen, an important focus in Marx's work was the role played by the criminal law and the interdependent relationship between capitalism and crime. Bonger, on the other hand, saw crime as a purely negative consequence of a 'bad' social system – one that would disappear once a morally sound socialism arrived. Hence, the analysis does not tease out the importance of the ever-changing definition of criminal acts, nor the ever-developing technological contest between the entrepreneurial criminal and the industrial environment. Rusche and Kircheimer's celebrated exploration of *Punishment and Social Structure* had already been somewhat undermined by events following the Russian Revolution insofar as the association between labour scarcity/surplus and severity of punishment appeared to break down. The genocide, imprisonment and/or transportation of peasant farmers, political opponents, cultural deviants and anyone else who came under Party suspicion could hardly be explained in terms of the negotiation between capitalist ruling classes and a more or less powerful proletariat. Moreover, explaining the attempted genocide of the Jews in Germany purely in terms of class conflict would require that the history of European Jewish settlement, racial prejudices and the peculiarly criminal political culture of Nazi Germany all be ignored entirely. Whilst Quinney and Chambliss both offer somewhat more grounded Marxist explanations of crime and crime control they nonetheless tend to adopt something of a bird's-eye view of crime problems. If crime and crime control are explained in terms of capital accumulation or powerful ruling-class interests there seems little for the ordinary man and woman to do other than tool up with Marxist theory and chase the revolution! The fact that many ordinary men and women view crime rather differently than do academic Marxists may suggest that a theory of crime needs to pay rather more attention to such perceptions and perhaps less attention to correct interpretations of Marx. Indeed, this is precisely the direction taken by **critical criminology**, feminism and left realism in the late 1970s and early 1980s.

See also: **critical criminology; feminism and criminology; realism**

Further reading: Chambliss (1975); Taylor, I., Walton, P. and Young, J. 'Marx, Engels and Bonger on Crime and Social Control', in Taylor *et al.* (1973)

MASS MEDIA

A medium serves as a conduit through which communication is transmitted. Mass media are large-scale and formally organised technologies of communication. They are distinguished, first, by their ability to enable a small number of people to speak to many thousands or millions of individuals. Second, by its very nature, mass media communication is a one-way process, with audiences able to receive but not respond to communication.

Mass media first developed in the form of print culture in the seventeenth century and grew rapidly during the era of industrialisation. The twentieth century saw a massive expansion of both the number and range of mass media, with the emergence of cinema, radio and television. Western industrial societies can be viewed as media-saturated, with inhabitants relying on these modes of communication for news, information, education and entertainment. Consequently, such media have formed a major focus across the social sciences, as they are seen to play a key role in shaping people's understandings of self, identity and the wider world. The power and influence of the media can be analysed from a number of different theoretical standpoints. *Liberal* and *pluralist* positions view the media as offering a diversity of competing perspectives from which audiences can select in order to construct their own understandings. In contrast, **Marxist** and critical theorists argue that the mass media converge on a set of common political and cultural viewpoints that help to reproduce the power of dominant classes.

Criminology has been interested in the mass media on a number of levels. First, analysts have examined the ways in which the media represent the nature and extent of crime problems. Numerous studies have highlighted the fact that media tend to consistently over-report crimes that in reality are quite rare (especially violent and sexual offences). At the same time, there is an under-reporting of those crimes that are the most commonplace (such as property crimes) and those associated with powerful social actors (such as corporate and **white-collar crimes**). In extreme instances, such distorted reporting may induce **moral panics** about particular forms of criminal activity. Second, criminologists have explored the role played by mass media in constructing stereotypes of criminality, thereby depicting certain groups (such as youth, minority ethnic groups and foreigners) as a fundamental threat to security and social order. Thirdly, **criminal psychology** has focused upon whether and to what extent media representations of crime, sex and violence might reinforce or encourage lawbreaking behaviour (the so-called *effects debate*).

The development of media and cultural studies has shaped in significant ways criminology's interest in media and their impacts. With the recent emergence of **cultural criminology**, media analysis has come to figure centrally within the discipline today.

See also: **critical criminology; cultural criminology; ideology; Marxist criminology; moral panic**

Further reading: Jewkes (2004); Reiner (2002); Sparks (1992); Thompson (1995)

MORAL PANIC

The concept of moral panic has developed in tandem with **labelling perspectives** on crime and deviance. Particularly important is the insight that classifications of deviant behaviour, and societal responses to it, will be shaped by the meanings that are applied to actors and their conduct. From this starting point, analysts of moral panics explore the ways in which unjustified social anxieties are created about certain types of individuals, groups and events. Particular emphasis is placed upon the role of **mass media** in defining danger and deviance, and the ways in which media representations are shaped by wider social, political and economic issues.

According to Stan Cohen (1972: 9) a moral panic occurs when

A condition, episode, person or group of persons emerges to become defined as a threat to societal values and interests; its nature is presented in a stylised and stereotypical fashion by the mass media; the moral barricades are manned by editors, bishops, politicians, and other right-thinking people; socially accredited experts pronounce their diagnoses and solutions; ways of coping are evolved or ... resorted to; the condition then disappears, submerges or deteriorates and becomes more visible.

Thus the term 'panic' denotes the fact that the representation of a supposed social problem is out of all proportion to the actual level of threat it entails. Indeed, it has been pointed out that even non-existent threats can nevertheless become the object of a panic and result in extreme societal reactions (for example, the 'witch hunts' that swept across Europe in medieval times). Furthermore, whether or not any given behaviour will be construed as a serious danger will depend upon cultural and social context; the selfsame conduct may at one point in time be considered unremarkable and relatively benign, only to suddenly become the object of a widespread panic (one such instance would be the emergence of a moral panic about marijuana use in the USA during the 1940s). Central to the creation of a panic is the role played by those whom Cohen calls *moral entrepreneurs*, agents who take it upon themselves to bring the supposed problem to the attention of wider society and who press for the condemnation and legal suppression of the behaviour in question.

Goode and Ben-Yehuda (1994) suggest that analyses of moral panic broadly fall into one of three kinds, each attributing their emergence to a different social location. First, they note those perspectives that view moral panics as engineered by *interest groups*, those who stand to benefit if a particular behaviour comes to be acknowledged as a serious social problem. Second, there are those accounts that view moral panics as *elite-engineered*, as ruling classes direct social concerns against those groups who might otherwise present a threat to elites' continued hold upon power. Third, there are those accounts that see moral panics as emerging from *grassroots* sentiments, such that wider public concerns drive an issue onto the political and law-enforcement agenda.

The concept of moral panic has been fruitfully used to examine the emergence of a wide range of crime problems, including youth delinquency, recreational drug use, child sex abuse, pornography and internet crime. However, the validity of the concept has been subject to criticism from a number of angles. Especially important is the critique developed by Waddington (1986) and others, which focuses on the question of whether or not a societal reaction to a problem is *disproportionate*. In other words, the concept of moral panic is generally understood as involving a reaction that is *out of proportion* to the actual seriousness of the problem. However, moral panic theorists do not specify what a *proportionate* reaction would be (i.e. just how much social concern is the right amount for any given crime problem?). Consequently, it is suggested that whether or not a reaction becomes classified as a panic has less to do with any objective criteria of disproportionality, and more to do with the political and social sympathies of the analysts themselves.

See also: **deviance amplification; labelling perspectives**

Further reading: Cohen (1972); Goode and Ben-Yehuda (1994); Waddington (1986)

NET-WIDENING

The debate about 'net-widening' needs to be set in the context of a long struggle in the 1960s and 1970s to introduce 'diversionary' strategies into the criminal justice systems of Britain and America – most often through forms of community service under probation supervision and, later, in programmes of 'intermediate treatment' that attempted to provide young offenders with alternative goals and skills as well as enhance their self-esteem (see Thorpe *et al.*, 1980). The 'diversion' movement was largely, but not exclusively, focused on young people and had supporters of remarkable renown (see Lemert, 1971). Amongst other things, the aim of the movement was to prevent the criminalisation of young people for minor offences by diverting them away from the 'hard' end of the criminal justice system towards a 'soft' end of treatment and support services. However, what in fact happened was that the diversionary programmes themselves acted as channels that funnelled young offenders into the criminal justice system in ever-increasing numbers. Dismayed by the apparent failures of the more welfare-oriented approaches, Lemert (1981) penned a critique of the approach with which he had for long been associated and, whilst diversionary projects continued to be used, they were no longer seen as the great progressive means of decriminalising youth.

In 1979 Stan Cohen published an essay called 'The Punitive City' (see also Cohen, 1985) in which he argued that the enormous increase in alternative treatments, punishments and rehabilitation regimes, far from reducing the reach of the criminal justice system, in fact acted to disperse social control even more widely throughout the social body. Drawing inspiration from Michel Foucault's (1977) *Discipline and Punish*, Cohen argued that the dispersal could be pictured in terms of the criminal justice system capturing more and more people in its 'nets'. In this argument the 'diversionary' programmes did not *substitute* for criminal justice interventions. Instead, they *supplemented* them – adding an increased menu of options for experts and decision makers to exert sanctions against (previously unsanctioned) activities. Thus, suggested Cohen, the attempt to divert young people had increased the size of the criminal justice system's nets. More agencies – notably social workers and community workers – had been drawn into administering criminal justice sanctions and, as a corollary, more individuals were ensnared in those nets as 'offenders'. At the same time, the kinds of behaviour that might lead a person to encounter criminal justice sanctions had altered – many more petty offences were now subject to criminal justice sanctions so that the 'mesh' of the nets had become progressively smaller. Finally, the range and kind of intervention had intensified – including more individualised and longer-term treatment regimes, and greater use of indeterminate sentences or sentence 'packages' made up of a number of components, meaning that the criminal justice system's nets had been strengthened.

So, far from diverting individuals away from criminal justice sanctions, Cohen argued, the diversionary welfare-oriented programmes of the 1970s had provided the system with wider and stronger nets consisting of a thinner mesh and led to an increase in the rate and variety of behaviours that were criminalised and subject to social control.

See also: **surveillance**

Further reading: Cohen (1985); Lemert (1981)

NEW MEDIA

A term used to denote the recent development of media that mobilise electronic and computer technologies to enable communication in digital form. The most notable such medium is the internet, a publicly accessible network of computers that emerged in the 1970s and came to span the globe by the late 1990s. New media differ from established mass media in a number of significant ways. First, while mass media such as television and radio only permit one-way communication between a single speaker and a large audience (one-to-many), new media enable two-way communication between large numbers of people (many-to-many). Second, digitisation has enabled words, sound and images to be flexibly manipulated and combined using powerful yet relatively inexpensive devices such as home computers. Third, media like the internet span geographical and political boundaries, enabling communication on a global scale. Taken together, it is suggested that these developments have democratised communication by allowing ordinary people to become the producers and not just consumers of media messages. However, criminological interest has focused upon the more negative aspects of these developments. In particular, the internet has seen the growth of a wide range of crime problems (so-called **cybercrimes**), such as computer hacking, child pornography, identity theft and fraud.

See also: **cybercrime; mass media**

Further reading: Lister *et al*. (2003)

NORMS

Norms are the shared rules that regulate behaviour in various social settings. Norms provide a set of guidelines and expectations about what is and is not acceptable or appropriate conduct. They are inculcated and reinforced through an on-going process of **socialisation**. For sociologists such as Durkheim, all societies are bound together by a normative structure that is essential for their continued existence, and the failure of normative regulation is closely linked to crime and social conflict. The role of norms in inhibiting criminality has been explored from a wide range of criminological perspectives, including **Chicago School criminology** and **social control** theories. Criminologists have also examined the ways in which norms at odds with those of mainstream society can support rule-breaking, especially in the context of deviant **subcultures**.

See also: **Chicago School criminology; community; crime and deviance; cultural transmission; differential association; Durkheimian criminology; social control perspectives; socialisation; subcultural criminologies**

OBSCENITY AND PORNOGRAPHY

Obscenity and pornography have become key concerns in studies of crime and deviance. Pornography denotes visual or written representations of a sexually explicit nature, whose primary aim or use is to stimulate sexual excitement. In Western societies the production and consumption of many kinds of pornography is not prohibited by law, although it may be condemned as deviant or unsavoury. However, some forms of pornographic representation are liable to be defined as obscene. Obscenity denotes representations and expressions that are held to be generally offensive and thus unacceptable by society at large. Obscenity is almost invariably subject to legal prohibition and formal, criminal sanctions. In recent years, particular attention has been focused upon child pornography, which has come to be seen as a major crime problem as new electronic technologies (such as the internet) have enabled such representations to be widely distributed. Most recently, concerns have been raised over violent sexual pornography, a phenomenon that has been linked (rightly or wrongly) to incidents of violent sexual victimisation. However, it must be borne in mind that what counts as either pornographic or obscene will vary widely across cultural and historical contexts, and whether or not any particular form of representation is considered pornographic and/or obscene may be deeply contested.

See also: **crime and deviance; cybercrime**

Further reading: Hyde (1964); Jenkins (2001); Procida and Simpson (2003)

ORGANISED CRIME

Until fairly recently, a widespread conception of organised crime has been the stereotypical image of the gun-toting gangster as part of a Mafia-type structure. The image is undoubtedly fuelled by popular media representations but the reality is more complex – and difficult to uncover with any certainty. Whilst criminologists know more about organised crime now compared to even the recent past there are two special problems in the attempt to paint an accurate picture of organised criminal activity. These are the problem of definition and the problem of sources of information.

All concepts, it goes without saying, are subject to varying interpretations but organised crime is especially problematic to define. Yet definitions are crucial since organised criminal activity has become a priority area for policy makers and law-enforcement agencies. There are many reasons for this, including the apparent growth in such activity across the last decade. However, there are several problems with arriving at a definition since definitions vary between countries, between agencies, and between academics. The issue is important because a definition can determine whether or not a problem is considered to be an organised crime issue. For example, in the 1960s it was thought that Germany had no organised criminal activity because this was understood using the official American view of organised crime as a rationally-designed, violent and powerful criminal organisation. Law-enforcement officials found this definition inadequate and when it was eventually changed Germany was able to note that there was indeed organised criminal activity within its borders (Von Lampe, 2001).

Definitions tend to be derived either from the legal system and criminal law or from perceptions of the characteristics of crime. The latter may be the type of activity (drug trafficking, internet fraud, or car-jacking rings, for example) and some countries, such as the Netherlands, Poland and Slovenia, derive their definitions in this way. Alternatively, the definition may be derived from the crime group and, in particular, its structure (see Albanese *et al.*, 2003). The Federal Bureau of Investigation (FBI), for example, defines organised crime as: 'A continuing criminal conspiracy, having an organised structure, fed by fear and corruption and motivated by greed' (ibid.: 4). The structure of the group is central to this definition yet the focus on the organisation of the group has created further difficulties since the concept of 'organisation' is even more problematic than that of 'crime'. Some conceive of organised crime as if it were carried out by 'an organisation' of criminals. That is, an illegal, hierarchical, bureaucratic corporation with a boss at the top and a line-management system. Others have argued against this conceptualisation and focused more on how the relationships between people involved are organised. In the extensive literature on organised crime this difference is frequently debated around a string of dichotomies: hierarchies versus networks; organised versus disorganised; traditional versus non-traditional. However, as organised crime exists in different forms and at different levels of sophistication the debate is bound to remain inconclusive. The United Nations (UN Office on Drugs and Crime, 2002) has tried to catalogue the variety through a pilot survey of organised crime in sixteen countries. The report states early on that 'The diversity of criminal actors and organisations has made consensus about the definition of "organised crime" difficult ... arguments as to what constitutes organised crime and what does not have occupied a central position in the debate, and are critical to efforts to monitor developments from an international level' (ibid.: 4). The results of the survey identified forty different types of organised crime group structures, ranging from the hierarchically organised to small, fluid clusters of persons coming together for particular 'projects'.

Defining organised crime according to the activity is also far from straightforward because there are many and varied types of such activity. For example, the following activities are considered to be organised criminal activities:

- trafficking: in arms, drugs, humans (especially women and children for the sex trade), hazardous wastes (e.g. plutonium and nuclear materials); human organs; wildlife

- smuggling – stolen vehicles, and other contraband (alcohol, tobacco)/ humans
- counterfeiting and piracy
- extortion and protection rackets
- fraud
- gambling
- racketeering
- loan sharking
- theft, robbery, hijacking, kidnapping
- prostitution
- pornography

Added to this variety are 'enabling activities': corruption of officials; money-laundering; violence and intimidation. Organised criminals are dependent upon and involved with personnel in the licit economic and political spheres, such as customs officials, police officers, politicians, business people and others. Organised crime represents not a pathological activity in a separate shadow economy but has widespread connections to legal society. This recognition has led to fears of destabilisation of economic and financial systems (through money-laundering), for example, and destabilisation of democracy in countries with 'weak' democratic systems (through corruption) (see Wright, 2006). These fears, in addition to the social harm caused by activities such as human trafficking, and, more recently, organised crime connections to insurgent groups, have ensured the political prioritisation of organised crime as a major, contemporary, international issue.

The second problem in trying to grasp organised crime and its consequences concerns source material. There are examples of good ethnographies (cf. Adler, 1993; Aries, 2006) but for the most part data tends to come from official agencies. This poses a number of problems for researchers as government and law-enforcement agencies have different agenda and priorities to academics so that accessing relevant data is often difficult if not impossible. Access to data is fiercely guarded and there will be gaps in any data secured. It will also have been selected by gatekeeper in the department or agency (see Dorn et al., 2005). Of course, some data is released for public consumption. For example, the National Criminal Intelligence Service in the UK (now absorbed into the Serious and Organised Crime Agency) and EUROPOL publish an Annual Threat Assessment. Whilst both of these contain useful information, they omit much data that is highly restricted. The problems involved in relying on official data are seen in the earliest criminological works on organised crime. Donald Cressey, for example, argued that 'if one understands the Cosa Nostra, he understands organised crime in the United States' (cited in Lyman and Potter, 2004: 4). The basis for this argument was official data Cressey obtained from Federal agencies. Cressey had discussed bow difficult and also dangerous it is to try and gain direct access to organised criminals and their operations and Lyman and Potter point out that in exchange for access to data Cressey had to agree to a positive representation of the agencies he was researching in, compromising the academic independence of his research.

Although organised crime is not a new phenomenon, since the early 1990s it appears to have become more mobile and sophisticated, taking advantage of the 'new' communication technologies, and exploiting political and economic changes within Europe and else-where. The last two decades have witnessed great changes in the political make-up of Europe: the collapse of Communism in 1989, and the enlargement of the European Union to 27 countries, have all contributed to the growth of organised crime. The opening up of borders for trade worldwide under neo-liberal policy agenda – often referred to as globalization – has expanded the possibilities for global economic activity and the mobility of goods, services and peoples, and has also opened up new opportunities for organised crime groups. These factors have led to organised crime becoming increas-ingly transnational in character, operating cross-border criminal activities with relative ease, and constituting a problem that affects nations across the world. Organised crime groups may have members living in different countries: they may source the illicit goods or ser-vices in one (usually economically disadvantaged) country or region and sell them on in other (richer) countries (Castells, 2000). There is also evidence to suggest that organised criminal groups in one coun-try are forging links with groups in other countries, and so extending their operations and broadening their markets. In this sense they operate as businesses aiming to make serious money, leading to the term 'enterprise crime' to describe their operations. For all of these reasons, methodological problems notwithstanding, criminological interest in organised crime seems set to intensify in the immediate future.

See also: **drug crime; state crime; terrorism**

Further reading: Lyman and Potter (2004)

PEACE-MAKING CRIMINOLOGY

Less a theoretical perspective and more a philosophy of non-violent conflict resolution, peace-making criminology draws together an eclectic range of approaches to the study of crime and criminal justice. Peace-making as an approach to understanding crime and justice came to the attention of criminology following the publication of a collection of essays edited by Harold Pepinsky and Richard Quinney entitled *Criminology as Peacemaking* (Pepinsky and Quinney, 1991). In his conclusion to the collected essays, Pepinsky suggested that peace-making drew on three sets of traditions – religious, feminist and critical traditions – although, in fact, its sources are much broader. Among other sources, contributors to the collection drew on anarchism, socialism, Marxism, mutualism and feminism; Buddhism, Quakerism and Gandhi; social psychology, functionalist sociology, post-structuralism, existentialism and psychoanalysis. Whilst the philosophical foundations of the peace-making approach are complex in the extreme, its moral perspectives on crime and criminal justice are not. It challenges the metaphor of 'war' in contemporary criminal justice policy – the 'war on drugs', or the 'war on crime', and so on – arguing that the relegation of criminals to the status of the 'enemy' is a form of dehumanisation that both prevents offenders from taking responsibility for the harms they perpetrate and reinforces society's unequal power relationships. The dominant approach to criminal justice in contemporary society is one of punishment and retribution, but this merely encourages offenders to be more efficient in order to avoid being caught (Fuller, 1998: 88) and does not go to the root of the causes of crime problem – which are to be found in the violent, unequal and exclusive organisation of modern society. Peace-making criminology is strongly linked to the **Restorative Justice** movement and shares many of the latter's proposals for dealing with problems of crime and justice.

Peace-making criminology begins in a distinction between 'negative' and 'positive' peace. Negative peace refers simply to the absence of violence. Positive peace refers to the presence of mutual support, humanism and freedom from oppression; that is, to the presence of those forms of human organisation that reduce motivations for violence. It is towards realising the second sense of 'peace' that peace-making criminology strives. In this regard, it is as much a critique of contemporary society as it is a branch of criminology. According to Barak (2005: 131), 'for positive peace to exist as a prevailing social reality, the dominant sources of violence – alienation, humiliation, shame, inequity, poverty, racism, sexism, and so on – would have to be substantially reduced, if not done away with'. Hence, the goal of peace-making is not simply to engage with offenders and make *them* more peaceful but to instil principles and practices of mindfulness, respect and reconciliation into the operations of all contemporary social institutions – including the institutions of criminal justice. A peaceful, or at least less violent, society cannot be built on the foundations of a violent and exclusive criminal justice policy. A society in which criminal justice is founded on punishment and retribution is one that upholds violence as a means of resolving conflicts. It sends out the signal that the way to deal with harms is to mete out equal or greater harms to their perpetrators. Such an approach turns the goal of reducing violence on its head because, according to Richard Quinney (2000: 27), 'the means cannot be different from the ends, peace can come only out of peace.' A violent and exclusive criminal justice system (CJS) offers no means through which offenders, victims and communities can be reconciled, reintegrated and enabled to devise useful and appropriate reactions to the criminal harms committed and suffered. Rather than

> escalating the violence in our already violent society by responding to violence and conflict with state violence and conflict in the form of penal sanctions such as death and prison, we need to de-escalate violence by responding to it through forms of conciliation, mediation, and dispute settlement.
>
> (Lanier and Henry, 2004: 329)

John Fuller (1998) has proposed a 'pyramid paradigm' for integrating peace-making principles and practices into the criminal justice system. At the pyramid's base is the principle of non-violence. This principle applies to premeditated violence on the part of the state as much as to the violence perpetrated by individual offenders: the goal of a criminal justice system should not be to meet violence with more violence but to reduce the total levels of violence in society as a whole. Built on top of the commitment to non-violence are five further sets of commitments – a commitment to *social justice* in which the CJS actively works towards diminishing its inherent ethnic, class and sex discriminations; to *inclusion*, where the CJS incorporates offenders, families and communities into negotiations about the most suitable outcomes of criminal justice procedures; to the use of *correct means* in order to ensure that neither victims nor offenders are forced to accept resolution by the imposition of inappropriate sentences; to *ascertainable criteria* so that all parties involved are able fully to understand the procedures used and options available; and to the *categorical imperative* in which criminal justice procedures are designed to uphold the dignity and respect of all parties involved – including the offender and the victim.

Although peace-making criminology is a relatively new perspective, it has attracted its fair share of criticism. Gibbons (1994) welcomed the emphasis on conflict resolution and techniques of mediation as alternative strategies in law enforcement but expressed some scepticism about the potential of the overall project. With reference to the United States, Gibbons went on to observe that it seemed a bit of a tall order to propose a fundamental overhaul of all social institutions as a means of delivering a more humane system of criminal justice. Given all of the political and economic problems that beset the modern United States – including an eye-wateringly enormous budget deficit and 'runaway entitlement program costs' – it would be all but impossible to achieve a fundamental transformation in America's social and criminal justice institutions. Moreover, whilst peace-making criminology is keen to emphasise the road to a mindful criminal justice policy, it is somewhat short on instructions for how to get there. Small-scale initiatives in victim–offender reconciliation and the inclusion of peace-making perspectives in education and training courses are all very well, but they do not point in any obvious way to the 'grand scale changes' that would be needed (Gibbons, 1994: 172).

Akers (2000) agrees with Gibbons that there is a contradiction between peace-making criminology's ends and its means – that is, there is a disjuncture between its political goals of a fair, just and peaceful society, and its practical recommendations for revising criminal justice policies. Many of its proposed alternative methods – of mediation, rehabilitation, restitution, and so on – have been part of the criminal justice mainstream for a long time and, it might be added, there is, as yet, no sign that a peaceful society is about to develop in their wake. Moreover, he argues that whilst it may be an interesting and ethically laudable standpoint on injustice it does not offer a theory of crime that can be tested nor a convincing explanation of why the systems of criminal justice in modern societies operate as they do. Instead, it appears that the peace-makers' account of crime and criminal justice is a 'just-so' story of the malaise of modern society.

See also: **restorative justice; victimology**

Further reading: Fuller (1998); Pepinsky and Quinney (1991)

POLICING AND THE POLICE

Policing denotes a wide range of regulatory practices that serve to monitor social behaviour and ensure conformity with laws and normative codes. Policing can be informal as well as formally organised, and can involve a wide range of social actors and institutions. The police, in contrast, comprise a formally organised institutional apparatus that is charged with upholding laws on behalf of society and is ultimately directed by and accountable to the state. Thus the police are but one of the many agencies that undertake policing across various walks of life. The history of policing in modern times is largely one of the formalisation and centralisation of law enforcement, a process in which policing functions have been gradually monopolised by specialised and professional crime-control agencies.

The origin of the modern police force in England and Wales is usually located in the late eighteenth and early nineteenth centuries. Before this period policing was undertaken by a 'patchwork' of local agencies and individuals, including watchmen, part-time parish constables and private 'thief-takers' who would recover property or apprehend wanted felons for financial reward. The early 1800s saw attempts to reorganise policing in London, creating parish-based groups of constables whose activities were regulated by a body of magistrates, and whose work was funded in part by the government (this arrangement was based upon the model of the so-called 'Bow Street Runners' which had been established by Henry and John Fielding in the mid-eighteenth century). The watershed year of 1829 saw the creation of the Metropolitan Police Force by the then home secretary Robert Peel. This marked a significant step in the organisation of public policing as well as instituting a system of accountability and centralised control. Over the next few decades, the Metropolitan force set the template for the development of mandatory county-based forces across England and Wales. These forces were funded by a combination of local revenues and central monies from the treasury, and were subject to performance monitoring by government inspectors who would report annually to Parliament. The period from the 1850s to the early decades of the twentieth century was also characterised by an incremental professionalisation of the police, with its officers becoming full-time paid public employees and the development of standardised methods of recruitment, training and supervision.

The emergence of modern policing has been explained in a number of different ways. The conventional (so-called 'Whig') histories of crime control view these developments as a rational and progressive response to a range of problems including the inefficiency of the 'patchwork' system, the high levels of corruption amongst constables and other law-enforcers, the lack of proper accountability, and the inability of the old system to cope with a rising tide of crime in London and the other rapidly expanding cities. However, more critical (so-called 'revisionist') historians have located the drive to reorganise policing in more political motivations. The period in question was a time of significant social upheaval and conflict, with a growing and impoverished industrial working class rebelling against exploitative working conditions, grinding poverty and their exclusion from political participation. This manifested itself in numerous strikes, protests and 'riots' that were viewed by those in power as a threat to the existing social, economic and political order. The development of the 'new police' can thus be seen as an attempt to more effectively suppress revolutionary movements that would inevitably have threatened the power and privilege of a small and highly privileged ruling class. It is certainly true that the Metropolitan and other newly established forces were frequently used in a military manner (sometimes alongside the army) to suppress political protest, to break strikes, and to tighten control over the working classes. This politicised use of the police remains controversial to this day, with for example the use of the police to suppress the miners' strike by the Thatcher government in the 1980s.

More broadly, it has been argued that the police do not in fact have a single clearly defined public role. Initial claims to justify the development of centralised policing focused upon the goal of crime prevention through patrolling and visible deterrence. However, it is a matter of considerable doubt as to whether and to what extent the police are able to effectively prevent crime, as opposed to reacting to it after it has occurred. A second supposed role of the police is to investigate crimes and bring offenders to justice. Again, given the very small proportion of crimes that result in arrests and convictions, the ability of the police to discharge this responsibility has been questioned. It has been suggested that the police are caught between the goals of prevention and response. For example, the 1960s saw aconcerted move away from foot patrols towards rapid reaction to crime incidents using patrol cars. While this was deemed to create a greater efficiency in use of police personnel, it has also been criticised for removing police from the community and undermining visible deterrence, resulting in renewed calls for a return to 'bobbies on the beat'.

A further tension arises from the contrasting imperatives of 'coercion' and 'consent'. On the one hand the police are deemed to be servants of the people and to be responsive to the needs of citizens. On the other side, they are often called upon to use force against those same citizens, thereby engendering public distrust and hostility towards officers. Problems of legitimacy and trust have come to the fore in recent decades through a combination of scandals including miscarriages of justice, accusations of police racism and brutality, claims by serving black and women officers about a police culture of discrimination, and a sense of grievance around what has been perceived as heavy-handed treatment of minority communities. This culminated with the inquiry into the Metropolitan Police's handling of the racist murder of black teenager Stephen Lawrence, which concluded that the force itself was 'institutionally racist'. In response the police have been subjected to an ongoing process of reform aimed at creating a force that is more properly representative of and responsive to society, and which might command the confidence of all sections of the community.

Perhaps the most significant change in the organisation of policing in recent decades has been an ongoing process of *pluralisation* and *privatisation*. Pluralisation entails the redistribution of crime-control and law-enforcement activities from the police to a range of other public and private agencies (such as local authorities, community groups and private contractors). Local authorities now operate a vast network of CCTV monitoring systems and employ street patrols and community safety wardens, while citizen groups organise neighbourhood watch schemes, and the contractors such as Group 4 take responsibility for transporting prisoners to and from court. Privatisation, a related development, entails the increasing performance of policing functions by private commercial organisations motivated by profit. Such organisations offer an increasing range of security services, including the provision of private security guards, the provision and maintenance of crime-prevention devices and alarm systems, the operation of electronic tagging and offender monitoring systems, the creation and maintenance of criminal intelligence and records systems for the police, specialised training for police officers, and drug testing and background checks for companies on potential employees. These changes can be seen as the result of a number of pressures. First, the post-World War II period saw a massive increase in recorded crime, and an upsurge that the police seemed unable to curtail despite substantial increases in personnel and funding. This produced a widespread perception that the police were unable to effectively prevent crime, and encouraged individuals, communities and organisations to seek alternatives. Second, the political shift to the right under the Conservative Thatcher government in the 1980s placed emphasis on limiting public spending and finding market solutions to public policy challenges. This actively encouraged private provision of goods and services that had previously been provided from within the public sector. Third, this period saw an ever-greater range of demands placed upon the police, creating the problem of balancing crime prevention, public safety, public reassurance, tackling antisocial and nuisance behaviour, and investigating crime. Fourth, processes of social, political and economic change saw the emergence of a range of new offences that the police, as traditionally constituted, were ill equipped to tackle, including hi-tech crimes, intellectual property crimes, and transnational crimes. Taken together, these changes marked the end of the public monopoly on policing. Criminologists such as Bayley and Shearing (1996) have argued that we now face a reversion to the pre-modern system in which policing is provided by a wide range of actors, many of whom are located outside the public sphere. Many criminologists have been critical of recent trends, suggesting that they raise some serious difficulties. First, they note problems in assuring that private providers are publicly regulated or accountable (an issue that has been especially notable in relation to the hiring and behaviour of private security personnel). Second, they point out that access to policing and security through the market inevitably discriminates against those with the least financial resources, thereby leaving the poorest most vulnerable to criminal victimisation. Third, there can arise overlaps and conflicts between the various agents involved in policing, making the system less not more efficient. It remains to be seen whether these developments mark a permanent reordering of policing and crime control, or whether this plurality of activity will eventually be reabsorbed under more centralised regulation.

See also: **community crime prevention and community safety; risk; social control; surveillance**

Further reading: Foster and Bowling (2002)

POSITIVIST CRIMINOLOGY

In the first instance, positivism refers not so much to a particular theoretical perspective, as to a philosophical and methodological approach to producing knowledge. Positivism originated in the early 1800s, and was shaped by the development of the natural sciences in the preceding century. Enlightenment science viewed the natural world as subject to universal laws of cause and effect, which it held could be uncovered through careful observation and experimentation. The knowledge produced through scientific investigation would be objectively true, and based solely upon demonstrable facts rather than opinion, speculation or superstition. Early nineteenth-century social positivists such as Auguste Comte (1798–1857) were inspired by the methods of natural science to propose a science of society that would provide objective knowledge about the forces that shaped society and the behaviour of individuals within it (it was Comte who first coined the term 'positivist philosophy', as well as 'sociology'). Positivists viewed human beings as fundamentally no different from the objects studied by other sciences, insofar as people's actions were similarly determined by objective causes. Just as the behaviour of a falling stone could be explained through the force of gravity acting upon it, the actions of human individuals and groups could be explained by uncovering the social forces behind them (a 'social physics', as Comte termed it). Breaking with tradition, positivists rejected the notion of human free will, and insisted that humans were determined in their actions by the forces that acted upon them. These forces, they insisted, could be discovered by copying the observational methods of the natural sciences, most especially through the careful and systematic collection and analysis of facts about society.

The impact of positivism upon the study of crime manifested itself relatively rapidly, with the work of the Belgian statistician Adolphe Quételet (1796–1874) standing as an early important example. From the 1820s to the 1840s he authored a number of influential works outlining his vision of a 'social mechanics', including his book *On Man and the Development of his Faculties, or an Essay on Social Physics* (1935). In such works, he suggested that a law-like regularity could be identified amongst social phenomena, and sought to relate such phenomena (such as mortality and ill health) to other determining social and demographic factors. In respect to crime, he noted that rates for different types of crime remained remarkably constant over time, thereby suggesting that criminal behaviour was subject to ordered and regular causes, and not simply a random outcome of human free will. Through an analysis of official crime statistics he also identified social factors (such as youth, poor education, low income and unemployment) that appeared to have a strong connection with criminal conduct. Similar work was conducted in France by Quételet's collaborator A. M. Guerry, and later in the nineteenth century, in England, by R. W. Rawson, Joseph Fletcher and John Glyde.

Criminological positivism is today most closely associated, however, not with Quételet but with the Italian physician Cesare Lombroso (1835–1909) and his followers. Lombroso founded the self-styled *Il Scuolo Positivo* ('The Positive School') of criminology in the late nineteenth century. In adopting this label, Lombroso demonstrated his commitment to developing a 'science of criminality' based upon positivist principles (it is Lombroso who is commonly attributed with first coining the term 'criminology' to describe his studies). He took issue in particular with earlier classicist accounts of crime that held to the idea of human free will and choice. For Lombroso, humans could not be exempted from the laws of nature and its causes, and crime had to be explained in an objective manner by identifying those characteristics or traits that disposed certain individuals or groups towards criminality. Unlike Quételet, Lombroso focused not upon social, economic or demographic factors, but upon biological characteristics. By carefully examining and cataloguing the physical traits of hundreds of convicted felons, he sought to uncover those biological peculiarities that marked out 'born criminals' and which accounted for their lawbreaking behaviour.

The positivist method has exerted an enduring influence over social and natural scientific studies of crime. For example, Emile Durkheim (1858–1917), one of the so-called 'founding fathers' of sociology and an early sociological analyst of crime and punishment, borrowed from the objective 'social mechanics' of Quételet (something he acknowledged in his famous book *Suicide* (1897)). Proponents of biological and psychological explanations of crime have likewise sought to identify the objective causes of crime. The analysis of large aggregates of statistical crime data, in the search for factors that correlate with the propensity to offend, continues to be a dominant trend in criminological research, something readily apparent in the pages of leading criminological research journals.

However, almost from its inception, positivism has come under sustained criticism from alternative perspectives. Interpretive social scientists in particular have objected to positivists' attempts to equate humans with other objects and entities to be found in the world of nature. They point out that, unlike stones or trees, humans are capable of understanding the world in which they live and of interpreting the situations in which they find themselves. Human conduct is, they insist, meaningful – how someone acts will depend crucially upon the meanings they attach to their own experiences and actions, and those of others.

They accuse positivists of reducing humans to unthinking 'puppets' who are blindly propelled this way or that by forces over which they have no control. The interpretive critique within criminology reached its high point in the work of labelling theorists such as Howard Becker. Becker and others insisted that the objective causes of crime could not be found because crime itself is a social construct, and whether or not an act is deemed criminal will be the result of labels or meanings attached to people's actions. Rather than vainly searching for the objective causes of criminal behaviour, we should instead uncover the subjective interpretations through which particular individuals and certain actions become identified as criminal in different social contexts. This critique of criminological positivism has been revived, most recently, by **cultural criminology**. Thus for example Jock Young (2004) dubs positivist, statistically oriented analysis to be a kind of 'voodoo criminology', one which makes spurious connections between actions and their supposed causes by playing a 'numbers game' complete with scientific-looking equations, charts and tables. This rhetoric of science, he suggests, hides the fundamental wrong-headedness of a criminology that treats humans as dumb objects rather than the reflexive and self-aware beings that they in truth are.

See also: **biological criminology; classical criminology; crime data; Durkheimian criminology; labelling perspectives**

Further reading: Beirne (1987); Garland (2002a); Hughes and Sharrock (1990); Yar (2004); Young (2004)

POSTMODERNITY/POSTMODERNISM

There are two distinct senses of the term 'postmodern' that should not be conflated. The first construes the postmodern as a type of society or historical era ('postmodernity') that has transcended the modern industrial world. In this meaning, postmodern society is said to be characterised by a shift from a manufacturing and industrial economy to a service and information economy, from mass solidarities based on shared social experiences to fragmented allegiances based on cultural distinctions, from a world of fixed hierarchies and traditions to a world of 'hyper-differentiated' lifestyles characterised by a deep-seated moral relativism (see Crook *et al.*, 1992). The second sense construes the postmodern as an altered way of seeing or understanding the world ('postmodernism'): a movement in the arts, sciences, architecture and in cultural outlooks more generally. In this meaning, the postmodern is characterised as a series of challenges to dominant ways of describing and explaining the social world: by showing how structures of gender and racial inequality were built into the very foundations of European industrial and colonial development (McClintock, 1995) or constitute a cornerstone of contemporary welfare and legal systems (see Copjec, 1991; Fraser, 1995). Both meanings (but especially the second) are contentious in social science generally, and criminology specifically, because they tend towards relativism: that is, postmodern explanations of social phenomena construe the world from a specific point of view. They challenge the assumption of neutral (social) scientific knowledge and proclaim that 'suppressed' or 'subjugated' knowledges are equally valid accounts.

Criminological debates about the postmodern generally follow the two different senses outlined above. On the one hand there are debates about whether criminal justice systems have moved beyond modern goals of universal justice, proportionate sentencing and economy of punishment to selective (even arbitrary) application of law, disproportionate sentencing for petty misdemeanours and excessive reliance on penal and criminal justice expenditures at the expense of welfare and social expenditures (see Hallsworth, 2002; Penna and Yar, 2003). On the other hand, there are debates about the very rationality of contemporary criminal justice systems and their historical relationship to colonial and imperial European projects. Biko Agozino (2003), for example, challenges the discipline to 'decolonise' its theories and methods and produce a criminology capable of exposing fully the wide-scale suffering and harm embedded in the contemporary global order. Dragan Milanovic (1997), similarly, not only suggests that the world has tipped into a period of 'postmodernity' but also seeks to use a range of new outlooks (notably chaos and catastrophe theory and psychoanalytic semiotics) to develop a version of criminological postmodernism.

See also: **constitutive criminology; discourse; idealism; realism**

Further reading: Hallsworth (2002); Penna and Yar (2003)

PRISONS AND IMPRISONMENT

Imprisonment entails the incarceration of offenders within specialised institutional settings (prisons), and has come to figure as the dominant form of punishment across Western industrialised societies. However, this use of imprisonment only emerged in the modern era, from the seventeenth century onwards. Prior to this time imprisonment was largely used to detain those accused of crimes prior to trial and sentencing. Once convicted, the offender would be punished using either corporal or capital measures (physical punishments ranging from whipping and branding to execution). It was with the declining use of such physical punishments that imprisonment came gradually to the fore. Michel Foucault (1977) has argued that this shift represented a critical change in thinking about how best to deal with deviant populations. First, it came to be believed that corporal and capital punishments failed to act as effective deterrents, as the era of modernisation and urbanisation saw large increases in crime. Second, there emerged at this time a new humanitarian consciousness that balked at the cruelty and excess entailed in physical punishment. Third, the Enlightenment belief in freedom as one of the most important features of a fully human existence meant that the loss of liberty entailed in imprisonment could now be viewed as a sufficiently harsh punishment in its own right. Fourth, the Enlightenment era also brought with it new scientific understandings of humanity that viewed deviance as the result of flawed reasoning, irrationality or illness, rather than as the expression of an innate and irremovable evil. As such, offenders could be 'corrected' through rationally engineered interventions, and thereafter returned to a society in which they would then be able to play a productive role. Consequently, rather than punishing offenders by acting upon the body, the new regime sought to capture the 'soul' or mind of the offender, and in doing so hoped to change, reform or rehabilitate the deviant through structured regimes of prison discipline.

Over the course of the nineteenth and twentieth centuries there developed a new regime of imprisonment whose organisation was driven by a reforming and progressive imagination. Rather than seeing prisons simply as storehouses where society's undesirables could be contained (often in terrible conditions of squalor and neglect), reformers saw them as sites in which the misguided and wayward could be re-educated and redeemed. New prisons were designed to implement planned programmes of correction for inmates, were subject to central state inspection and supervision, and were separated into an array of institutions meant to cater for the needs of different populations (male and female, the young and old, the more and less dangerous offender, and so on). However, significant shifts began to occur from the mid-twentieth century. First, the decades after World

War II saw a steady increase in prison populations, a trend that sha-
dowed the substantial upward trend in incidents of recorded crime.
Second, there emerged a loss of faith in the rehabilitative ideals of an
earlier generation, as those released from prison showed extremely
high rates of recidivism or reoffending. This failure to rehabilitate has
been linked to the cluster of social and personal problems that often typify
those in custody. For example, a significant proportion of the offender population is likely to be poor, have low levels of educational
attainment (down to the level of functional illiteracy), to have been
unemployed prior to detention, to have drug and alcohol addictions,
and to suffer from mental illness. Insofar as prisons have proven
unable to tackle these underlying problems (in fact often exacerbating
them), many hold out little hope for effective rehabilitation.

In the UK the period from about 1990 to the present has seen a
steady decline in recorded crime levels. However, the trend in prison
numbers has continued upward, raising concerns that the criminal
justice system (and society generally) is becoming more punitive and
placing excessive emphasis upon the use of imprisonment in com-
parison to other non-custodial forms of punishment. In 2006 the
adult prison population in England and Wales passed 80,000, the
highest rate of incarceration since statistics began in the 1870s and a
near doubling of the figure over the previous twenty-five years. In
addition, there are now record numbers of juveniles held in detention
in Young Offender Institutions (YOIs). The current imprisonment
rate is the highest in Western Europe, and has raised very real fears
that the UK is heading towards a system of 'mass incarceration' like
the USA (which has the second highest prison population in the
world after China, with almost 2 million Americans presently in
detention). There are also serious concerns for the well-being and
safety of both prisoners and prison staff. Many commentators
increasingly see prisons as dangerously overcrowded and under-
resourced, with prisoners of necessity held for long periods of time in
locked cells or poorly supervised by inadequate numbers of prison
staff. Incidents of violence, drug use, self-harm and suicide all indicate
that the prison system may now have reached a crisis point.

In addition to the issues of rehabilitation, prison numbers and
conditions, controversy has also raged around other developments
within the operation of the system, most especially the trend towards
privatisation. Following similar developments in the USA, the UK saw
in the 1980s the introduction of prisons privately run by businesses
for profit. The rationale of the right-wing Conservative government
of the time was that such services could be delivered more efficiently

and cheaply within a competitive market, and handing over the running of prisons to private contractors would ease the financial burden upon the taxpayer, especially in the context of rising prison populations. Private prisons are just one component of a growing commercial market in the provision of 'security services', what Christie (1993) has called the 'crime control industry'. Critics argue that handing over the supervision and care of suspects and convicted offenders to companies driven by profit will undermine proper standards of care for inmates, adequate and safe levels of staffing, suitable levels of expertise and training amongst prison workers, and the assurance of public accountability. As an alternative, many critically minded criminologists have renewed calls for 'decarceration' and a move away from reliance upon imprisonment, favouring instead non-custodial and less punitive community-based programmes such as **restorative justice**.

See also: **community sentences and community punishments; punishment; restorative justice; surveillance**

Further reading: Christie (1993); Foucault (1977); Garland (2002b); Mathiesen (2000)

PROPERTY CRIME

Crimes against property take a wide variety of forms. Familiar instances include burglary, robbery, motor vehicle theft, and criminal damage (e.g. arson and vandalism). In addition to such relatively 'low level' offences, property crimes are also committed by powerful organisations and institutions such as corporations and states, and can include crime such as the illegal appropriation of land and the extraction of valuable natural resources. Property crime may be committed by a variety of means, variously making use of *force*, *stealth* and *fraud*. Some types of property crime will also entail other kinds of criminal offence, as in the case of robbery that uses violence against the person in order to deprive people of their property.

According to official statistics property offences account for a majority of reported crime, comprising around 80 per cent of crimes. The increasing number of property crimes has been held responsible for the strong upward trend in recorded crime that occurred across many Western societies in the post-World War II decades. One widely cited explanation for this rise has been the massive increase in property ownership, especially the proliferation of portable, high-value goods such as home electronics and consumer durables, along with the massive increase in car ownership. These developments increase the availability of potential targets suitable for criminal predation. However, while economic motivations are typically offered as explanations for property crime, criminologists have also noted that not all such offences offer material or financial rewards. Consequently, **cultural criminology** has suggested that we need to understand the emotional satisfactions that offenders enjoy from participating in activities such as arson and graffiti.

The prevalence of property offences amongst the overall pattern of crime has inevitably shaped both the formal and informal organisation of policing, criminal justice and crime control. Significant proportions of police resources are devoted to dealing with property crimes, as are those of courts, prisons and probation services. A rapidly growing private sector in crime control also focuses to a great extent upon the protection of property, utilising private security guards and CCTV, as well as a range of technical devices such as burglar alarms and car immobilisers. As such, property offences have come to comprise and define to a large degree what is considered by many to be 'the crime problem'.

See also: **crime data; critical criminology; cultural criminology; intellectual property crime; routine activity theories; violent crime**

Further reading: Indermauer (1995); Trickett *et al.* (1995)

PUNISHMENT

The use of punishment as a sanction against rule-breaking is a universal feature of all human societies. Punishment may be organised informally, as for example when parents chastise a misbehaving child. However, it is also organised on a formal basis with socially empowered actors passing judgement on lawbreakers and punishment being administered on behalf of society as a whole.

While the rationale for punishing offenders may appear self-evident, there are in fact a number of justifications for its use. The three major such justifications are:

1 *Deterrence.* Punishment is justified by its perceived ability to prevent further offences from occurring. First, it is held that the

experience of punishment will deter offenders from committing further crimes, as they will now be aware of the unpleasant consequences that will follow should they again be apprehended and sentenced. Second, it is claimed that the sight of offenders being punished will deter other potential lawbreakers, as it will serve as an example of the dictum that 'crime doesn't pay'. At the heart of punishment as deterrence is a **rational choice** model of action, one that supposes that individuals will weigh up the likely costs and benefits of lawbreaking before choosing whether or not it is in their interests to act. Provided that the punishment is sufficiently severe and likely to occur, individuals will decide that the costs (pain, suffering, deprivation, loss of liberty) outweigh the gains and choose not to offend. However, the evidence for the deterrent effect of punishment is scant; for example, a large percentage of those released from prison will reoffend and be reconvicted within a couple of years, suggesting that the experience of punishment does little to disincline offenders from further crimes.

2 *Incapacitation.* This rationale is based upon the idea that punishment prevents the offender from being able to commit further crimes. Incapacitation can be temporary in character, as for example by denying the offender opportunities to offend through imprisonment or other measures such as electronic tagging or home detention. It can also be permanent in character. For example, recent years have seen controversial calls for the 'chemical castration' of sex offenders, rendering them physically incapable of committing rape. The most extreme form of incapacitation is provided by the death penalty, which permanently removes any possibility of reoffending.

3 *Retribution.* This justification is not based upon the goal of preventing further offences from being committed. Rather, it is based on a notion of 'just deserts', the idea that individuals who have inflicted suffering upon others should themselves be made to suffer in turn. From this position, the failure of punishment to deter or incapacitate is not a sufficient reason to not punish – retribution is considered a justification in and of itself. Following Durkheim's insights about the social functions of punishment, retribution can be viewed as an important mechanism for cementing society's commitment to key norms about proper behaviour and reinforce the solidarity amongst its members. Recent years have seen an ongoing criminological debate about whether society has in fact become more punitive and supportive of retribution, at the expense of rehabilitation of offenders.

Viewed historically, punishment has taken a wide variety of forms and there have occurred important shifts in the ways in which society elects to deal with offenders. As Michel Foucault (1977) notes, pre-modern punishment tended to be centred upon the body of the offender, with a range of mortifications being visited upon the flesh in dramatic public spectacles. These included the use of stocks, stoning, whipping, branding and mutilation, as well as execution by hanging, beheading, disembowelling, and drowning. However, during the transition to modern society such punishments fell increasingly out of favour, being gradually replaced by the use of imprisonment. This shift can be explained in a number of different ways. At one level, the turn against the infliction of physical pain upon offenders can be seen as symptomatic of a new consciousness that saw such punishment as cruel and inhumane. However, it has also been argued that it was the failure of such punishments to act as an effective deterrent that underpinned their discontinuation. Despite the widespread abolition of physical punishment across Western societies, there remain notable exceptions (such as the USA) that persist with the use of the death penalty, using means such as electrocution and gassing, forms of punishment that many now consider morally unacceptable.

See also: **classical criminology; Durkheimian criminology; prisons and imprisonment; rational choice**

Further reading: Foucault (1977); Garland (1990); Hudson (2003b)

RACISM

Racism denotes any utterances, representations or actions that discriminate against an individual or individuals on the basis of their real or perceived 'race' or ethnicity. Racism has been and continues to be deeply entrenched across Western societies, and has long-standing roots in colonial relations of exploitation with the non-Western world. Criminology has a long-standing, and not altogether progressive relationship with issues of racial and ethnic difference. Early **biological criminologists** (such as Lombroso) claimed that 'inferior', non-European races were innately disposed towards criminality. More recently, Herrnstein and Murray (1994) have controversially linked race with low-IQ and criminal tendencies. In contrast, critical criminologists have been concerned with the ways in which minority groups suffer racially motivated crimes, and with the racism that permeates the police, courts and prison system. Racism has been identified as a key factor behind the disproportionate rates at which members of minority ethnic groups figure in the crime figures and in prison custody.

See also: **biological criminology; hate crime; policing and the police; punishment**

Further reading: Bowling and Phillips (2002)

RATIONAL CHOICE

Rational choice refers to the view that human actions are directed by individuals' calculations of self-interest. For those favouring a rational-choice perspective, all conduct can be traced to a free choice based upon the actor's estimation of the rewards or benefits that will accrue from the behaviour. The concept has shaped criminology in important ways, especially in promoting the notion that the inevitability of punishment will effectively deter individuals from crime, as the costs promise to outweigh the benefits.

See also: **classical criminology; positivist criminology; routine activity theories**

Further reading: Clarke and Felson (1993); Cornish and Clarke (1986)

REALISM

In philosophical terms 'realism' refers to the doctrine that there is a reality beyond our perception or classification of it. In other words, that how we name things, what we believe about them, what associations they carry for us has no impact on the real nature of the things themselves. For example, I see a colour as green and you see it as blue – this is merely a disagreement between us about how to correctly label the colour. It does not mean that we are observing two different real things. What this example shows is that our labels, beliefs, classifications of the world are only approximations: they do not capture reality perfectly. However, a central tenet of realism is that over time our approximations of the objective world will continuously improve.

In criminology 'realism' has come to be associated with a view that 'crime' is the consequence of identifiable real-world causes: the realist's concern is not with how crime is labelled or defined but in the causal forces that lead to its perpetration. 'Right' realists – inspired by James Q. Wilson (1985) – argue that crime is caused by a lack of individual self-control. People commit crimes because such activities offer immediate gratifications – financial or material rewards or emotional ones – and individual criminals lack the internal restraints that prevent most of us from acting out our criminal impulses. 'Left' realists, inspired by Jock Young (see Young, 1992), argue that crime is caused by the interactions between four sets of social actors: the police (and other agencies of social control), the public, the offender and the victim. According to Young, the efficacy of policing is determined by the relationships between the police and the public and the impact of crime is determined by the relationships between the victim and the offender. Moreover, the public themselves sustain the informal economy that motivates burglary, for example, whilst the state's criminal justice and welfare policies are the major factor behind recidivism.

See also: **critical criminology; environmental criminology; idealism; social control**

Further reading: Wilson (1985); Young (1992)

RESTORATIVE JUSTICE

Restorative justice (RJ) shares a family of ideas about crime and crime control with **peace-making criminology**. Like the latter, some in the RJ movement aim not only to transform the operations of the criminal justice system itself but through this to achieve a more positive, humane and community-centred society. Others are less ambitious, seeking rather to foster more integrative and less retributive models of justice into contemporary crime-control policies. Its modern origins are traced variously to Eglash (1977) and Barnett (1977) although the ideas developed are much older (see Wright, 1991; Zehr, 1995). Zehr (1995), for example, traces notions of restorative justice back to (primarily Christian) religious doctrine, and much inspiration has been drawn from traditional approaches to justice found among the indigenous populations of New World nations – the Aboriginal Court Day in Australia and Maori Justice in

New Zealand, as well as examples of Native American Sentencing Circles. There have been many different attempts to depict the essence of a restorative justice approach to problems of crime and criminal justice, and these are indicative of the debates about what its adherents are trying to achieve. Other labels for the same (or related) intellectual agenda have included 'transformative justice', 'positive justice' and 'relational justice'. Whilst the differences of opinion about an appropriate label may seem unimportant they go to the heart of what 'restorative' means in relation to dominant paradigms of modern criminal justice. Nonetheless, what they all imply is an attempt to re-imagine what 'justice' might look like if it were not the sole province of a state-sponsored, monolithic, punishment-oriented 'criminal justice system'.

Whilst the restorative justice movement is clearly an attempt to develop an alternative philosophy of justice in modern society it is also associated with a collection of techniques and strategies aimed at resolving the conflicts and addressing the criminal harms that blight many (especially inner-city) communities (see below). If there were a slogan to sum up the RJ approach in general – encapsulating both its philosophical and practical features – it would be 'restoration not retribution'. It is important to recognise here that the idea of 'restoration' carries several different meanings. Within RJ there is certainly a focus on repairing the damage that crimes cause in communities. An important part of this focus is to ensure that offenders make reparation for the harms they have committed, but even this straightforward axiom is not as simple as it seems. On the one hand there is a commitment to ensuring that individual victims of crime receive suitable recompense for the harms they have suffered. In RJ this reparation is not understood primarily in terms of financial or other direct compensation. Rather, the 'reparation' is more importantly understood as *recognition* on the part of the offender that a harm has been committed and their self-avowed *practical commitment* to enabling the victim to live their lives without fear of intimidation or further harm. Thus, the victim's sense of security and value needs to be 'restored'. On the other hand there is a commitment to restoring the community's wider sense of control and authority over threats posed by offenders: the community's own moral and ethical pre-rogatives need to be revalidated in order to strengthen the bonds of attachment that encourage law-abiding behaviour. Finally, and most importantly, the goal of RJ is to *restore the offender* to a positive social status within their community. Restoration, or reintegration, of an offender's previously positive identity back into the community's values and ways of life, stands as a reaffirmation of the community's own security and cohesion.

RJ's ethical and philosophical commitments are, in part, a critique of labelling theory. The critique is most forcefully articulated by Braithwaite (1989: 20) when he accuses the **labelling perspective** of fostering 'a debilitating nihilism that gave no advice about the limits of tolerating diversity'. 'A labelled person', he argues, 'far from being pushed into a deviant self-conception, may, through confronting the low regard expressed by others, decide that she has a problem [...] and needs help. Then she may be motivated to rehabilitate herself.' The label, in other words, need not be the final or self-fulfilling outcome of a process of judgement and justice. Instead of construing the label 'deviant' or 'offender' as entirely negative it is possible to view the label as a *temporary* stigma which, through negotiation, mediation and reconciliation with the affected parties, can be left behind as its wearer moves into a more mature and accepted (i.e. restored or reintegrated) status within their community.

Braithwaite's contribution to the RJ paradigm has been highly influential but also highly controversial. In his (1989) *Crime, Shame and Reintegration* he laid out a 'family model' of justice and proposed that formal and informal methods for the 'reintegrative shaming' of offenders might buttress both their own internal resistance to the temptations of crime and the community's sense of responsibility for and involvement in dealing with crime problems. In Braithwaite's (1989: 81–82) words:

> Because shaming is a participatory form of control, compared with formal sanctioning which is more professionalised than participatory, shaming builds consciences through citizens being instruments as well as targets of social control. Participation in expressions of abhorrence toward the criminal acts of others is part of what makes crime an abhorrent choice for us ourselves to make.

A key insight of the perspective is that all individuals (including offenders) are members of social groups, and as such others' opinions about their conduct will matter to them. Others have the ability to induce in us strong (at times almost unbearable) feelings of guilt and shame if they publicly judge us to have behaved wrongly. This in turn can shape our subsequent conduct in important ways. Reintegrative shaming seeks to condemn the deviant act but not the person who commits it. Shaming requires those close to the offender (such as family, friends, peers, and neighbours) to publicly express their disapproval of the conduct in question and their disappointment in the individual. If performed appropriately, this reaction will induce feelings of shame and remorse on the part of the offender. Once the offender has made amends for the harm they have caused, they can be forgiven and symbolically readmitted to the community. Indeed, the expectation of public shaming can act as a significant deterrent in the first instance, as individuals must contemplate the emotional distress and loss of face they would experience if publicly chastised.

Although 'naming and shaming' has made some limited appearances in criminal justice initiatives, it has not proved popular or effective as a response to problems of predatory or **street crime** in the UK. However, there remains an important debate about its role in tackling problems of **white-collar crime** and/or **corporate crime**. Braithwaite's own research (Braithwaite, 1984, 1985; Fisse and Braithwaite, 1983) appears to show that business enterprises fear bad publicity more than they fear penal sanctions. They are more likely to comply with regulations and 'good practice' to avoid tarnishing their reputation than they are to avoid paying (often paltry) fines or other legal penalties.

Braithwaite is a hugely influential figure but his writings tend to focus on only part of the RJ agenda – specifically, issues of crime prevention and control. Other important issues in RJ include the interests of the victim and questions of consistency and standards of justice. If decisions about how offenders are to be treated are passed to communities and groups outside of the tightly regulated criminal justice system, there is a real danger of wide inconsistencies between outcomes for similar offences. Not only might this represent a threat to the rights of defendants, but it might also undermine the expectations of any given victim that their suffering should not be seen to be treated differently to that of other victims of similar crimes. RJ practitioners (and theorists) are well aware of these potential dilemmas, but they point out that inconsistency of outcomes is already widespread and the needs and expectations of victims are hardly taken into account in contemporary criminal justice processes.

See also: **peace-making criminology; victimology**

Further reading: Ahmed *et al.* (2001); Braithwaite (1989); Dignan (2004); Johnstone (2003)

RISK

Risk is everywhere in contemporary social science, although its precise meaning is far from clear. David Garland (2003) points out that risk is used to describe both the idea of threat or insecurity as well as the idea of pleasure and thrill-seeking; it refers to what is objectively real and scientifically measurable and what is subjectively felt and socially constructed; it refers to a governmental strategy or technique and an uncertain global context to which governments must respond. Criminologists must grapple with all of these meanings simultaneously, but there are two elements of the idea of risk that are of particular interest.

The first is the widespread use of the term 'risk' in criminal justice practice and research – this is the 'actuarial' use of risk as a (supposedly) objective measure or indicator of the likelihood of criminal victimisation. This actuarial use is to be found in the effort to discover what factors in an individual's life correlate with offending behaviour and, in particular, with those factors that lead to the onset or aggravation of such behaviour. For example, in the Home Office study on gender differences in risk factors for offending, Farrington and Painter (2004) point to low family income, large family size, nervous and/or poorly educated fathers and mothers, harsh or erratic parental discipline and low social class, among an extensive list of potential triggers to offending lifestyles. The idea of risk is also firmly embedded in the operations of criminal justice agencies themselves. For example, probation service practitioners are required to demonstrate competence in the use of OASys (Offender Assessment System), SRA (Structured Risk Assessment) and RPM (Risk Prediction Monitoring) as well as Risk Matrix 2000 and the use of Acute Risk Checklists (Probation Circular, 2005). Practitioners are also required to familiarise themselves with the RAG (Red, Amber, Green) code for allocating risk scores to potential sex offenders. According to Reiner (2006) the essence of these risk-based approaches 'is usually seen as their instrumentalism, replacing attribution of blame, rehabilitating offenders or meting out retributive justice with pragmatic, business-like calculations of what works in terms of cost-effective harm reduction'. In these cases, criminal justice interventions are based on risk scores or risk factor correlations rather than on the judgement of the practitioner or the moral personhood of the (actual or potential) offender (see Wandall, 2006).

Beyond these technical senses of the term there are wider issues about the extent to which 'risk' has become much more than part of the specialised language of protected professional approaches to crime and justice. In Loader and Sparks' (2002: 93) words, 'risk "seeps out" from such protected spaces to become part of the very idiom of our contemporary moral and political conversations'. In this second sense, risk has become a key element in the governance of contemporary societies insofar as it involves 'bringing possible future undesired events into calculations in the present, making their avoidance the central object of decision-making processes, and administering individuals, institutions, expertise and resources in the service of that ambition' (Rose, 2000: 332). This ambition is clearly articulated in the risk factor analysis referred to above and is a clear goal of **developmental criminology**. On a planetary scale, the same kind of ambition is visible in the debate currently raging about the impacts of global climate change and the means that must be adopted now to forestall the worst of the future risks that it heralds. In this regard, it has been claimed that we live in a 'risk society' (Beck, 1992) where the object of governance is not to cut up the cake of progress and distribute its goods but to manage the 'bads' that progress has delivered and prevent their unregulated escalation. In Barbara Hudson's (2003a: 46) pithily astute words, 'though risks might not be able to be eliminated, they can be kept within reasonable levels'. Thus, in criminal justice as in climate change, the language of 'risk' is said to signal an ambition to regulate rather than eliminate the problems that modern society has itself created.

See also: **actuarial justice; developmental criminology; governance and governmentality**

Further reading: Loader and Sparks (2002)

ROUTINE ACTIVITY THEORIES

The famous criminologist Edwin Sutherland drew a distinction between two types of criminological perspective, what he called the *dispositional* and the *situational*. Dispositional criminology focuses upon the offenders, and attempts to uncover those factors (biological, psychological, social, economic or cultural) that dispose or incline them towards committing crimes. Situational criminology, in contrast, directs its attention to the wider contexts that influence and shape offending. Routine activity perspectives begin by noting that the vast majority of criminological theories are dispositional in their orientation. By centring their inquiries on the offender's background, experiences and motivations, such theories tend to neglect the immediate situation or context in which crime occurs. Consequently, routine activity perspectives seek to shift attention away from the offender and towards the ways in which situational factors play a crucial role in shaping crime. Routine activity theorists draw upon **classical criminology** to suggest that human beings are utility- or pleasure-seeking by nature, and as such the motivation to commit crime is no mystery. If the potential rewards of offending seem to outweigh the costs incurred in committing the crime, then we are all prone to take the offending option in order to satisfy our wants and desires. Therefore, they suggest, there is nothing special or peculiar about offenders that makes them different from 'the rest of us', and which will explain why they turn to crime. The difference between the offender and non–offender lies in the situations they encounter, and whether or not these situations offer the prospect of rewards and benefits at little risk or cost. It is these criminogenic situations that routine activity analysts take as their main focus.

The routine activity perspective was first developed by Lawrence Cohen and Marcus Felson in their article 'Social Change and Crime Rate Trends: A Routine Activity Approach' (1979). They argue that a criminogenic situation (one likely to lead to crime) occurs when three distinct elements are present. These are (i) a motivated offender, (ii) a suitable target, and (iii) the absence of a capable guardian:

1 The presence of a *motivated offender*. As we have already seen, routine activity theorists hold that there will always be a large pool of individuals who have motivations to offend, given that we are all inclined to choose offending if it promises to easily satisfy our desires. Therefore, they tend to take for granted the presence of motivated offenders.

2 The presence of a *suitable target*. Whether or not a potential target is suitable for criminal predation will depend, according to Cohen and Felson, upon a combination of four characteristics. The first is the *value* of the target. The more valuable it is, the more tempting it will be. Value can be monetary in nature (what the target is worth on the market, how much it might subsequently be sold for). However, value is also shaped by factors such as style and fashion. When particular goods become highly prized or fashionable, then this increases their value (a good contemporary example is the ipod music player, which has become both a highly esteemed personal accessory, and the target of many thefts). The second

element of suitability is that of *inertia*. This refers to the physical properties of the target, and whether or not these properties make it easy for the target to be removed. Items that are small, light and portable (such as cash, jewellery, mobile phones and laptop computers) will offer much less resistance than those that are large and heavy (such as furniture). The third element defining target suitability is that of *visibility*. The more readily visible the item is to potential offenders, the more likely it is to be targeted. Conversely, if an item is hidden from view then it is much more unlikely that its existence will be known to potential offenders. The fourth and final dimension of suitability is that of *accessibility*. This refers to the ease with which the target might be accessed by potential offenders. For example, an unlocked door or window on the ground floor of a building makes for high accessibility.

3   The absence of a *capable guardian*. Capable guardianship refers to the ability of either persons or objects to prevent a crime from occurring. A guardian may be an individual formally charged with protecting potential targets, such as a police officer or security guard. Such individuals' presence will serve to deter potential offenders from acting on their criminal impulses, and they can intercede to disturb a crime in the course of its commission. However, Cohen and Felson note that the presence of such a guardian is unlikely in most crime situations. Therefore, it is much more likely that guardianship will be exercised by ordinary citizens in their homes, workplaces or on the streets. The very presence of witnesses will serve to exert control over the behaviour of others, making it less likely that a crime will be perpetrated. This notion of informal guardianship can be found at work in schemes such as Neighbourhood Watch, where residents of particular streets and locales help each other by 'keeping an eye out' for suspicious activities or persons. However, guardianship can also be exercised by objects as well as people. Technologies such as locks, alarms, security lights and CCTV all serve to place barriers in the way of predation, thereby reducing the likelihood of crime.

For Cohen and Felson, a crime-prone situation is created when these three elements *converge in space and time*. In other words, a motivated offender and a suitable target have to come together at a particular place at the same time, without the presence of a guardian, for the crime situation to exist. Whether or not a convergence will happen will be shaped by the ways in which people organise their everyday *routine activities*. For example, if individuals habitually leave portable valuables on clear display on the seat of a car, overnight when there are few people around to deter a potential break-in, then a crimino-genic situation has been created. Cohen and Felson use their theory to explain long-term trends and patterns of crime. For example, rates for property crime in the United States underwent a long and sus-tained increase in the post-war years. This sharp rise posed great difficulties for motivational theories of crime, especially those that proposed a link between criminal motivation and the experience of poverty; after all, the post-war era was one of sustained economic growth and increasing prosperity for a great part of the American population. Cohen and Felson claim that their theory can explain this crime increase by looking at how social and economic change impacted on the situational contexts in which crime is able to occur. First, they note that prosperity brought with it a massive increase in personal possessions, especially those of a compact and portable nature. As Americans had more disposable income, they accumulated new consumer goods such as televisions, radios, stereo systems, elec-tric toasters, and so on. Consequently, there was a massive increase in targets suitable for crime. Moreover, the post-war period saw social changes that brought many more American women out of the home and into the workplace. This pattern of having more adult family members in work had a profound impact on guardianship over property. Previously, when most women tended to remain at home during working hours, there existed a natural guardianship within houses and on the streets of residential neighbourhoods. However, with many more homes empty during working hours, this created a situation in which domestic property and personal possessions were left regularly unguarded, making them more vulnerable to theft. In this way we see how changes in both target suitability and capable guardianship can shape the patterns and levels of crime.

The routine activities approach has been widely adopted, and subsequently developed both by Felson and others. For example, Richard Felson (1996) had used the theory to examine individuals' likelihood of becoming the victims of inter-personal violence. He suggests that such violence is more likely to occur when the potential offender enjoys an advantage in terms of physical strength over the potential target (victim). This becomes particularly significant for explaining the sex differences in violent victimisation, as men on average are likely to have more physical strength than women, thereby making women more 'suitable' targets for violent attack.

One of the great advantages of the routine activity perspective is that it can be used by criminologists to inform practical measures to reduce crime by limiting opportunities for offending. For example, individuals can be advised to use money belts worn under their clothing so that their cash will not be visible to potential pickpockets, and guardianship can be maximised by fitting window locks to homes and immobilisers to cars. Nevertheless, the theory does have numerous detractors. A first criticism is that we cannot assume that potential offenders will behave rationally, assessing the costs and benefits of a situation before deciding whether or not to offend. A significant proportion of crimes may be committed on impulse, and an individual's judgement may further be clouded by the effect of alcohol, drugs or overwhelming emotions. Second, the theory has been criticised for assuming that all individuals have the motivation to offend; after all, not all people will respond in the same way in a given situation, therefore suggesting that there *are* important differences between people that will make their offending more or less likely (something clearly evident from **crime data** which show significant differences between men and women, and young and old, when it comes to involvement in crime). As a result, while the theory may be useful for understanding why certain people at certain times and places are more likely to become the **victims** of crime, it is of limited use for understanding the complex range of factors that might lead people to become offenders.

See also: **classical criminology; victimology**

Further reading: Birkbeck and LaFree (1993); Clarke and Felson (1993); Cohen and Felson (1979); Felson (1996); Felson (1998)

SEX CRIMES

Sexual offences are amongst the most high-profile crimes, garnering large amounts of media attention, public concern and political action. Crimes involving a sexual element take a wide range of officially recognised forms, including rape, indecent assault, familial sex offences (incest), child sex abuse, obscenity, sexual grooming, unlawful intercourse, sexual trafficking, and offences of 'procurement' such as prostitution. In 2002–3 almost 50,000 sexual offences were recorded by the police in the UK. Of these, about 50 per cent were sexual assaults against women, and about 4 per cent were sexual offences involving children. Sexual offences account for a very small amount of the crimes recorded by police, comprising only 0.8 per cent of crimes recorded in 2002–3. However, against this we must bear in mind that, first, **victimisation** surveys and *self-report studies* suggest significant levels of under–reporting of such crimes, so the true figures may be much higher. Second, while sexual offences may only make up a very small amount of crime in percentage terms, it must be remembered that they are generally accepted to be much more serious than those many more 'low-level' crimes making up the bulk of the statistics.

The legal framing and policing of sexual offences has had a long and complex history, very much reflecting wider social and cultural shifts in understandings of sex and sexuality. For example, it was only with the rise of the feminist movement that the criminal justice system was forced to take more seriously sexual offences against women. Feminist academics and campaigners argued that historically women victims of rape had been ill served by the system. Women found themselves reluctant to come forward to report sexual victimisation due to widespread assumptions that to admit such occurrences was a source of shame and stigmatisation. Where women reported such offences, they often came up against sexual stereotypes that saw women as responsible for their victimisation through inappropriate dress and 'provocative behaviour'. There was also a notable reluctance for police to become involved in what they considered as essentially 'domestic' conflicts, situations that they felt were best dealt with privately by those concerned rather than a matter for formal intervention. This was reflected in the legal provisions around rape and sexual assault, with rape within marriage only becoming a criminal offence in 1994. This was a belated acknowledgement that the majority of sexual abuses against women were committed not by strangers but by family members.

Another area that has seen major shifts over time is the response to sexual offences involving children. It must be appreciated that understandings of children and childhood are neither universal nor unchanging. Rather, our contemporary classification of children as distinct and different from the adult population is historically speaking a relatively recent phenomenon. It was not until the nineteenth century that, along with a new view of children as a uniquely vulnerable social group, efforts were made to afford them legal protection from sexual exploitation. This was driven by journalistic exposés documenting the extent of child prostitution in Victorian society. However, despite these reforms, there continued to be a widespread neglect of sexual abuse committed 'behind closed doors' – in homes by parents, in orphanages by carers, in schools by teachers and in churches by priests. Recent decades have witnessed renewed efforts to expose and pursue those who sexually victimise children. Attention has focused in particular upon those who abduct and abuse children, as well as those guilty of producing and consuming child pornography and of 'grooming' children for abuse on the internet and elsewhere. However, some criminologists have suggested that, first, the political and public outcry has been exaggerated, a case of **moral panic** in which suspicions and accusations of abuse may be levelled based upon little compelling evidence. Second, they have noted that the legislative and law-enforcement agenda has been driven in considerable part by a concern with strangers preying upon children (so-called 'stranger danger'). However, they point out that, as in cases of sexual victimisation of adults, the greatest threat of sexual abuse faced by children comes from members of their own families. The narrow focus upon internet groomers and individuals loitering by the school gates may do little to protect children from the threat of domestic abuse.

A third area upon which the criminal justice system has historically focused is the activity of sexual minorities, especially homosexual men engaging in consensual acts. In common with many other countries, **homophobia** has traditionally been institutionalised through a range of formal sanctions prohibiting same-sex relationships. Through criminal offences such as 'buggery', 'sodomy', and 'gross indecency', British law made homosexual activity punishable by imprisonment. It was only in 1967 that homosexual acts were decriminalised, provided that the parties involved were over twenty-one years of age and the acts undertaken in private. In 1994 the age of consent for homosexual acts was reduced to eighteen, and in 2001 further reduced to sixteen, finally placing homosexual and heterosexual consent on a par. However, despite the great strides made by gay rights activists and civil libertarians in driving the decriminalisation of homosexuality, there remain significant disparities in the ways in which the criminal justice system treats sexual minorities. For example, recent moves to criminalise the possession of 'violent sexual pornography' have raised concerns that it is homosexual representations of consensual sadomasochistic acts that will in fact feel the weight of enforcement activity.

See also: **crime data; hate crime; homophobia; moral panic; sexism; violent crime**

Further reading: Phoenix and Oerton (2005); Thomas (2006)

SEXISM

Sexism denotes any utterances, representations or actions that discriminate against an individual or individuals on the basis of their sex or gender. Sexism may be institutionalised across a wide range of institutional and social settings, including labour markets, education, politics and family life. Through the work of feminist criminologists it has become apparent that the criminal justice system has been and continues to be sexist in terms of the unequal treatment of women as compared to men, and in the ways in which sexual stereotypes shape understandings of crime and deviance. The discipline of criminology has likewise been criticised for sexism, by turns ignoring or grossly misrepresenting women both as offenders and victims of crime.

See also: **biological criminology; feminism and criminology; gender; sex crimes**

SOCIAL CONTROL

Social control is a widely used although rather ill-defined concept. In its most general sense it refers to the various means by which conformity to social rules and norms is achieved. These means can include **socialisation**, parenting, peer-group pressure and ideology as well as more formal mechanisms associated with policing and punishment. In recent years the most widely discussed use of the concept has been developed from the work of Michel Foucault. Foucault examined the ways in which modern societies institutionalise networks of control through mechanisms of surveillance, discipline, treatment and punishment. These ideas have been mobilised by criminologists such as Cohen (1985) and Garland (2002b) to uncover the array of control strategies deployed by state agencies concerned with crime and welfare. They suggest that, more than ever before, society is saturated with webs of control that penetrate both the public and private lives of individuals, and which aim to produce a high degree of behavioural conformity.

See also: **ideology; socialisation; surveillance**

Further reading: Cohen (1985); Garland (2002b); Foucault (1977)

SOCIAL CONTROL PERSPECTIVES

A great number of criminological theories start from an assumption that offenders are in some way fundamentally *different* from other members of society. Such perspectives then attempt to identify those factors or causes that account for such individuals' criminal propensities. These underlying causes might variously be biological, psychological, social or economic in nature. Control theories, in contrast, approach the question of crime in a rather different manner. Instead of asking why *they* (the offenders) turn to crime, control theorists ask instead why *we* (the majority of people) *do not* offend. In other words, they seek to uncover the factors that prevent or inhibit most people, most of the time, from breaking the laws and rules of society. Their interest lies in understanding the mechanisms that produce conformity with norms of behaviour. In other words, they are oriented towards those features of society that control our everyday behaviour.

Control theories are based upon the assumption of human nature as fundamentally self-interested and pleasure seeking. As such, society needs to place constraints and limits upon its members if their actions are to be regulated. This view originates in the work of the philosopher Thomas Hobbes (1588–1679), who suggested that human life in its 'state of nature', before social regulation was in place, would be a 'war of all against all'. In other words, each and every individual would be interested only in satisfying their own desires, whatever the cost to others. This understanding was echoed by the sociologist Emile Durkheim, who held that individuals possessed potentially 'infinite desires', and it was only society's norms that set limits on their yearnings. If such limitations failed in their effectiveness, criminal and deviant behaviour would likely result. In short, control theorists take a rather 'pessimistic' view of human beings, in that we are all by nature inclined to criminal behaviour, and it is only the controls put in place by society that prevent us from acting upon our inclinations.

One of the earliest instances of a control perspective in criminology was that proposed by Albert J. Reiss (1951). Through an examination of probation records for juvenile offenders, he concluded that those diagnosed as having 'weak egos' were most likely to be drawn into repeat offending. Such individuals suffered from a weakness of personal controls that would ensure they sought to satisfy their needs in a manner consistent with the rules of their community. F. Ivan Nye (1958) shifted the focus from personal to social controls over behaviour. In his book *Family Relationships and Delinquent Behavior*, Nye identified a range of different forms taken by control mechanisms:

direct controls, *indirect* controls, *internalised* controls and controls over *opportunity.* Direct controls are those formalised constraints over behaviour imposed by law-enforcement and other institutions. Indirect control refers to those informal social relationships, especially close ties to family members, which serve to shape an individual's conduct. Internal controls, on the other hand, comprise beliefs and values learned by the individual and regulate actions through the workings of conscience. Finally, controls over opportunity shape behaviour by making available more or less viable chances to offend. Nye stressed that, on the whole, the most influential of these factors were the indirect and internal controls. It was family relationships and learned codes of behaviour, rather than law and law enforcement, that played the crucial role in deterring young people from offending. A similar perspective was developed by Walter Reckless (1961) in his article 'A New Theory of Delinquency and Crime'. Reckless suggested that there were internal factors that would insulate juveniles from offending. These included a positive self-image; a goal-oriented personality, which gave individuals clearly defined ambitions; a clear set of moral beliefs; and a high tolerance to frustration when individuals found their goal-achieving efforts temporarily thwarted. Similarly he proposed a number of important external control factors. These included the provision of a consistent set of values by parents and other influential agents; the presence of positive, law-abiding role models; the clear demarcation of the limits of acceptable behaviour and of the individual's responsibilities to others; and a developed sense of belonging amongst peers and the wider community. Weakness across a combination of these dimensions would make delinquent and criminal behaviour more likely.

The most influential formulation of the control perspective appeared in Travis Hirschi's book *The Causes of Delinquency* (1969). In his *social bond theory,* Hirschi proposed four dimensions of control which taken together would serve to direct young people away from offending: *attachment, involvement, commitment* and *beliefs.* Attachment denotes the individual's sensitivity to the needs and interests of others. The stronger this sense of attachment, the less likely the individual will damage others through offending. Particularly important here are the young person's emotional ties to parents and family members. The youth who is sensitive, responsive and emotionally close to their family will fear the disapproval, rejection and upset that offending may cause, and so will be less likely to act on temptations to delinquency. Commitment refers to the individual's investment in realising conventional goals and aspirations. If he or she has sacrificed time, energy and other resources in pursuit of such goals (for example through educational achievement), they will be loath to jeopardise this through improper behaviour. The more they have to lose, the less likely they will put it at risk. Involvement refers to the amount of time spent in conventional activities. The more of the person's time that is committed to these, the less will be available for potential participation in delinquent acts. The fourth and final dimension, that of beliefs, denotes the strength of an individual's identification with obeying society's rules and regulations – the weaker this is, the less inhibitions he or she will have about breaching such requirements. Hirschi tested his theory by questioning some 4,000 Californian juveniles about their family relationships, friendships, studies, hobbies and other activities. He claimed that the strength of social bonds uncovered in the study was central as to whether or not the boys offended. Contrary to common criminological understandings, Hirschi found that neither social class nor ethnic background were significant indicators of an individual's likely involvement in offending. Much more important was the overall strength of bonds, in particular that of attachment, which Hirschi concluded was the single most important control mechanism.

Hirschi's theory, while highly influential, has been criticised on a number of grounds. First, like many other social control theorists, Hirschi's attempts to empirically verify his claims centre upon the study of juveniles who engage in relatively low-level offending. Consequently, there is little evidence that the perspective could successfully explain adult offending and/or participation in more serious crimes. Second, Hirschi's exclusive focus upon males means that the perspective remains gender-specific, and does little to illuminate the ways in which social bonds might impact upon female offending rates. Third, it has been suggested that while Hirschi may be correct in identifying a correlation between weak bonds and delinquency, he may well have mistaken the nature of the causal relationship between them. In other words, it is plausible to argue that it is not weak social bonds that lead to delinquent behaviour, but that it is engaging in such conduct that subsequently causes the individual's bonds to become weakened (for example as family and friends seek to distance themselves from the offender, and the offender himself feels increasingly disinvested from conventional ways of life). Fourth, there are some counter-examples that challenge the claim that strong bonds (such as those of attachment and commitment) necessarily insulate individuals from the temptations of crime. An obvious instance of this kind is that of **white-collar crime**, where persons with strong family attachments (including children), community ties and professional careers at stake nevertheless choose to abuse their occupational position by turning to crime. How can the social bond theory account for such offending?

A recent attempt to deal with such weaknesses, especially the latter, is Charles Tittle's *control balance theory* (1995). Tittle argues that it is not so much a weakness of control that leads to offending as an *imbalance between two types of control* – the degree of control an individual is subject to from others, and the degree of control the individual can exert over others. If the individual is highly controlled, but has little capacity for exercising control or influence over others, this will lead to feelings of powerlessness. Consequently, this may result in what Tittle calls *repressive deviance*, as the individual seeks to establish more autonomy or control over their situation. Examples of repressive deviance would include predation upon others (e.g. assault, robbery) and defiance of others' norms and values (e.g. sexual promiscuity, drug taking, vandalism). On the other hand, if an individual enjoys considerable control over others, but is not subject to a great deal of control by others, this may result in what Tittle calls *autonomous deviance*. Here individuals have the capacity to exploit, abuse and humiliate others while they themselves are relatively free from control over their behaviour. By splitting the concept of control in this way, Tittle's perspective can help account for a wide range of offences, ranging from the rebellions of the over-controlled youth to the abuses perpetrated by large and powerful corporations.

See also: **Durkheimian criminology; white-collar crime**

SOCIAL EXCLUSION

The idea of 'social exclusion' emerged in the 1980s through the activities of the European Union – notably through the establishment of the European Community Programme to Foster Economic and Social Integration of the Least Privileged Groups, which was followed in the early 1990s by the European Observatory on Policies to Combat Social Exclusion (Berghman, 1995: 11). Whereas the anti-poverty programmes of the 1960s and 1970s had focused almost exclusively on the problems of inadequate income, the emerging social exclusion programmes, as Room (1995: 5) explains, focused 'primarily on relational issues, in other words, inadequate social participation, lack of social integration and lack of power'. Social inclusion/exclusion refers to the extent to which individuals are incorporated within a wider moral and political community. Such incorporation is achieved through the acquisition of certain rights; to a basic standard of living, for sure, but also to participation in the major social and occupational institutions of the society. Thus, 'Where citizens are unable to secure their social rights, they will tend to suffer processes of generalised and persistent disadvantage and their social and occupational participation will be undermined' (ibid.: 7). Social exclusion is therefore understood within what Room (1995) calls a 'vocabulary of disadvantage'. It encompasses both lack of adequate access to resources and lack of integration into key social institutions. In the United Kingdom, the New Labour government established the Social Exclusion Unit almost immediately after coming to power in 1997. Its purpose was to coordinate the approaches of different government departments to ensure that their work delivered integrated approaches to securing improvements for the most disadvantaged and marginalised groups in society, as well as carrying out independent research into social exclusion. The unit was renamed the Social Exclusion Task Force in 2006 and is now under the authority of the Cabinet Office.

There are undoubted connections between social exclusion and crime problems. For example, in 2002 the Social Exclusion Unit published its own research on reoffending by ex-prisoners in which it noted that, amongst other indicators of exclusion:

- 72 per cent of Britain's prison population were on state benefits prior to their incarceration compared with 13.7 per cent of the general population;
- 4.7 per cent were sleeping rough compared with 0.001 per cent of the general population;
- 27 per cent had been in local authority care as children compared with 2 per cent of the general population;
- 52 per cent of the male prison population and 71 per cent of the female population had no educational qualifications whatsoever, compared with just 15 per cent of the general population.

Moreover, social exclusion is associated not just with the commission of crimes. It is also strongly correlated with criminal victimisation. Lone parent households and the unemployed are twice as likely to be victims of burglary than the average person; and people on low incomes, in rented accommodation and living in inner-city areas, are all much more likely to be very worried about victimisation than average. At the same time, the greater the degree of social exclusion the more that people encounter problems in achieving redress for wrongs through the criminal or civil justice system. In short, whilst social exclusion cannot account for all problems of crime and victimisation, it is clear that it greatly exacerbates the individual and community impacts of those problems.

Further reading: Grover (2008); Jones Finer and Nellis (1998)

SOCIAL HARM

The concept of social harm is intended to signal a wider intellectual and political agenda than the focus on crime alone. Although it has only recently become an important subject of debate in criminology, its antecedents can be traced back to Edwin Sutherland (1949), who observed that the criminal justice system discriminates unfairly between crimes of the powerful and crimes of the powerless. Whilst tax evaders and corporate malpractitioners clearly do significant harm to the economy and society, they are treated far more leniently, often under civil law, than many petty offenders whose behaviours are regularly criminalised. Herman and Juliet Schwendinger (1970) took Sutherland's observations a step further by asking whether criminologists were interested merely in the problem of social order at the expense of a broader concern with human rights. If the latter is central to criminology's self-definition, then the concept of 'crime' is insufficient to grasp the many harmful processes and structures that threaten such rights. The fact is that death or injury by avoidable accident and treatable illness, for example, is far more common than death by murder or injury by assault, yet the system of regulation and the penalties attached to responsibility for the first pair are far less serious than those attached to responsibility for the second pair.

Adopting a concept of social harm implies that criminologists concern themselves with a much wider range of personal, social and environmental issues than is involved in the traditional focus on crime as infractions of criminal law. These might include anything from pay and job discrimination to environmental degradation and the activities of the arms industry. Whilst there may be a tendency to dismiss such a broad focus as being more about politics than crime, it needs to be remembered that the exploitation of labour, land theft, drug cultivation, civil strife, human trafficking, toxic-waste dumping, species extinction and climate change are not disconnected phenomena (see Hillyard *et al.*, 2004). The impoverishment of African and Asian populations and the over-exploitation of their natural

resources are, in part at least, consequential on the paths to industrialisation and consumerism taken by developed nations. In turn,
these processes fuel the demand for more exploitable land and
resources which, according to the Stern Report, is responsible for
global climate change. In turn again, such change alters the patterns
of rainfall and desertification and intensifies the struggle for arable
land and water – a key factor in many civil wars and a driver of
economic migration and human trafficking.

Indeed, it is not just academic criminologists who have become
interested in the idea of social harm. This concept is also coming to
play an increasing role in the operation of several government agencies,
and is summed up neatly in the UK government's alcohol Harm
Reduction Strategy which refers explicitly to the 'social harm' attendant
on problematic alcohol use (Department of Health *et al.*, 2007: 49,
66). The same phrase recurred repeatedly in the House of Commons
(Select Committee on Science and Technology) (2006) report on
drug classification. By 'social harm' the government intended to refer
primarily to the behavioural consequences of intoxication and the
healthcare burden of problematic consumption; but it is telling that the
House of Commons report included the category 'other social harms' –
even if these were not defined. Whilst government departments and
criminologists do not share the same meanings when they invoke
'social harm', it is clear that this notion is coming to occupy a more
central place in both criminological research and government policy.

See also: **corporate crime; environmental crime; justice; state crime**

Further reading: Hillyard *et al.* (2004); Muncie (2000)

SOCIALISATION

Socialisation refers to the process through which individuals learn to
become members of society and its social groups. Socialisation imparts
not only shared norms and values, but also the knowledge and skills
needed to perform various social roles. As socialisation is associated
with the production of conformity it is of central importance to
criminology, and it is the failure of the socialisation process that is
often held responsible for individuals' criminal or deviant behaviour.
In particular, criminologists have focused upon the role played by
family, school and peer association in shaping individuals' tendency
towards rule-breaking. However, there is disagreement amongst

criminologists about the extent to which socialisation determines behaviour. Biological criminologists, for example, see 'nature' rather than 'nurture' as the most important determinant of criminal conduct. Others have suggested that criminology has tended to view individuals as 'over socialised' (i.e. excessively determined in their conduct by social forces), thereby downplaying the degree of freedom people are able to exercise. Despite such disagreements, socialisation remains a concept central to criminological inquiry.

See also: **biological criminology; developmental criminology; Durkheimian criminology; ideology; positivist criminology; subcultural criminologies**

STATE, THE

There is no single agreed definition of the state. In common parlance, the state is used to refer to the institutions and agencies – the 'instruments' – through which political power is exercised, whilst 'government' refers to the means by which access is gained to those institutions and agencies. In this 'neutral' sense, the state is simply a collection of (more or less) open organisations to which anyone, in theory, can gain access. In modern industrial societies it is clear that intensive political participation is not widespread. This has led some scholars to argue that whilst, in theory, access to state power is open to anyone, in reality the state provides an arena only for periodic competition between leaders for election. In this 'pluralist' outlook, the state is the societal vehicle through which competing interest groups negotiate and bargain with each other to achieve political ends (see Dahl, 1973). However, more critical definitions construe the state less in organisational terms and more in terms of politics and strategy.

Karl Marx, for example, claimed that the state was 'but a committee for managing the common affairs of the whole bourgeoisie'. In this case, the state was seen as being tied to the interests of the ruling class rather than as an arena for negotiating gains and losses across classes. Elsewhere, Marx argues that the state comprised a vast 'bureaucratic and military organisation', a 'frightful parasitic body' comprising an immense machinery of political control intended to secure the social and economic subordination of the proletariat. Max Weber, on the other hand, defined the state as the organisation that has 'the monopoly of legitimate violence within a defined territory'. In Weber's view, rather than being subordinated to the demands of the ruling class, the bureaucratic state was simply the political expression of 'rule by officialdom in modern industrial societies' – a form of rule that would overtake both public and private organisations (King, 1987: 70, 71).

For a short time in the 1970s and early 1980s there was a concerted cross-disciplinary effort to develop a comprehensive theory of the state that could be used in the fields of legal studies, criminology and jurisprudence (see Fine *et al.*, 1979, for example). The most famous example of this effort was Hall *et al.*'s (1978) *Policing the Crisis*. In this text Hall and colleagues argued that the state was a site of political struggle through which a range of social and economic problems were resolved. The resolution of problems does not imply that they are solved positively. Instead, what Hall *et al.* pointed to was the hegemonic coalition of political, industrial and media organisations and the ways that this coalition sought to exert control in times of crisis. In relation to the state's response to urban disorder in the 1970s, Hall and colleagues described the hegemonic strategy as one of 'authoritarian populism', a strategy which expressed

> a blind spasm of control: the feeling that the only remedy for a society which is declared to be 'ungovernable' is the imposition of order, through a disciplinary use of law by the state.
>
> (Hall, 1988: 3)

Here, the concern is with the means by which the state secured consent for its increasingly authoritarian polices by using the figure of urban disorder and the problem of 'street crime' as the *real* crises that needed to be addressed – thereby subordinating the economic, political and social crises that underpinned the perceived problems of disorder and crime in the first place. Indeed, one might similarly argue that the threat of 'terrorism' today provides a new vehicle through which increasingly draconian and authoritarian state policies are being mobilised.

More recently, criminological interest in the state has turned on the problem of 'state crime' – that is, crimes committed by or on behalf of the institutions of political administration – rather than on developing a cross-disciplinary approach to a theory of state power.

See also: **critical criminology; hegemony; state crime**

Further reading: Fine *et al.* (1979); Hall *et al.* (1978)

STATE CRIME

State crime refers to those offences and violations committed by **the state** and its agents or officials.

The criminological study of state crime is a very recent development. The historical neglect of such crimes can be viewed as the result of criminology's close relationship (both intellectual and political) with the state and its agendas. Criminology had tended to take as its starting point those laws and sanctions created *by* the state to control and punish the behaviour of its citizens, and the crime–control activities undertaken by state agencies such as the police. Thus the state is seen as the primary actor in the fight *against* crime, rather than a potential or actual *perpetrator* of crime. Insofar as criminology takes for granted that crime is that which is criminalised by the state, the state itself disappears from criminological view, since it is in a unique position to exclude its own harmful behaviour from the array of legally prohibited actions. For these reasons, the state-as-criminal has been largely absent from criminological analysis.

William Chambliss (1989: 184) defined state crime as comprising 'acts defined by law as criminal and committed by state officials in the pursuit of their job as representatives of the state'. He later extended this definition to include 'behaviour that violates international agreements and principles established in the courts and treaties of international bodies' (1995: 9). Kramer and Michalowski (2005) go a step further and include within their understanding not only criminal acts committed by state agents acting on the orders of or on behalf of the state, but also those criminal acts committed by officials over which the state fails to exercise appropriate control or diligence. Thus state crime would encompass illegal acts committed by state-empowered actors (for example, police, judges, civil servants, ministers) even if they act without explicit or tacit authorisation for their actions, and insofar as the state fails to adequately control or prevent such conduct.

State crimes can take a variety of forms, including:

1 Those crimes committed by state officials in the course of securing or maintaining political control of the state and its apparatus. Examples would include the fixing of elections, bribery and coercion, intimidation or silencing of political opponents (for example through censorship of other political parties). Such practices have been identified in states worldwide, with one of the most notable recent instances being the alleged electoral fraud committed during the US presidential election in 2000.

2 Those crimes committed on behalf of the state by military and police forces, and by paramilitary organisations that are supported by the state. In such cases the state may use its monopoly over the legitimate use of violence to engage in torture, assassination, 'ethnic cleansing', genocide and **war crimes** against civilians. Such crimes may be committed within the territory governed by the state, or against other states and their citizens. Thus Kramer and Michalowski (2005) argue that the US-led invasion and occupation of Iraq constitutes a state crime, as it was undertaken in violation of international law, and resulted in the deaths of tens of thousands of innocent civilians, and continues to result in violations of human rights by occupying forces, such as the torture and ritual humiliation of prisoners by US and British military personnel. Such state crimes may also be committed covertly, as in cases such as the US-sponsored military coup that overthrew the democratically elected socialist government in Chile in 1973.

3 Economic crimes committed by the state, either acting alone or in partnership with business corporations (so-called state-corporate crimes). This again can take a wide variety of forms, and examples would include: the forced use of prison labour (a practice that human rights groups have condemned in China); the violation of health and safety regulations resulting in death or injury to workers; and the illegal expropriation of land or other material resources from their rightful owners.

Given the power of states to commit crimes and the difficulty in holding them accountable, it can be suggested that the problems of crimes perpetrated by states against citizens far outweigh in scope and seriousness those offences committed by citizens against each other. However, it is the latter that remain the primary focus of criminology to the present day.

See also: **corporate crime; state, the; war crimes**

Further reading: Chambliss (1989, 1995); Friedrichs (1998); Green and Ward (2004); Kramer and Michalowski (2005)

STREET CRIME

Street crime is a term that is regularly invoked but poorly defined. In common parlance street crime is understood to include all manner of offences – assault, graffiti, vandalism, motor-vehicle theft or damage, robbery, and so on. Indeed, this broad range of crimes is often invoked by criminologists themselves as a catch-all category to capture the mundane, everyday crimes of (especially) urban existence. In fact, there is no agreed definition of 'street crime' and few criminologists have seen any merit in interrogating the concept seriously. Hallsworth (2005: 4) notes that there are several different approaches – including the 'omnibus' use of the term to depict various offences from theft to gun crime – but that most of these approaches do not refer to the way the term is used by the police. The 'official' (UK) definition was coined by the Home Office in its Street Crime Initiative that began operation in March 2002 in an attempt to reduce headline crime figures for street robbery. Here:

> the term 'street crime' includes robbery and snatch theft. A 'robbery' involves violence or the threat of violence. A 'snatch theft' is when property is stolen from the physical possession of the victim with some degree of force directed to the property, but not to the victim.
>
> (Home Office, 2003)

Using this approach, the Home Office claims that street crime has fallen consistently every year since the initiative was introduced and, specifically, fell by 12 per cent in the year 2004–5 (Home Office, 2006). These figures need to be treated with considerable caution, since it is always possible to code arrest and disposal figures in different ways – a reduction in offences may be achieved by a reduction in the recording of offences rather than a reduction in the actual criminal events. Similarly, changes in offence rates may have less to do with criminal justice efforts and more to do with changes in criminal enterprise. For example, Curran et al. (2005) report that one of the largest increases in 'street crime' offences that had stimulated the Street Crime Initiative was mobile phone theft. This offence was already declining by the time the initiative was developed and the subsequent fall in street crime statistics owes much to the shrinking popularity of this offence. In turn, the reduction in this type of offending can be explained by expansion of mobile phone ownership leading to reduced demand for stolen items and reduced prices on their illegal resale. To add further confusion, since July 2007 the category 'street crime' has no longer been used by the police in gathering statistics. Instead, the focus is now (at the time of writing) on 'robbery' – 'where force is intimated or used to steal property' – whilst 'snatch theft' is no longer even publicly recorded (Metropolitan Police, 2007). In this reframing of policing priorities, 'robbery' now refers to robbery of personal *and* business property, so that the figures for 2007 onwards do not refer to the same thing as the figures collected up to and including 2006.

Even if the Metropolitan Police have abandoned the category 'street crime' the general public are very likely to continue associating the streets – i.e. exposed public places and thoroughfares – as potential sites of criminal and antisocial behaviour. Indeed, the lawlessness of street life and the urban milieu generally as a potentially dangerous series of spaces is a well-established part of the popular imagination (and fear) of crime. Here, 'street crime' refers less to a statistical category and more to a feeling of insecurity and lack of control over the social environment. From the 'dangerous [urban] classes' of the Victorian era evoked by Stedman Jones (1971) to the moral panic over black youth crime so meticulously deconstructed by Hall *et al.* (1978), the urban street crime and personal danger have for long been closely associated in popular constructions of modern life.

In a wider sense, criminologists often contrast the term 'street crime' to 'suite crime' in order to draw attention to the way that mainstream criminology has tended to focus on the predatory and acquisitive crimes of the powerless rather than on the corporate and **white-collar crimes** of the powerful (Box, 1983: 31; See and Khashan, 2001). Here 'street crime' is less a concept and more an orienting device to remind criminologists that theories of crime need to be able to explain the whole range of criminal and quasi-criminal enterprises that characterise modern society rather than simply explaining why some poor people are more violent than others or end up getting caught for breaking the law whilst others do not.

Further reading: Hallsworth (2005); See and Khashan (2001)

SUBCULTURAL CRIMINOLOGIES

The term 'culture' is generally used within the social sciences to denote the ways in which a society represents the world, including the everyday beliefs, values, symbols and truths that support the practices of its members. Culture thus refers to all those facets of human existence that are of people's own making, and do not owe their existence to any innate biological origins. As anthropologists have consistently demonstrated, societies are subject to great cultural variation, each having its own modes for making sense of experience. The term 'subculture', which originated within anthropology, refers to the existence of a 'culture within a culture', a set of values, symbols and meanings that is noticeably different from, and often at odds with, that of the rest of society. Members of subcultures will consequently hold to beliefs that may well contest those of the wider community, and may equally support forms of behaviour that others see as peculiar, incomprehensible, deviant or socially unacceptable.

The criminological use of subcultural analysis originates in the work of Edwin H. Sutherland (1883–1950) in the 1930s and 1940s. Sutherland, an associate of the **Chicago School** sociologists, is generally recognised as the most important criminological thinker of his time. His interest in delinquent subcultures developed from the studies of deviant youth produced by fellow Chicagoan Henry Shaw during the 1930s. Particularly important was Shaw's concept of **cultural transmission**, by which he designated the ways in which delinquency-supporting beliefs and knowledge would be passed across generations of youth. Shaw argued that in so-called *delinquency areas*, younger boys would be socialised into crime by acquiring the skills and techniques of offending from their older associates. In this way, particular neighbourhoods would become the centres for delinquent activity over many years. From this insight, Sutherland developed his concept of **differential association**. By this he referred to the importance of an individual's peer associations, especially during the formative years of childhood, for establishing subsequent patterns of thought and behaviour. It was by association with delinquent others that individuals came to invest themselves in similar conduct. The effectiveness of associations in socialising individuals into crime and delinquency would depend on four factors: their *frequency, duration, intensity* and *priority*. Thus if an individual engaged frequently, for long periods of time, with others whom he/she considered important, during the formative childhood period, it was very likely that this individual would adopt the behaviour and outlook of those associates. In this way, Sutherland sought to reject the idea that delinquency was either (a) the result of individual pathology, or (b) a biologically inherited disposition. Rather, it was a social learned phenomenon.

The subcultural perspective was developed further by the American sociologist Albert Cohen in the 1950s. Cohen began his analysis by borrowing from Robert Merton's theory of *anomie*, in particular the claim that the lack of access to socially approved avenues for success could lead to criminal conduct. However, Cohen was highly critical of

Merton on two counts. First, he took issue with Merton's *individualism*, in that he appeared to view people's responses to anomie as unaffected by social relationships. Second, Cohen felt that Merton over-emphasised the *material* goals that individuals sought to rea-lise. Putting these two points together, Cohen argued that youth in lower-class communities were blocked not so much from acquiring material success, as from gaining recognition or *status* in the eyes of a society dominated by middle-class ideas of respectability – what Cohen termed *status frustration*. This frustration would lead such youth to form their own alternative means for gaining status and esteem, inverting the wider society's values in the process. If working-class youth could not be recognised for 'doing good' (e.g. succeeding in education), then they could instead be recognised by their peers for 'doing bad'. They would gain esteem from each other by engaging in rule-breaking activities that would offend the sensibilities of the middle-class world that refused to value them. Thus, for example, if the dominant middle-class ethos emphasised respect for property, the delinquents' subculture would give symbolic rewards for damaging other people's property through theft and vandalism. In this way, the exclusion of the working class from society's vision of success would breed subcultures committed to resisting that vision by celebrating and encouraging delinquent and disreputable behaviour.

Merton's perspective was further elaborated in the work of Cloward and Ohlin (1961). They agreed with the idea that lack of access to opportunities for material success could result in the development of delinquent and criminal subcultures. However, they further claimed that whether or not people would use 'innovative' criminal means to secure their goals would depend upon their degree of access to *illegitimate opportunities*. Not all frustrated youth had equal oppor-tunities to access the knowledge, skills and social support needed to pursue success via crime. In those relatively stable working-class communities where such opportunities and bonds existed, a *criminal subculture* was likely to develop, enabling its members to engage in professional criminal activity as a way of life. However, in *socially dis-organised* areas, where bonds were weak and opportunities for learning were limited, it was more likely that frustration would stimulate the development of a *conflict subculture*, one that encouraged the indivi-dual use of violence to acquire a 'reputation' for toughness. Finally, amongst those who could attain *neither* rewards of wealth through crime *nor* status through violence, there would emerge a *retreatist subculture*. The culture of such a group would support withdrawal from community life and a surrender of the search for wealth or status, and instead involve its members in activities such as immersion in alcohol and drug-taking. Through this account, Cloward and Ohlin sought to demonstrate how a *variety* of subcultural forms could emerge from the initial experience of exclusion from the legitimate opportunity structure.

Thus far we have considered the development of subcultural approaches in the United States from the 1930s to the 1960s. However, beginning in the late 1960s, a distinctive tradition of subcultural criminology also emerged in the UK. In contrast to Cohen, David Downes (1966) found little support for status frustration amongst British working-class youth. Instead he argued that these youth distanced themselves from the world of middle-class aspirations by channelling their energies into *leisure pursuits*. The problems of crime or deviance only emerged later if working-class leisure activities became the object of middle-class concern, which could result in their *criminalisation*. This idea set the stage for a number of subsequent studies that focused upon the ways in which dominant societal interests constructed certain subcultures as deviant because of their distinctive leisure and consumption patterns. Influential analyses included Jock Young's study of middle-class marijuana smokers (1971), and Stan Cohen's (1972) account of **moral panics** about 'mods' and 'rockers'. The interest in subcultural *resistance* re-emerged, however, in the influential work of the Centre for Contemporary Cultural Studies, based at Birmingham University. Scholars such as Stuart Hall, Tony Jefferson and their colleagues claimed that subcultures constituted ritualised forms of resistance in a society increasingly polarised by class divisions and racial discrimination. This theme was also taken up by Dick Hebdige (1979) who analysed working-class subcultures such as the punks as expressions of resistance via their styles of music and fashion. The focus upon subculture, leisure, style and criminalisation continues to be a feature of British criminology, exemplified by the work of Mike Presdee (2000) that examines working-class youth practices such as recreational drug use and joyriding as inversions of dominant values.

Despite its popularity across the fields of criminology, sociology and cultural studies, the subculture concept has been subjected to criticism. Perhaps the most criminologically significant is that proposed by David Matza in his book *Delinquency and Drift* (1964). Matza challenged the idea that delinquent behaviour was the result of a subcultural membership entailing values and beliefs at odds with those of society as a whole. He claimed to have found that the normative commitments of delinquents were largely indistinguishable from those of their non-delinquent peers. In other words, delinquents shared wider cultural understandings of 'right' and 'wrong', 'proper' and 'improper' behaviour. As such, their participation in delinquency could not be attributed to some set of beliefs that endorsed, supported or rewarded such behaviour. He suggested instead that those engaging in rule-breaking in fact felt guilt at breaching the codes of behaviour to which they, like other members of society, were committed. Delinquency became possible *in spite* of their cultural commitments, not *because* of them. Specifically, Matza argued that delinquents were forced by the situation of offending to temporarily suspend or 'neutralise' their beliefs; it was only in this way that they could excuse themselves from what they otherwise felt to be 'wrong' or 'bad' behaviour and so overcome their moral inhibitions. This perspective suggests that there in fact do not exist any delinquent subcultures whose members hold to beliefs that are radically different from the social mainstream. Despite this telling criticism, however, subcultural analysis continues to be an important feature of much criminological research to date.

See also: **Chicago School criminology; critical criminology; cultural criminology; Durkheimian criminology; labelling perspectives; moral panic; techniques of neutralisation; youth crime**

Further reading: Cloward and Ohlin (1961); Cohen (1955); Downes (1966); Hall and Jefferson (1993); Hebdige (1979); Matza (1964); Presdee (2000); Sutherland (1949)

SURVEILLANCE

The debate about surveillance in criminology goes far beyond questions of police powers to keep track of and monitor lawbreakers. It is, in effect, a debate about the implications of technological systems for recording, storing and using personal information for the purposes of social control. This information is derived from an enormous number and extensive range of sources – from CCTV cameras to credit and debit cards, from driving licences to DNA samples – all of which raise questions about privacy, human rights and the powers of states and corporations. In modern societies, from before the moment you are born to beyond the moment of your death, your personal details are recorded, stored, exchanged between organisations and used to determine your social entitlements and responsibilities. The potential for modern surveillance systems to monitor your national and international movements, your consumer preferences and your leisure and work habits is virtually unlimited. Indeed, you may well be shocked if you were aware of just how much information about your most personal preferences is being kept by private and public organisations.

Criminological interest in surveillance developed from the 1970s onwards. Inspired, primarily, by the work of the French philosopher Michel Foucault (1977) that interest turned initially on a thorough critique of modern surveillance as a new kind of insidious power. In Foucault's work the surveillance of populations was one component of a 'disciplinary matrix' – that is, the unrelenting exercise of control over people's behaviours in order to turn them into 'useful bodies'. Everything from school uniforms and tightly controlled curricula through institutional timetables to prison inmate training regimes was analysed in terms of its role in generating conformity and compliance. At the centre of this regulated system stood the 'panoptic gaze' – the capacity of a single agent to monitor the behaviour of a huge number of individuals simultaneously. The term 'panoptic' refers to Jeremy Bentham's design for a prison (the panopticon – which was never in fact built) in which a central watchtower overlooks and makes visible all of the prison cells at once. In this system, the inmates would never know whether or not they were being watched, and would be induced to behave *as if* they were under constant surveillance in order to avoid punishment for any misdemeanour. As David Lyon (2006: 44) puts it:

> The panoptic urge is to make everything visible; it is the desire and the drive towards a total gaze, to fix the body through technique and to generate regimes of self-discipline through uncertainty.

It was this (alleged) power to induce conformity that underpinned criminology's early critical engagement with surveillance.

Indeed, the intrusive scope of modern surveillance systems has, naturally, given rise to fears about the growth of an Orwellian 'surveillance state' in which each individual is constantly monitored to ensure loyalty and compliance. Some contemporary technologies do offer the capacity to track individual movements – the 'Oyster' travel card in London, for example, can track an individual across the public transport network whilst the congestion charging system's cameras can follow the movements of individual vehicles. At a wider level, 'cookies' (files attached to hard drives by internet advertisers) can (and do) track an individual's surfing patterns on the World Wide Web. Perhaps more worrying than these instances of surveillance are the trends towards 'data matching' – that is, comparing electronic data sets held by different organisations. For example, in 1998, The Audit Commission's National Fraud Initiative matched data sets held by over 400 local authority councils, police and fire services, as well as the NHS Pensions Agency and the Civil Service Pension Scheme, in order to combat benefit fraud – an exercise that is conducted bi-annually. Other data-matching enterprises include the Serious Organised Crime Agency's access to a very wide range of databases – including Her Majesty's Revenue and Customs and the Driver and Vehicle Licensing Agency. Roger Clarke (1988) coined the term 'dataveillance' to describe this mining and use of personal electronic information for institutional purposes. In the fight against crime of all kinds there is obvious support for data-sharing schemes, but there are real dangers of 'function creep', where 'subsequent novel uses are devised for existing technical systems' without, necessarily, any public debate or democratic control over the extended surveillance capacities (Lyon, 2005: 67). Moreover, surveillance systems are not neutral in relation to their targets but have a tendency to operate along established lines of inequality and prejudice. Norris and Armstrong (1999), for example, found that CCTV operators were more likely to scrutinise young black men than any other social group and sometimes used the cameras for voyeuristic purposes – zooming in and lingering on 'attractive' women. Commenting on Canadian CCTV, Haggerty and Ericson (2006: 14) note instances in which 'titillating incidents were occasionally recorded, with videotapes being traded across shifts much like playing cards'.

One of the key dilemmas of surveillance technologies, in these scenarios, is that they are always amenable to more and more uses. It is, to all intents and purposes, impossible to restrain their functional expansion. One important consequence of these developments is that social control becomes 'deterritorialised'. Where, in the past, the primary means of surveillance and control were linked with dedicated institutions – prisons, asylums and schools, for example – now social control, says Bogard (2006: 59), is an 'inclusive, continuous and virtual function, traversing every level and sequence of events'.

Whilst there is no doubt that modern technologies offer unprecedented possibilities for monitoring populations and recording an enormous range of behaviour patterns, there is also a growing recognition that such technologies are woven into the very fabric of modern societies. Without them, so much of what is taken for granted about housing, taxation, health, schooling, and so on, might well collapse. Some of the very technologies that provoke suspicion of a totalitarian state watching our every move are crucial to ensuring that we get the right wages for working, that the general practitioner knows whether we are allergic to a particular drug, that (at least in theory) some public places are safer at night, and so on. For surveillance is not simply about social control in a negative sense. It might also be said that surveillance contributes to social control in some positive senses. Rather than thinking of these technologies as the realisation of an Orwellian nightmare, it may be more appropriate to recognise that they are, in fact, rather fragmented and often incoherently controlled, performing several different roles in monitoring personal needs and preferences as well as public spaces and social trends. Far from a 'panoptic', all-seeing system, contemporary surveillance technologies might better be understood as an 'assemblage' (Haggerty and Ericson, 2000) – a disconnected and only partially coordinated array of different schemes, driven by different needs and performing a variety of potentially positive, as well as potentially negative, functions.

Further reading: Haggerty and Ericson (2006); Lyon (2004)

TECHNIQUES OF NEUTRALISATION

Techniques of neutralisation is a concept developed by Gresham Sykes and David Matza, as a part of a critique of subcultural theories of deviance. Subcultural theorists argue that offending (especially amongst youth) is a result of membership of delinquent subcultures. These subcultures are united by a shared commitment to oppositional norms and values, beliefs that invert dominant social codes about right and wrong behaviour and which support their members' commitment to rule-breaking. Sykes and Matza, however, argued that delinquents in fact hold to the same mainstream beliefs and norms as their non-delinquent peers. Delinquent behaviour does not result from an investment in alternative norms, but from the ability of actors to temporarily suspend their beliefs while engaged in rule-breaking. This suspension is achieved through techniques of neutralisation that serve to deflect the guilt that delinquents would otherwise feel about engaging in activities they know and feel to be wrong. Sykes and Matza identified five such techniques:

1 *Denial of responsibility*: offenders deflect guilt by maintaining that they were not responsible for the act in question.
2 *Denial of injury*: offenders maintain that no real harm occurred as a result of their actions, thereby excusing them.
3 *Denial of the victim*: here the offenders insist that the victim of their crime somehow deserved what happened to them, that they brought their victimisation upon themselves.
4 *Condemnation of the condemners*: offenders turns accusations of immorality back upon their accusers, suggesting that those who condemn are in fact themselves guilty of greater wrongs.
5 *Appeal to higher loyalties*: offenders deny any personal or selfish motive for their actions, arguing instead that they were undertaken for the benefit of others.

Taken together, these techniques provide offenders with the mechanisms needed to at least temporarily release themselves from normative constraints on their behaviour, enabling them to justify their involvement in illicit activities.

See also: **subcultural criminologies**

Further reading: Sykes and Matza (1957)

TERRORISM

Prior to the attacks on the World Trade Centre on 11 September 2001, criminologists had expressed little interest in the subject of terrorism. The field had been left largely to political scientists and political sociologists, and even here interest was not widespread (see Schmid and Johgman, 1988). Following the destruction of the Twin Towers, however, academics of many stripes began to take a keener interest and debates about terrorism began to spread across the social sciences.

The term 'terrorism' stems from the time of the French Revolution (1789–95). Between 1789 and 1794 the French government, headed by Robespierre, executed, arrested or deported hundreds of thousands of 'enemies of the state' during what became known as the Reign of Terror. The sense of a wilful abandonment of legal and moral principles in the pursuit of political ends survives to this day in both popular and official understandings of terrorism. Yet there is, currently, no agreed definition. Definitions differ between nation states and even between departments within nation states. Some definitions emphasise the groups responsible for terrorist incidents, some the motives of the perpetrators, others the means by which attacks are carried out. The United Nations defines terrorism as:

> any act intended to cause death or serious bodily injury to a civilian, or to any other person not taking an active part in the hostilities in a situation of armed conflict, when the purpose of such act, by its nature or context, is to intimidate a population, or to compel a government or an international organisation to do or to abstain from doing any act.
>
> (Article 2(b) of the International Convention for the Suppression of the Financing of Terrorism, 5 May 2004)

In this sense, terrorism has an inherent criminological concern insofar as it is a matter of national (and international) security as well as personal safety.

However, it must be remembered that there is an intrinsic dilemma in deciding who is and who is not a 'terrorist' since it depends whose point of view is adopted. The British and American governments, for example, funded and supported (including by supplying arms) the Afghani mujahideen in their struggle against the Soviet occupation of Afghanistan between 1979 and 1989 – even going so far as to describe the Afghan forces as 'freedom movements' (see East, 1995). In contrast, following the Anglo-American invasion of Afghanistan in 2001, some of the very same groups who had been armed and supported previously now became 'terrorists'. Moreover, there is a long history of American and British support for extra-governmental armed groups – in Africa and South America, in particular – in order to destabilise regimes considered unfriendly or politically dangerous to Anglo-American interests.

Notwithstanding the difficulties of defining what and deciding who is a 'terrorist', there remain some important connections between terrorist and criminal activities that are understood to have extended and deepened in the contemporary world. Indeed, many official agencies propose that there is a clear link between terrorism and organised crime. The UK Home Office (2004: 7), for example, argues that 'the threat from organised crime, often operating across international frontiers and in support of international terrorism, has probably never been greater', and that

> organised crime groups share many characteristics with terrorists, including tight-knit structures and the preparedness to use ruthless

measures to achieve their objectives. In Northern Ireland and many parts of the world like Colombia, the boundary between the two is increasingly blurred. Many other terrorist groups use the techniques of organised crime to fund their activities.

Whilst everything from video and audio piracy to human trafficking has been linked with terrorist activities, the greatest concern has been over the link between drugs and terrorism and, in particular, 'narcoterrorism'.

'Narcoterrorism' is generally understood to mean attempts by drug traffickers to influence the policies of a government or a society through violence and intimidation, as has been the case in Colombia, in particular. The term has expanded to mean known insurgent/guerrilla organisations that engage in drug trafficking activity to fund their operations and gain recruits and expertise. Examples of these organisations include the Revolutionary Armed Forces of Colombia–People's Army (FARC) and a paramilitary group, the United Self-Defenses of Colombia (AUC) in Colombia, Hezbollah in Lebanon, and Al-Qaeda throughout the Middle East, Europe and Central Asia. The AUC and the FARC have raised a lot of money from the drug industry – FARC collects money from 'taxing' people who cultivate or process illicit drugs in the areas it controls, and others such as Hezbollah and the AUC are said to traffic drugs themselves. Narco-terrorism became a major issue in the 1980s, first in Peru in relation to the Shining Path movement and then with the United States' fight against the Colombian Medellín cocaine cartel. The Medellín cartel exemplifies the notion of 'narcoterrorism'. Led by the famous Pablo Escobar, the cartel was responsible for at least a decade of narcotics-related violence, triggered by the Colombian government's crack-down on drug trafficking and agreement to an extradition treaty with the USA. From 1984 the cartel began a campaign of assassinations of members of the Colombian political and judicial systems (a justice minister; the attorney-general), and kidnappings (see Narcoterror, 2002). Under a special deal with the Colombian authorities, Escobar finally surrendered in June 1991 and was imprisoned in a facility constructed to his personal specifications.

Some criminologists are less concerned with the objective threats posed by terrorism itself and more interested in how individuals come to adopt the terrorist identity (Arena and Arrigo, 2006). Here, the research question turns on how to explain a person's willingness and commitment to engage in acts that, by definition, are likely to cause harm to many non-combatant civilians and, in the case of suicide terrorists, lead to the death of the terrorist him/herself. These questions have, of course, been posed by psychologists (see Silke, 2003), but criminologists seek to integrate the psychology of group attachment, the cultural processes that solidify 'insider' and 'outsider' (or 'enemy') status and the socio-economic conditions under which 'terror' becomes a viable option (see Hoeksema and Ter Laak, 2003), as well as paying attention to the unequal international structures and relationships that establish the political soil in which terrorism, and responses to it, are sown.

Given the dynamic character of terrorist organisations, new challenges are being posed all the time – not least the challenge of responding to attacks against computers and networks and the information they contain for the purpose of crippling political and social infrastructures: cyberterrorism.

See also: **cybercrime; drug crime**

UNDERCLASS

'Underclass is an ugly word', wrote Charles Murray in 1990, 'with its whiff of Marx and the lumpenproletariat.' To get away from its 'ugliness', Murray went on immediately to propose that it 'does not refer to degree of poverty, but to a type of poverty'(see Murray, 1996: 32). The idea that there exists an identifiable underclass in industrial societies has a long history. In the Victorian era social commentators remarked on the 'disrespectable' or 'undeserving' poor – sometimes collectively referred to as the 'dangerous classes' (see Morris, 1994). In more recent times, sociologists have attempted to define the term with more rigour. For Giddens (1973) 'underclass' referred to the chronically unemployed, semi-employed or those in the lowest-paid occupations whilst Runciman (1990) reserved the label for the chronically unemployed alone. What was distinctive about Charles Murray's approach was that it shifted attention away from problems of employment and income and towards problems of values: in Murray's vision the underclass refers to a collection of licentious, parasitic, criminal and feckless individuals whose moral turpitude has been caused by the demise of traditional values, the breakdown of conservative social norms and the rise of a culture of welfare dependency that undermines self-reliance and family independence. The consequence has been large-scale disengagement from the labour force, rising rates of illegitimacy and lone-parent households, a propensity to feral and predatory criminal behaviour and a disregard for the feelings and rights of the wider community. Murray's use of the concept, in fact, harks back to those Victorian meanings that combined moral judgement and social classification in a single phrase.

It is certainly the case that common-sense conceptions of the underclass have informed a great deal of public rhetoric about crime and the breakdown of law and order, but specifying precisely what role such a group plays in contemporary criminality is a more difficult task. It is certainly true that poverty and *certain kinds of crime* are linked: petty drug-dealing and domestic burglary, for example, are far more likely to be perpetrated by members of low-income groups. On the other hand, tax evasion, large-scale financial fraud or corporate malpractice are far more likely to be perpetrated by members of high-income groups. Why the former, rather than the latter, should be seen as the greater ill or the more pressing sign of social breakdown is unclear. At the same time, some of the assumptions on which the underclass concept rests are themselves dubious. For example, far from there being an 'epidemic' of illegitimacy caused by the wanton promiscuity of the underclass, most lone-parent households are temporary arrangements and very many are the result of divorce rather than casual sexual liaisons (see Lister, 1996). Moreover, the evidence on the culture of welfare dependency and long-term unemployment does not sit easily with the assumption of large-scale voluntary withdrawal from the labour market. Bradshaw and Holmes (1989) and Gallie (1994), for example, both report little difference in attitudes to work, independence and self-reliance between families affected by long-term unemployment and families in stable employment. What they did find were differences in opportunities and the deleterious impact of the growing gap between the well-off majority and the minority left behind in increasingly desperate poverty.

Further reading: Hayward and Yar (2006); Morris (1994)

VICTIMOLOGY

It can be suggested that every crime necessarily involves two parties, an offender and a victim. Therefore, it may be surprising that criminology has historically tended to focus upon the offender, having little to say about the victims of crime and the process of victimisation. Victimology attempts to redress this imbalance by studying the relationships between offenders and victims, by examining how and why certain individuals and groups become prone to criminal victimisation, and by considering the ways in which crime impacts upon those who suffer it.

Victimology first emerged in the late 1940s in the work of Von Hentig, who sought to treat victims as active participants in crimes. He suggested that victims played a causal role in crimes, variously consenting, cooperating, conspiring or provoking the offence. Thus victims could be differentiated or classified according to those characteristics or behaviours that they contributed towards the crime. The classification of victims was further developed in the work of Mendelsohn (1956). Mendelsohn argued that victims could be differentiated according to their degree of culpability for the crime that was committed against them. In other words, he felt that individuals were to varying degrees responsible for their own victimisation, and that this needed to be reflected when it came to judging and punishing offenders. This kind of analysis has proven politically controversial, since it effectively 'blames the victim' by suggesting that they have brought crime upon themselves. One of the most widely criticised analysis of this kind is Amir's (1971) study of rape, in which he argues that some women are to blame because they might dress in a 'provocative' manner or behave in a way that invites men to assault them.

In the decades following the pioneering work of Von Hentig and Mendelsohn, numerous studies were undertaken examining the dynamics of victim–offender interactions involved in a wide range of crimes including homicide, robbery, assault, fraud and blackmail. However, over time victimology has directed its attention away from the micro-level interactions between individuals and towards the social and structural factors that shape patterns of victimisation. Hindelang *et al.* (1978) examined the ways in which lifestyles and everyday routines subject people to varying risks of criminal victimisation. For example, regular presence in city centres at night, where copious quantities of alcohol are being consumed, will carry with it a heightened vulnerability. Insight into such patterns was afforded by large-scale victimisation surveys that identified the socio-demographic characteristics of those targeted by various crimes, as well as helping to establish the overall volume, trends and patterns in criminal victimisation.

The social and structural analysis of victimisation has been further developed by critical and feminist victimologists, such as Mawby and Walklate (1994). First, such analysts draw attention towards those 'hidden' and traditionally neglected experiences of victimisation that occur within the private sphere of the home, such as domestic violence and child abuse. Second, they argue that vulnerability to such crimes will reflect structural differences and power inequalities between social groups, so that factors such as gender, 'race', class and disability will all impact on patterns of victimisation. In this way, they suggest that proneness to victimisation is not so much an outcome of individual choices and behaviour as the result of powerlessness and inequality organised on the societal level.

During the early decades of its development victimology was a largely theoretical enterprise. However, from the 1970s onwards a more applied orientation became apparent. This was driven in considerable part by a growing concern for the victims of crime and the realisation that the criminal justice system had largely neglected their needs and failed to take account of their experience of crime. Again, feminist activists played an important role here, taking up the cause of women subjected to domestic violence and sexual assault. The work of applied victimologists helped to uncover the manifold ways in which crime impacted upon its victims. Most obviously, victimisation might result in physical injury (in cases of violent assault) and/or material losses (in cases of theft and robbery). However, victimisation might also have longer-term psychological and emotional consequences, such as fear and depression that would affect individuals' ongoing quality of life. Likewise, victimisation might have ongoing financial implications, as when victims of crime are left unable to work and earn a living. The impact of crime also extends beyond the immediate victim to affect the families of those victimised, often causing considerable distress, hardship and strain for those closest to victims. Awareness of these consequences helped victimologists to identify a range of needs that must be met if victims are to successfully come to terms with their experience of crime. For example, victimisation creates a need for both immediate and longer-term assistance, be it in the form of medical attention, comfort, support, counselling or practical help in dealing with material damage. Victims also express a need for information about the progress of their case, and the desire to have some involvement or 'say' in how the offender is dealt with. Over recent decades an array of initiatives has been established to help meet such needs; victims' support organisations offer advice and assistance, police and other criminal justice agencies have sought to inform and consult victims, and various charters of victims' rights have granted them a greater say in the judgement and punishment of their victimisers. Such developments have converged with the movement for **restorative justice** that favours the involvement of victims in the justice process, and places emphasis upon the need for offenders to both understand the impact that their crimes have upon victims and to make restitution to victims. In short, victimology has had a significant impact in refocusing both criminology and criminal justice institutions away from their fixation on the offender so as to encompass those on whom the offender's actions have the greatest effect.

See also: **crime data; feminism and criminology; restorative justice; sex crimes; sexism**

Further reading: Hindelang *et al.* (1978); Karmen (1990); Mawby and Walklate (1994); Von Hentig (1948)

VIOLENT CRIME

At its simplest, violent crime refers to acts of bodily harm, directed towards a person or persons by others, that are subject to legal prohibition and punishment. Violence is legally understood through a scale of categories organised by their supposed lesser or greater seriousness. A violent crime may be classified, for example, as homicide, grievous bodily harm, wounding, actual bodily harm, or common assault. More broadly, such crimes may also be differentiated according to the setting in which they take place or according to the social characteristic of the perpetrators and/or victims, for example domestic violence, street violence, gang violence, violence against women, child abuse, racist violence, and so on. Crimes of a sexual nature (rape, indecent assault) can also be classified as crimes of violence (although they are usually treated separately in official statistics). However, what may or may not be considered as an instance of violence is open to considerable variation. For example, some criminologists might wish to consider as violent crimes various forms of *verbal* harassment, threat and abuse, and so understand racist, sexist, and homophobic discourse as instances of symbolic, psychological and emotional assault.

The overall scale of violent crime is difficult to establish, as research evidence indicates that a majority of such offences do not in fact get reported to the police, and are dealt with by victims through more informal mechanisms. In fact, criminologists have suggested that violence needs to be understood not as an exceptional occurrence but as an integral part of everyday social life and interactions. Violence may be used in an organised and premeditated way for strategic purposes (e.g. so as to secure material gains, in instances such as robbery-assaults). It may also be an integral part of the ways in which social actors establish status and authority within their social groups, and exercise social control over others (e.g. the ritualised violence of gang fights and football hooliganism, or assaults by individuals against their children, partners or other family members). In some contexts, violence may be seen as a 'normal' mechanism for resolving a range of disputes, disagreements and conflicts. Violence may be undertaken for ideological and political reasons (for example racist assaults by political extremists). Violence also has the ability to erupt in a relatively spontaneous manner, fuelled by alcohol and other intoxicants (a phenomenon seemingly on the rise in the UK as part of the growing night-time leisure economy).

Common understandings of violence tend to dwell upon the threat of victimisation presented by strangers. However, research has shown that victims usually know the perpetrators of violence. For example, Francis *et al.* (2004) found that in over 70 per cent of homicide cases in England and Wales the victim had known their killer; in over 30 per cent of homicides the offender was the partner or a member of the victim's family. The most likely perpetrators of violent crimes are young males from lower-socio-economic-class backgrounds. However, again contrary to popular perceptions, it is young working-class males who are most likely to be the victims of violence, and not women as is often supposed (although the likelihood of serious and repeated violent assaults is considerably higher for women when we focus upon domestic settings). The risk of violent victimisation will also vary according to ethnic background, with those from minority groups suffering the highest incidence of violent attacks. The rates for violent victimisation also vary significantly according to place of residence, with more crimes being reported in urban than in rural areas. Young people are generally at greater risk of violence, a fact that is attributed by many criminologists to the distinctive lifestyle patterns of the young, patterns that will more likely place them in situations where the risk of violence is high (for example regular drinking in busy city-centre pubs, bars and clubs). The relative powerlessness of potential victims will also crucially affect the likelihood of victimisation, with the very young being especially vulnerable (although there is also now a growing literature documenting apparently high levels of violence directed at the elderly in domestic and care settings – so-called elder abuse). In short, the likelihood of being either a victim or a perpetrator of violence will depend upon a wide range of social, cultural and economic factors that combine in a variety of ways to produce distinctive distributions and patterns of crime.

Given the variety of types and contexts of violence noted above, it is unsurprising that there is no agreement amongst criminologists about how such crimes can best be explained. Broadly speaking, explanations fall into one of three kinds: biological, psychological and socio-cultural. Biological accounts seek to identify some physiological abnormality or anomaly that is held to dispose individuals towards violent behaviour. Biological criminology has suggested, variously, that violence can be traced to hormonal imbalances, brain injury, genetic inheritance, and chromosomal irregularity. Like biological explanations, psychological perspectives tend to focus upon individuals, and locate the propensity to violence in the distinctive 'mental make-up' of offenders. Psychologists may suggest, for example, that violence is the result of a particular 'personality type', or the outcome of 'conditioning' processes through which the individual has learned to respond to particular conditions or stimuli with violence. Those favouring socio-cultural explanations in contrast reject the biological reduction of social behaviour to built-in dispositions, and likewise reject psychology's focus upon the human individual. Instead, they understand the propensity to violence as something embedded in the cultural orientations and beliefs of social groups, as a reflection of shared norms about conduct, and as an integral part of the social worlds that people inhabit.

See also: **biological criminology; criminal psychology; family crime; sex crimes; subcultural criminologies**

Further reading: Levi and Maguire (2002); Stanko (1990)

WAR CRIMES

The term 'war crimes' refers to offences that are committed in times of war, and which are not considered 'legitimate' acts of warfare or related military activity. Given that war crimes are largely committed by military personnel in the context of inter-state conflicts, there is inevitably a close relationship between war crimes and **state crimes**.

Illegal acts committed during the prosecution of war include: deliberate targeting of civilian persons or property; coercion, abuse, torture or other maltreatment of civilians or of detained enemy combatants (so-called 'prisoners of war'); and use of outlawed weapons (e.g. biological weapons). Such activities have in fact been a consistent feature of wars across the span of human history, up to and including attempts to deliberately eradicate whole populations (*genocide*). However, it was only in the mid-nineteenth century that the notion of war crimes was introduced in order to distinguish between legitimate and illegitimate behaviour on the part of military and other state personnel. The rules of war are codified in the *Geneva Conventions*, a series of international treaties that require all signatory nations to establish criminal laws covering offences committed during wartime. Instances of war crimes in the twentieth century include: the murder of French and Belgian civilians by German troops during World War I; the Holocaust in World War II, involving the murder of 7–10 million Jews and other minorities by the German Nazis; mass killings, rapes, looting and maltreatment of prisoners by the Japanese during World War II; and genocide committed in Bosnia by Serb forces in the Yugoslav Civil War in the 1990s.

In the past, those charged with war crimes have been tried in ad hoc hearings convened after the end of conflicts (for example the Nuremberg and Tokyo trials after World War II). In 2002 the International Criminal Court came into existence as a permanent forum for the prosecution of war crimes. However, despite the cumulative extension of international mechanisms for dealing with such offences, there remain significant problems in bringing war criminals to justice. First, it has been historically apparent that those from the losing party or nation in a conflict are much more likely to face prosecution than the victors. Thus, for example, while senior German and Japanese military and government officials were tried after World War II, no such charges were brought against the Allies, despite the fact that acts such as the deliberate area bombing of German cities were arguably war crimes. Such instances exemplify a general reluctance by states to bring to account those individuals who act in their name. A second problem arises because of some nations' refusal to acknowledge the legitimacy of institutions such as the International Criminal Court or to surrender their nationals to that court for trial (at present these include the USA, China and Israel). Finally, the concept of war crimes is limited by the fact that it only constrains states and their agents from committing certain types of harms, leaving untouched . those many acts of large-scale violence, death and destruction which states claim as their legitimate right in the context of war.

See also: **human rights; state crime**

Further reading: Bartov *et al.* (2003); Kramer and Michalowski (2005); Ruggiero (2006)

WHITE-COLLAR CRIME

The term white-collar crime was first coined by the famous **Chicago School** criminologist Edwin Sutherland in the early 1940s, in order to identify:

> a crime committed by a person of respectability and high social status in the course of his occupation.

By drawing attention to such activities, Sutherland wished to challenge the overwhelming criminological and law-enforcement focus upon 'street crimes' and other offences committed by those from lower socio-economic groups. Sutherland claimed that dominant understandings of 'the crime problem' significantly misrepresented the reality of offending, and that in fact criminal activity was widespread amongst the more privileged and supposedly respectable members of society. A second motivation for broadening the scope of criminology to include such offences was a realisation that white-collar crimes often produced more harm to society than low-level offences such as petty theft and robbery. For example, offences such as tax evasion will deprive the state of valuable revenues that are needed for providing citizens with services such as education, healthcare and welfare; the production of sub-standard and adulterated food and drugs will place public health in jeopardy; unsafe working conditions will place employees in jeopardy; fraudulent accounting practices can ultimately lead to the collapse of businesses and the loss of work for an organisation's employees (as happened in the recent case of the Enron Corporation in the USA). For these reasons, Sutherland felt that sociologists and criminologists needed to broaden their agenda and examine those crimes committed by society's elites.

One of the notable features of Sutherland's definition is that he included within the scope of white-collar offences not only those activities that are prohibited by *criminal law,* but also those that fall afoul of *civil* and *administrative* law. Subsequent criminologists have broadened their understanding even further, incorporating within white-collar crime activities that may not be subject to any legal regulation whatsoever, but which may nevertheless be viewed as sources of **social harm**. Sutherland's sociological definition was criticised by Paul Tappan (1947), who argued that only those acts subject to formal criminal sanctions should be included within white-collar crime, and not those what the criminologist might find morally objectionable or undesirable. However, Sutherland provided a compelling reason for going beyond the scope of criminal law in defining crime, in that he felt such laws inevitably reflected the interests and influence of the more powerful members of society. It is precisely for this reason that many harmful behaviours by businesses and corporations are allowed to go unchecked. An integral part of Sutherland's project was to uncover the ways in which the privileged were able to evade condemnation and punishment for their crimes.

For Sutherland, white-collar crime was distinguished by the social characteristics of those who commit it. It is the status and position of the *offender* that make a crime 'white-collar'. Given his desire to refocus criminology away from the disadvantaged criminal, his offender-based definition is understandable. However, other analysts have taken issue with this approach, and suggested that criminology needs instead to home in on the particular characteristics of the offence rather than the offender who commits it. Thus, for example, Edelhertz (1970) defines white-collar crime as 'an illegal act or series of illegal acts committed by nonphysical means and by concealment or guile, to obtain money or property, to avoid the payment or loss of money or property, or to obtain business or personal advantage'. Similarly, Shapiro (1990) argues that white-collar crime is distinguished by the illegal exploitation of *trust* that is embedded in institutional and professional roles. In this way, those positions that carry a maximum of trust and autonomy will offer greater opportunities for abusing that trust for illegitimate advantage or gain. However, it has also been suggested that it is not only positions of high trust that offer opportunities for crime, and that almost all people are potentially able to exploit their occupational position in this way. Commonplace instances of such work-based crime include the use of employers' time and resources for personal business (for example: time taken off work under the guise of sickness leave, use of the internet or telephone for personal and leisure activities, or the fabrication of work-related expenses claims). In this way, the study of white-collar crime has moved away from Sutherland's original emphasis upon 'status' and 'respectability' to centre upon the kind of opportunities that occupational activities offer for criminal endeavour. This shift has been reflected in the development of new terminology, with many criminologists preferring to now use terms such as *business crime, economic crime* and **corporate crime** to characterise such offences.

See also: **corporate crime; crime and deviance; criminal justice system; social harm**

Further reading: Croall (2001); Edelhertz (1970); Shapiro (1990); Sutherland (1949); Tappan (1947)

YOUTH CRIME

Offending by youth comprises a central concern in contemporary society, and provides a significant focus for law, policing and punishment. The relationship between age and offending is borne out by official crime statistics, which suggest that the 'peak age' for offending by males is eighteen, and for females just fifteen. After these ages, there appears to be a steady decline (or pattern of *desistance*) in terms of individuals' tendency to offend. This relation between youth and crime is also confirmed by *self-report studies*. For example, Flood-Page *et al.* (2000) found that 60 per cent of males aged 16–17 admitted to having committed a crime. The crimes committed by youth are predominantly property offences, such as theft, burglary, handling of stolen goods and criminal damage. The correlation between youth and crime is also reflected in patterns of imprisonment, with almost 25 per cent of inmates in UK adult prisons being under twenty-one years of age, in addition to those incarcerated in juvenile detention facilities tailored to those under eighteen years of age.

Criminologists have offered a wide range of explanations for youth offending. Psychological criminologists have argued that adolescence is a period of inevitable turmoil and crisis, suggesting that such disturbance helps account for youthful participation in crime. Theories of developmental psychology claim that individuals, as they move from childhood to adulthood, pass through a number of stages of moral learning; it is only with maturity that individuals are fully able to appreciate and apply moral principles to regulate their own and others' behaviour. As such, juveniles occupy a space of moral immaturity in which they are likely to act upon their impulses with limited regard for the impact of their actions upon others. From a more socially oriented perspective, developmental criminologists claim a strong correlation between youth offending and experiences of parental neglect, parental conflict and family disruption and breakdown. Therefore, youth crime is seen as the result of failed **socialisation** and the absence of appropriate controls ordinarily provided by family relationships. **Subcultural** and **differential association** perspectives on delinquency, in contrast, stress the need to situate crime in the context of social group membership. The groups to which individuals belong will have distinctive shared beliefs, attitudes and values, and it is this distinctive subculture that both licenses and rewards behaviour at odds with mainstream social norms and rules. It is through association with criminal and deviant subcultures that young people will learn not only the techniques for carrying out crimes but also the attitudes and values that support and validate such behaviour. Sub-cultural explanations have also been given a social class dimension by those criminologists who view working-class youth cultures as expressions of *status frustration*. Youth from lower socio-economic backgrounds, who find themselves denied access to the socially approved paths to attain recognition and status, instead formulate their oppositional values that stress rule-breaking as a source of social esteem. Conservative criminologists have in contrast claimed that a generational change in cultural attitudes is responsible for large increases in youth crime, with writers such as Charles Murray arguing that today's youth are no longer committed to hard work and civic responsibility, preferring instead to lead lives of idleness and crime.

However, other criminologists have challenged the notion that young people in fact have a special propensity to behave in a criminal or deviant manner. Instead they argue that society's preoccupation with youth offending has its roots in a tendency to scapegoat young people and to view youthful behaviour as delinquent, antisocial and dangerous. Geoffrey Pearson (1983) charts the ongoing waves of **moral panic** about young people that can be traced back to the eighteenth and nineteenth centuries. The kinds of views about moral decay amongst the young expressed by Murray and others can in fact be seen as a recurrent feature of social concerns in every generation. The subsequent targeting of the young by politicians, lawmakers and law enforcers serves to demonise and criminalise what might other-wise be considered fairly innocuous behaviour. Given such fears, a disproportionate amount of time, energy and resources are expended in policing the young, inevitably resulting in more offences by young people being detected, thereby inflating the presence of youth in crime statistics. It is certainly true that recent decades have seen a whole raft of new offences being created that are focused upon youth culture and young people's everyday activities. Well-known instances in the UK include the criminalisation of 'rave' parties in the 1980s and the introduction of **Antisocial Behaviour** Orders (ASBOs) in the 1990s. By creating criminal offences out of young people's pre-sence and leisure activities in public places, more and more juveniles are brought into the criminal justice system (a process of **net-widening**), which in turn simply reinforces the public perception that youth crime is a problem 'out of control' and that even more harsh measures are required to curtail it. As a result critical crimin-ologists tend to favour the decriminalisation of youth, arguing that this is the best way in which young people can be kept away from imprisonment and punishment, processes that merely serve to further exclude the young from the social mainstream.

See also: **crime data; deviance amplification; labelling perspectives; moral panic; subcultural criminologies**

Further reading: Muncie (2004); Newburn (2002); Pearson (1983),

ZERO TOLERANCE

The term 'zero tolerance' is most commonly associated with a series of initiatives instigated by the New York Police Department in the mid-1990s under the leadership of Police Commissioner William Bratton. The initiatives did not require the passing of new laws. Instead, a 'zero-tolerance' approach meant much stricter application of existing laws and a greater emphasis on minor crimes. Coupled with the development of new technologies and practices – such as **crime mapping** to provide solid information about crime trends across different city districts   Bratton encouraged beat officers to retake control of the streets and neighbourhoods and to arrest and process perpetrators of *all* offences within their remit rather than ignoring petty misdemeanours or leaving many offenders to other more specialist squads. However, whilst the term has been picked up by the media, and by some criminologists, it is a rarity indeed to find a law-enforcement agency that explicitly promotes zero tolerance as an operational stance on law enforcement. As Ken Pease (1998) observes, in the real world of policing 'zero tolerance' is hardly anywhere to be found. Instead, the idea has come to stand in for a wide range of policing (and related) practices that focus on relatively minor crimes and low-level disorder.

The origins of the 'zero-tolerance' approach are to be found in the coming together of two independent trends in (American) criminal justice and criminology in the 1980s. One was the stance of the Reagan and Bush administrations' (1981–93) 'war on drugs'. In this campaign there was a marked shift of emphasis from the policing of dealers and suppliers to the policing of users – on the grounds that users generate the market from which suppliers and dealers profit. Thus, if the criminal justice system could make a significant impact on the American market, the suppliers would either give up their business or take it elsewhere. So whilst there was a seemingly rational core to the campaign, its underlying popular moral appeal also needs to be considered: possession and/or use of any measurable amount of a proscribed drug is illegal and the 'war on drugs' intimated that American society would no longer 'tolerate' the casual disregard for its laws. The zero-tolerance approach to drug use put the responsibility squarely on the shoulders of the individual user and some rather draconian measures were applied – such as confiscation of commercial fishing boats and other property on the basis of trace evidence of marijuana. In this regard 'zero tolerance' was more a symbol of government determination to be seen to be tough on drug use than a practical framework for law enforcement (see also Newburn and Jones, 2007, on the symbolism of zero tolerance).

The second strand in zero tolerance law enforcement is associated almost exclusively with an essay by Wilson and Kelling (1982) – later updated by Kelling and Coles (1996) – entitled 'Broken Windows: The Police and Community Safety'. In this short, but quite brilliant, essay Wilson and Kelling argued that communities invited crime and criminals into their midst by failing to care for and repair the physical and social environment. Where communities tolerated broken windows, vandalised bus shelters, graffiti-strewn walls, groups of vagrants drinking in public, antisocial behaviour among young people and other low-level signs of disorder, they sent out signals to the effect that the community did not care for itself. Consequently, the community was likely to witness an influx of criminal groups and steady but certain rises in crime rates. It follows from this analysis that the solution to crime is to be intolerant of low-level disorder and incivility in order to prevent more serious criminals from gaining a foothold in the first place. Therefore, according to Wilson and Kelling, policing is and should be more about maintaining order than fighting crime: the need to fight crime is a consequence of tolerating disorder.

Of course, neither Wilson and Kelling nor any other proponent of 'order-maintenance' policing suggests that *all* crime arises out of petty disorder. What is suggested is that the kinds of crimes that regularly blight the urban landscape – including assaults, vehicle crime and burglaries – can be drastically reduced by caring for and taking responsibility for a community's physical and social environment. In line with other shifts in criminal justice policy in the USA and the UK, such approaches ostensibly focus on the criminal act rather than on the circumstances, background or context of the act or the person who commits it. However, as with so many street-level criminal justice initiatives, the ideal is rather different from the reality.

First, as Barbara Hudson (2003a: 69) points out, such initiatives have the effect of 'defining up' delinquency such that the 'distinction between illegal and unpleasant behaviour, crime and nuisance, delinquency and disorderliness is being eroded'. Thus, order-maintenance policing has a **net–widening** and mesh-thinning effect. Moreover, modern surveillance systems, exclusion orders and community demands for action tend to be 'directed at certain types of people whatever they are doing'. In particular, young black people are more often defined as the problem when in reality they are most likely to be victims of crime and disorder.

Second, it is far from clear that zero-tolerance/order-maintenance policing has any real impact on either crime or disorder. In William Bratton's New York, crime certainly fell during the implementation of more aggressive policing styles, but crime also fell in other cities where such styles were not adopted. The fact is that, with appreciable degrees of regional and contextual variation, crime rates have been falling across Western societies for some considerable time regardless of the policing styles adopted in different cities and countries.

Finally, the order maintenance approach to policing does, as Hudson suggests, have the effect of 'defining up' delinquency but it also has the effect of 'defining down' crime. No amount of order maintenance on the streets of Western nations is going to alter the propensity to fraud or corruption, corporate or state crime, environmental destruction or illegal trading in toxins, endangered species or humans. If the zero-tolerance approach to crime symbolises anything it is that contemporary law-enforcement agencies are still charged with looking down at street crime rather than up at suite crime.

See also: **crime mapping; net–widening; street crime; surveillance**

Further reading: Kelling and Coles (1996); Newburn and Jones (2007)

BIBLIOGRAPHY

Adler, F. (1975) *Sisters in Crime*, New York: McGraw-Hill.

Adler, P. A. (1993) *Wheeling and Dealing: An Ethnography of an Upper-level Drug Dealing and Smuggling Community*, New York: Columbia University Press, 2nd edn.

Agozino, B. (2003) *Counter-Colonial Criminology: A Critique of Imperialist Reason*, London: Pluto Press.

Ahmed, E., Harris, N., Braithwaite, J. and Braithwaite, V. (2001) *Shame Management Through Reintegration*, Cambridge: Cambridge University Press.

Ainsworth, P. (1999) *Psychology and Crime: Myths and Reality*, Harlow, UK: Longman.

Akers, R. L. (2000) *Criminological Theories: Introduction, Evaluation and Application*, 3rd edn, Los Angeles: Roxbury.

Albanese, J. S., Das, D. K. and Verma, A. (2003) *Organized Crime: World Perspectives*, New Jersey: Prentice-Hall.

Amen, D. G., Yantis, S., Trudeau, J., Stubblefield, M. S. and Halverstadt, J. S. (1997) 'Visualising the Firestorms of the Brain: An Inside Look at the Clinical and Physiological Connections between Drugs and Violence Using Brain SPECT Imaging', *Journal of Psychoactive Drugs* 29(4): 307–19.

Amir, M. (1971) *Patterns of Forcible Rape*, Chicago: University of Chicago Press.

Arena, M. P. and Arrigo, B. A. (2006) *The Terrorist Identity: Explaining the Terrorist Threat*, New York: New York University Press.

Arias, E. D. (2006) *Drugs and Democracy in Rio-de-Janeiro: Trafficking, Social Networks, & Public Security*, Chapel Hill: University of North Carolina Press.

Baldwin, J. and Bottoms, A. E. (1976) *The Urban Criminal*, London: Tavistock.

Barak, G. (1998) *Integrating Criminologies*, Boston MA: Allyn and Bacon.

——(2005) 'A Reciprocal Approach to Peace-Making Criminology: Between Adversarialism and Mutualism', *Theoretical Criminology* 9(2): 131–52.

Barnett, A., Blumstein, A. and Farrington, D. P. (1987) 'Probabilistic Models of Youthful Criminal Careers', *Criminology* 25: 83–107.

Barnett, R. (1977) 'Restitution: A New Paradigm for Criminal Justice', *Ethics* 87(4): 279–301.

Bartov, O., Grossmann, A. and Nolan, M. (eds) (2003) *Crimes of War: Guilt and Denial in the Twentieth Century*, New York: The New Press.

Bauman, Z. (2001) *Community: Seeking Safety in an Insecure World*, Cambridge: Polity Press.

Bayley, D. and Shearing, C. (1996) 'The Future of Policing', *Law and Society Review* 30: 585–606.

Beccaria, C. (1995) *On Crimes and Punishments and Other Writings*, R. Bellamy (ed.), Cambridge: Cambridge University Press.

Beck, U. (1992) *Risk Society: Towards a New Modernity*, London: Sage.

Becker, H. (1963) *Outsiders: Studies in the Sociology of Deviance*, New York: Free Press.

Beirne, P. (1987) 'Adolphe Quételet and the Origins of Positivist Criminology', *The American Journal of Sociology* 92(5): 1140–169.

Beirne, P. and South, N. (eds) (2007) *Issues in Green Criminology: Confronting Harms against Environments, Humanity and Other Animals*, Cullompton, UK: Willan.

Benton, T. (1998) 'Rights and Justice on a Shared Planet: More Rights or New Relations?', *Theoretical Criminology* 2(2): 149–76.

Bequai, A. (1999) 'Cybercrime: The US Experience', *Computers and Security* 18(1): 16–18.

Berghman, J. (1995) 'Social Exclusion in Europe: Policy Context and Analytical Framework', in G. Room (ed.) *Beyond the Threshold: The Measurement and Analysis of Social Exclusion*, Bristol, UK: Policy Press.

Bertrand, M.-A. (1969) 'Self Image and Delinquency: A Contribution to the Study of Female Criminality and Woman's Image', *Acta Criminologica*, 2(1): 71–138.

Bianchi, H. and van Swaaningen, R. (1986) *Abolitionism: Towards a Non-Repressive Approach to Crime*, Amsterdam: Free University Press.

Birkbeck, C. and LaFree, G. (1993) 'The Situational Analysis of Crime and Deviance', *Annual Review of Sociology* 19, 113–37.

Block, A. A. and Scarpatti, F. R. (1985) *Poisoning for Profit: The Mafia and Toxic Waste in America*, New York: William Morrow and Company, Inc.

Blumstein, A. and Cohen, J. (1979) 'Estimation of Individual Crime Rates from Arrest Records', *The Journal of Criminal Law and Criminology* 70(4): 561–85.

Blumstein, A., Cohen, J., Roth, A. and Visher, C. A. (eds) (1986) *Criminal Careers and 'Career Criminals'*, 2 vols, Washington DC: National Academy Press.

Bogard, W. (2006) 'Welcome to the Society of Control: The Simulation of Surveillance Revisited', in K. D. Haggerty and R. V. Ericson (eds) *The New Politics of Surveillance and Visibility*, Toronto: University of Toronto Press.

Bonger, W. (1969) *Criminality and Economic Conditions*, Bloomington: Indiana University Press. (Abridged edition with an introduction by Austin Turk.)

Bowling, B. (1993) 'Racial Harassment and the Process of Victimization: Conceptual and Methodological Implications for the Local Crime Survey', *British Journal of Criminology* 33(2): 231–50.

——(1999) *Violent Racism: Victimization, Policing and Social Context*, Oxford: Oxford University Press.

Bowling, B. and Phillips, C. (2002) *Racism, Crime and Justice*, Harlow, UK: Longman.

Box, S. (1983) *Power, Crime and Mystification*, London: Tavistock.

Bradshaw, J. and Holmes, H. (1989) *Living on the Edge*, Tyneside, UK: Child Poverty Action Group.

Braithwaite, J. (1984) *Corporate Crime in the Pharmaceutical Industry*, London: Routledge and Kegan Paul.

——(1985) *To Punish or Persuade: Enforcement of Coal Mine Safety*, Albany NY: State University of New York Press.

——(1989) *Crime, Shame and Reintegration*, Oxford: Oxford University Press.

Brownlee, I. D. (1998) *Community Punishment: A Critical Introduction*, Harlow, UK: Longman.

Bulmer, M. (1984) *The Chicago School of Sociology: Institutionalization, Diversity, and the Rise of Sociological Research*, Chicago: University of Chicago Press.

Burney, E. (2005) *Making People Behave: Anti-social Behaviour, Politics and Policy: The Creation and Enforcement of Anti-social Behaviour Policy*, Cullompton, UK: Willan.

Carlen, P. (2002) 'Critical Criminology? In Praise of an Oxymoron and Its Enemies', in K. Carrington and R. Hogg (eds) *Critical Criminology: Issues, Debates and Challenges*, Cullompton, UK/Oregon, USA: Willan.

Carrington, K. and Hogg, R. (eds) (2002) *Critical Criminology: Issues, Debates and Challenges*, Cullompton, UK/Oregon, USA: Willan.

Carson, R. (1962) *Silent Spring*, New York: Houghton Mifflin.

Castells, M. (2000) *End of Millennium*, Vol. 3 of *The Information Age*, Oxford: Blackwell, 2nd edn.

Cavender, Gary (1999) 'Detecting Masculinity', in J. Ferrell and N. Websdale (eds) *Making Trouble: Cultural Constructions of Crime, Deviance and Control*, Hawthorne NY: Aldine de Gruyter.

Chainey, S. and Ratcliffe, J. (2005) *GIS and Crime Mapping*, London: John Wiley and Sons.

Chambliss, W. (1975) 'Toward a Political Economy of Crime', *Theory and Society* (2): 149–70.

——(1989) 'State Organised Crime', *Criminology* 27(2): 183–208.

——(1995) 'Commentary', *Society for the Study of Social Problems Newsletter* 26(1): 9.

Christie, N. (1993) *Crime Control as Industry: Towards Gulags, Western Style*, London: Routledge.

Clancy, A., Hough, M., Aust, R. and Kershaw, C. (2001) *Crime, Policing and Justice: The Experience of Ethnic Minorities. Findings from the 2000 British Crime Survey*, Home Office Research Study 223, London: Home Office.

Clarke, R. (1988) 'Information Technology and Dataveillance', *Communications of the ACM* 31(5): 498–512.

Clarke, R. V. (1997) *Situational Crime Prevention: Successful Case Studies*, 2nd edn, New York: Criminal Justice Press.

Clarke, R. and Felson, M. (eds) (1993) *Routine Activity and Rational Choice*, London: Transaction Press.

Clarke, Ronald V. G. and Mayhew, Patricia (eds) (1980) *Designing Out Crime*, Home Office Research and Planning Unit, London: HMSO.

Clarke, R. V. and Newman, G. R. (2005) *Designing Out Crime from Products and Systems*, Cullompton, UK: Willan.

Cloward, R. and Ohlin, L. (1961) *Delinquency and Opportunity: A Theory of Delinquent Gangs*, London: Routledge and Kegan Paul.

Cohen, A. (1955) *Delinquent Boys: The Culture of the Gang*, New York: Free Press.

Cohen, L. and Felson, M. (1979) 'Social Change and Crime Rate Trends: A Routine Activity Approach', *American Sociological Review* 44: 588–608.

Cohen, S. (1972) *Folk Devils and Moral Panics*, London: MacGibbon and Kee.

——(1979) 'The Punitive City: Notes on the Dispersal of Social Control', *Contemporary Crises* 3: 339–63.

——(1985) *Visions of Social Control: Crime, Punishment and Classification*, Cambridge: Polity Press.

Cohen, S. and Young, J. (eds) (1973) *The Manufacture of News: Social Problems and the Mass Media*, London: Constable.

Coleman, C. and Moynihan, J. (1996) *Understanding Crime Data*, Buckingham, UK: Open University Press.

Commons Hansard Debates (2004) 18 October 2004, Column 690, London: Stationery Office.

Copjec, J. (1991) 'The Unvermogender Other: Hysteria and Democracy in America', *Formations* 14: 27–41.

Cornish, D. and Clarke, R. V. (eds) (1986) *The Reasoning Criminal: Rational Choice Perspectives on Offending*, New York: Springer-Verlag.

Cottee, S. (2002) 'Folk Devils and Moral Panics: "Left Idealism" Reconsidered', *Theoretical Criminology* 6: 387–410.

Crank, J. P. (2003) 'Crime and Justice in the Context of Resource Scarcity', *Crime, Law and Social Change* 39: 39–67.

Crawford, A. (1998) *Crime Prevention and Community Safety: Politics, Policies and Practices*, Harlow, UK: Longman.

Cressey, D. R. (1969) *Theft of the Nation: The Structure and Operations of Organized Crime in America*, New York: Harper and Row.

Cressey, P. (1932) *The Taxi-Dance Hall: A Sociological Study in Commercialized Recreation and City Life*, Chicago: University of Chicago Press.

Croall, H. (2001) *Understanding White Collar Crime*, Maidenhead, UK: Open University Press.

Crook, S., Pakulski, J. and Waters, M. (1992) *Postmodernization: Change in Advanced Society*, London: Sage.

Crow, G. (2002) 'Community Studies: Fifty Years of Theorization', *Sociological Research Online* 7(3): www.socresonline.org.uk/7/3/crow.html

Crowe, Tim (2000) *Crime Prevention Through Environmental Design*, 2nd edn, Boston MA: Butterworth-Heinemann.

Curran, D. and Renzetti, C. (2001) *Theories of Crime*, 2nd edn, London: Allyn and Bacon.

Curran, K., Dale, M., Edmunds, M., Hough, M., Millie, A. and Wagstaff, M. (2005) *Street Crime in London: Deterrence, Disruption and Displacement*, London: Government Office for London.

Dahl, R. (1973) *Modern Political Analysis*, New York: Prentice-Hall.

Davies, M., Croall, H. and Tyrer, J. (2005) *Criminal Justice: An Introduction to the Criminal Justice System in England and Wales*, 3rd edn, Harlow, UK: Pearson Education.

Dawkins, R. (2006) *The God Delusion*, London: Bantam.

Deitch, D., Koutsenok, I. and Ruiz, A. (2000) 'The Relationship between Crime and Drugs: What We Have Learned in Recent Decades', *Journal of Psychoactive Drugs* 32(4): 391–97.

Delanty, G. (2003) *Community*, London: Routledge and Kegan Paul.

Del Olmo, R. (1998) 'The Ecological Impact of Illicit Drug Cultivation and Crop Eradication Programmes in Latin America', *Theoretical Criminology* 2 (2): 269–78.

Department of Health, Home Office, Department for Education and Skills and Department for Culture, Media and Sport (2007) *Safe. Sensible. Social. The Next Steps in the National Alcohol Strategy*, available at: www.dh.gov.uk/en/Publicationsandstatistics/Publications/PublicationsPolicyAndGuidance/DH_075218. Retrieved 2/9/07.

Dignan, J. (2004) *Understanding Victims and Restorative Justice*, Buckingham, UK: Open University Press.

Dobash, R. E., Dobash, R. P. and Noaks, L. (eds) (1995) *Gender and Crime*, Cardiff, UK: University of Wales Press.

Dorn, N., Levi, M. and King, L. (2005) *Literature Review on Upper Level Drug Trafficking. Home Office On-Line report 22/05*, London: Home Office Research Development and Statistics Directorate.

Downes, D. (1966) *The Delinquent Solution*, London: Routledge and Kegan Paul.

Drugscope (2004) 'How Much Crime Is Drug Related?' Available at: www.drugscope.org.uk/resources/faqs/faqpages/how-much-crime-is-drug-related.htm (retrieved 20/8/07).

Durkheim, E. (1970) *Suicide*, New York: Free Press.

——(1984) *The Division of Labour in Society*, Basingstoke, UK: Macmillan.

Eagleton, T. (1991) *Ideology: An Introduction*, London: Verso.

East, K. E. (1995) 'The Anglo-American Support Apparatus Behind the Afghani Mujahideen', *Executive Intelligence Review* 22(41), 13 October. Available at: www.larouchepub.com/eirtoc/1995/eirtoc_2241.html (retrieved 31/8/07).

Edelhertz, H. (1970) 'The Nature, Impact and Prosecution of White-collar Crime', report no. ICR 70–1, National Institute of Law Enforcement and Criminal Justice, US Department of Justice, Washington DC: US Government Printing Office.

Eglash, E. (1977) 'Beyond Restitution: Creative Restitution', in J. Hudson and B. Galloway (eds) *Restitution in Criminal Justice*, Lexington MA: Lexington Books.

Everett, C. (2003) 'Credit Card Fraud Funds Terrorism', *Computer Fraud and Security* 5(1): 1.

Farrall, S. (ed.) (2000) *The Termination of Criminal Careers*, Aldershot, UK: Ashgate.

Farrington, D. (1992) 'Criminal Career Research in the United Kingdom', *British Journal of Criminology* 32: 521–36.

——(1996) *Understanding and Preventing Youth Crime, Social Policy Research Findings*, no. 93, York, UK: Joseph Rowntree Foundation.

——(2002) 'Developmental Criminology and Risk-Focused Prevention', in M. Maguire, R. Morgan and R. Reiner (eds) *The Oxford Handbook of Criminology*, 3rd edn, Oxford: Oxford University Press.

Farrington, D. P. and Coid, J. W. (eds) (2007) *Early Prevention of Adult Antisocial Behaviour*, Cambridge: Cambridge University Press.

Farrington, D. P. and Loeber, R. (1999) 'Transatlantic Replicability of Risk Factors in the Development of Delinquency', in P. Cohen, C. Slomkowski and L. M. Robins (eds) *Historical and Geographical Influences on Psychopathology*, Mahwah NJ: Lawrence Erlbaum.

Farrington, D. and Painter, K. (2004) *Gender Differences in Risk Factors for Offending*, Home Office Findings 196, London: Home Office.

Fawcett Society (2004) *Report of the Commission on Women and the Criminal Justice System*, London: Fawcett Society.

Feeley, M. and Simon, J. (1992) 'The New Penology: Notes on the Emerging Strategy of Corrections and Its Implications', *Criminology* 30: 449–74.

——(1994) 'Actuarial Justice: The Emerging New Criminal Law', in D. Nelkin (ed.) *The Future of Criminology*, Thousand Oaks CA: Sage.

Felson, M. (1998) *Crime and Everyday Life*, 2nd edn, Thousand Oaks CA: Pine Forge Press.

Felson, R. (1996) 'Big People Hit Little People: Sex Differences in Physical Power and Interpersonal Violence', *Criminology* 34: 433–52.

Fenwick, M. (2004) 'New Directions in Cultural Criminology', *Theoretical Criminology* 8(3): 377–86.

Ferrell, J. (1996) *Crimes of Style: Urban Graffiti and the Politics of Criminality*, Boston MA: Northeastern University Press.

——(1999) 'Cultural Criminology', *Annual Review of Sociology* 25: 395–418.

Ferrell, J. and Hamm, M. S. (eds) (1998) *Ethnography at the Edge: Crime, Deviance and Field Research*, Boston MA: Northeastern University Press.

Ferrell, J., Hayward, K., Morrison, W. and Presdee, M. (eds) (2004) *Cultural Criminology Unleashed*, London: Glasshouse Press.

Ferrell, J., Milanovic, D. and Lyng, S. (2001) 'Edgework, Media Practices and the Elongation of Meaning: A Theoretical Ethnography of the Bridge Day Event', *Theoretical Criminology* 5(2): 177–202.

Ferrell, J. and Sanders, C. R. (eds) (1995) *Cultural Criminology*, Boston MA: Northeastern University Press.

Fine, B., Kinsey, R., Lea, J. and Young, J. (1979) *Capitalism and the Rule of Law: From Deviancy Theory to Marxism*, London: Hutchinson.

Fisse, B. and Braithwaite, J. (1983) *The Impact of Publicity on Corporate Offenders*, Albany NY: State University of New York Press.

Flood-Page, C., Campbell, S., Harrington, V. and Miller, J. (2000) *Youth Crime: Findings From the 1998/1999 Youth Lifestyles Survey*, Home Office Research Study no. 209, London: HMSO.

Foster, J. and Bowling, B. (2002) 'Policing and the Police', in M. Maguire, R. Morgan and R. Reiner (eds) *The Oxford Handbook of Criminology*, 3rd edn, Oxford: Oxford University Press.

Foucault, M. (1977) *Discipline and Punish: The Birth of the Prison*, London/New York: Allen Lane/Vintage.

Francis, B., Barry, J., Bowater, R., Miller, N., Soothill, K. and Ackerley, E. (2004) *Using Homicide Data to Assist Murder Investigations*, Home Office Research Study no. 26/04, London: HMSO.

Francis, B., Soothill, K. and Piquero, A. R. (2007) 'Estimation Issues and Generational Changes in Modeling Criminal Career Length', *Crime and Delinquency* 53: 84–105.

Fraser, N. (1995) 'Politics, Culture and the Public Sphere: Toward a Post-modern Conception', in L. Nicholson and S. Seidman (eds) *Social Post-modernism: Beyond Identity Politics*, Cambridge: Cambridge University Press.

Friedrichs, D. (ed.) (1998) *State Crime*, vols 1 and 2, Aldershot, UK: Gower.

Fuller, J. R. (1998) *Criminal Justice: A Peacemaking Perspective*, Boston MA: Allyn and Bacon.

Gabor, D. and Colombo, U. (with A. King and R. Galli) (1978) *Beyond the Age of Waste: A Report to the Club of Rome*, Oxford: Pergamon Press.

Gallie, D. (1994) 'Are the Unemployed an Underclass? Some Evidence from the Social Change and Economic Life Initiative', *Sociology* 28(3): 755–56.

Garland, D. (1990) *Punishment and Modern Society*, Oxford: Oxford University Press.

——(2002a) 'Of Crimes and Criminals: The Development of Criminology in Britain', in M. Maguire, R. Morgan and R. Reiner (eds) *The Oxford Handbook of Criminology*, 3rd edn, Oxford: Oxford University Press.

——(2002b) *The Culture of Control: Crime and Social Order in Contemporary Society*, Oxford: Oxford University Press.

——(2003) 'The Rise of Risk', in R. Ericson and A. Doyle (eds) *Risk and Morality*, London: University of Toronto Press.

Gibbons, D. C. (1994) *Talking About Crime and Criminals: Problems and Issues in Theory Development in Criminology*, Englewood Cliffs NJ: Prentice-Hall.

Giddens, A. (1973) *The Class Structure of Advanced Societies*, New York: Harper and Row.

——(1976) *New Rules of Sociological Method: A Positive Critique of Interpretive Sociologies*, London: Hutchinson.

——(1984) *The Constitution of Society: Outline of the Theory of Structuration*, Cambridge: Polity.

Giddens, A. and Held, D. (eds) (1982) *Classes, Power and Conflict: Classical and Contemporary Debates*, Berkeley CA: University of California Press.

Glueck, S. and Glueck, E. T. (1930) *500 Criminal Careers*, New York: Alfred A. Knopf.

Goffman, E. (1961) *Asylums: Essays on the Social Situation of Mental Patients and Other Inmates*, Harmondsworth, UK: Penguin, 1968. First published New York: Doubleday Anchor, 1961.

Goldstein, P. (1985) 'The Drugs-Violence Nexus: A Tripartite Framework', *Journal of Drug Issues* (fall): 493–506.

Goode, E. and Ben-Yehuda, N. (1994) *Moral Panics: The Social Construction of Deviance*, Oxford: Blackwell.

Gouldner, A. (1976) *The Dialectic of Ideology and Technology: The Origin, Grammar and Future of Ideology*, London: Macmillan.

Graham, G. (1991) 'Criminalisation and Control', in D. Whynes and P. Bean (eds) *Policing and Prescribing: The British System of Drug Control*, London: Macmillan.

Green, P. and Ward, T. (2004) *State Crime: Governments, Violence and Corruption*, London: Pluto Press.

Grover, C. (2008) *Crime and Inequality*, Cullompton, UK: Willan.

Haggerty, K. D. and Ericson, R. V. (2000) 'The Surveillant Assemblage', *British Journal of Sociology* 51: 605–22.

——(2006) 'The New Politics of Surveillance and Visibility', in K. D. Haggerty and R. V. Ericson (eds) *The New Politics of Surveillance and Visibility*, Toronto: University of Toronto Press.

Hall, S. (1988) *The Hard Road to Renewal: Thatcherism and the Crisis of the Left*, London: Verso.

Hall, S., Crichter, C., Jefferson, T., Clarke, J. and Roberts, B. (1978) *Policing the Crisis*, London: Macmillan.

Hall, S. and DuGay, P. (1996) *Questions of Cultural Identity*, London: Sage.

Hall, S. and Jefferson, T. (eds) (1993) *Resistance Through Rituals: Youth Subcultures in Post-war Britain*, London: Routledge.

Hall, S. and Scraton, P. (1981) 'Law, Class and Control', in M. Fitzgerald, G. McLennan and J. Pawson (eds) *Crime and Society: Readings in History and Theory*, London: Routledge and Kegan Paul.

Hallsworth, S. (2002) 'The Case for a Postmodern Penality', *Theoretical Criminology* 6: 145–63.

——(2005) *Street Crime*, Cullompton, UK: Willan.

Halsey, M. (2004) 'Against "Green" Criminology', *British Journal of Criminology* 44: 833–53.

Hanmer, J. (1990) 'Men, Power and the Exploitation of Women', *Women's Studies International Forum* 13(5): 443–56.

Hawkins, J. D. and Catalano, R. E. (1992) *Communities that Care*, San Francisco CA: Jossey Bass.

Hawkins, K. (1990) 'Compliance Strategy, Prosecution Policy, and Aunt Sally: A Comment on Pearce and Tombs', *British Journal of Criminology* 30 (4): 444–66.

Hayman, G. and Brack, D. (2002) 'International Environmental Crime: The Nature and Control of Environmental Black Markets', workshop report, November, London: Chatham House.

Hayward, K. J. (2004) *City Limits: Crime, Consumer Culture and the Urban Experience*, London: Cavendish.

——(2007) 'Situational Crime Prevention and Its Discontents: Rational Choice Theory Versus the "Culture of Now"', *Social Policy and Administration*, 41(3): 232–50.

Hayward, K. and Yar, M. (2006) 'The "Chav" Phenomenon: Consumption, Media and the Construction of a New Underclass', *Crime Media Culture* 2 (1): 9–28.

Hayward, K. J. and Young, J. (2004) 'Cultural Criminology: Some Notes on the Script', *Theoretical Criminology* 8(3): 259–73.

Hebdige, R. (1979) *Subculture: The Meaning of Style*, London: Routledge.

Heidensohn, F. (2002) 'Gender and Crime', in M. Maguire, R. Morgan and R. Reiner (eds) *The Oxford Handbook of Criminology*, 3rd edn, Oxford: Oxford University Press.

Henry, S., Barak, G. and Milanovic, D. (1997) 'Three By Three', *Critical Criminologist Newsletter* vols 2–3, special issue: 'Past, Present and Future'. Available at www.soci.niu.edu/~critcrim/CC/drag.html (retrieved 5 August 2007).

Henry, S. and Milanovic, D. (1996) *Constitutive Criminology: Beyond Post-modernism*, London: Sage.

Herrnstein, R. and Murray, C. (1994) *The Bell Curve*, New York: Free Press.

Hillyard, P., Pantazis, C, Tombs, S. and Gordon, D. (2004) *Beyond Criminology: Taking Harm Seriously*, London: Pluto Press.

Hinde, S. (2003) 'The Law, Cybercrime, Risk Assessment and Cyber Protection', *Computers and Security* 22(2): 90–95.

Hindelang, M., Gottfredson, M. and Garofalo, J. (1978) *Victims of Personal Crime*, Cambridge MA: Ballinger.

Hirschi, T. (1969) *The Causes of Delinquency*, Berkeley: University of California Press.

Hirst, P. Q. (1975) 'Marx and Engels on Law, Crime and Morality', in I. Taylor, P. Walton and J. Young (eds) *Critical Criminology*, London: Routledge and Kegan Paul.

Hobbs, D. (1995) *Bad Business: Professional Crime in Britain*, Oxford: Oxford University Press.

Hoeksema, T. and Ter Laak, J. (eds) (2003) *Human Rights and Terrorism*, Holland: NHC/OSCE.

Home Office (2002) *Statistics on Women and the Criminal Justice System: A Home Office Publication under Section 95 of the Criminal Justice Act 1991*, London: HMSO.

——(2003) 'Crime Reduction: Street Crime', available at: www.crimereduction.gov.uk/streetcrime/streetcrime10.htm (retrieved 23/08/07).

——(2004) *One Step Ahead: A 21st Century Strategy to Defeat Organised Crime*, Cm6167, London: HMSO.

——(2006) 'Crime and Victims: Robbery and Street Crime', available at: www.homeoffice.gov.uk/crime-victims/reducing-crime/robbery/ (retrieved 20/08/07).

——(2007a) 'Reducing Crime: Hate Crime', available at: www.homeoffice. gov.uk/crime-victims/reducing-crime/hate-crime (retrieved 18/08/07).

——(2007b) 'How We're Reducing Crime: Drug-related Crime', available at: www.homeoffice.gov.uk/crime-victims/reducing-crime/drug-related-crime (retrieved 20/08/07).

Hood, R. (ed.) (1974) *Crime, Criminology and Public Policy: Essays in Honour of Sir Leon Radzinowicz*, London: Heinemann.

House of Commons (Select Committee on Science and Technology) (2006) Fifth Report: *Drug Classification: Making a Hash of It?*, available at: www.publications.parliament.uk/pa/cm200506/cmselect/cmsctech/1031/103102.htm (retrieved 02/09/07).

Hudson, B. (2003a) *Justice in the Risk Society*, London: Sage.

——(2003b) *Understanding Justice: An Introduction to Ideas, Perspectives and Controversies in Modern Penal Theory*, Buckingham, UK: Open University Press.

Huff, C. R. (ed.) (1990) *Gangs in America*, Newbury Park CA: Sage.

Hughes, E. (1937) 'Institutional Office and the Person', *American Journal of Sociology* 43: 404–13.

Hughes, G. and Edwards, A. (eds) (2002) *Crime Control and Community: The New Politics of Public Safety*, Cullompton, UK: Willan.

Hughes, J. and Sharrock, W. (1990) *The Philosophy of Social Research*, 3rd edn, Harlow, UK: Longman.

Hyde, H. (1964) *A History of Pornography*, New York: Farrar, Straus and Giroux.

Inciardi, J. A. (1999) 'Legalizing Drugs: Would It Really Reduce Violent Crime?' In J. A. Inciardi (ed.) *The Drug Legalization Debate, Second Edition*, Thousand Oaks CA: Sage.

Inciardi, J. A. and McBride, D. (1989) 'Legalisation: A High Risk Alternative in the War on Drugs', *American Behavioural Scientist* 32(3): 259–89.

Indermauer, D. (1995) *Violent Property Crime*, Annandale, NSW: Federation Press.

Jacobs, J. (1961) *The Death and Life of Great American Cities*, New York: Vintage.

Jacobs, P., Brunton, M., Melville, M., Brittain, R. and McClermont, W. (1965) 'Aggressive Behaviour, Mental Subnormality and the XYY Male', *Nature* 208: 1351–352.

Jenkins, P. (2001) *Beyond Tolerance: Child Pornography Online*, New York: New York University Press.

Jewkes, Y. (2004) *Media and Crime*, London: Sage.

Johnstone, G. (2003) *Restorative Justice: Ideas, Values, Debates*, Cullompton, UK: Willan.

Jones Finer, C. and Nellis, M. (eds) (1998) *Crime and Social Exclusion*, London: Blackwell.

Kane, S. C. (2004) 'The Unconventional Methods of Cultural Criminology', *Theoretical Criminology* 8(3): 303–21.

Karmen, A. (1990) *Crime Victims: An Introduction to Victimology*, Pacific Grove CA: Brooks Cole.

Katz, J. (1988) *Seductions of Crime: Moral and Sensual Attractions in Doing Evil*, New York: Basic Books.

Kelling, G. and Coles, C. (1996) *Fixing Broken Windows*, New York: Free Press.

Kelly, L., Lovett, J. and Regan, L. (2005) *A Gap or a Chasm? Attrition in Reported Rape Cases*, Home Office Research Study 293, London: HMSO.

Kemp, V., Pascoe, P. and Balmer, N. (2007) 'The Problems of Everyday Life', King's College, London: Centre for Crime and Justice Studies. Available at: www.crimeandjustice.org.uk/tpoelstructure241007.html (retrieved 28/11/07).

Kersten, J. (1996) 'Culture, Masculinities and Violence Against Women', *British Journal of Criminology* 36(3): 381–95.

King, R. (1987) *The State in Modern Society: New Directions in Political Sociology*, London: Chatham House Publishers.

Kramer, R. C. and Michalowski, R. J. (2005) 'War, Aggression and State Crime: A Criminological Analysis of the Invasion and Occupation of Iraq', *British Journal of Criminology* 45(4): 446–69.

Lanier, M. and Henry, S. (2004) *Essential Criminology*, Boulder CO: Westview Press.

Lavine, R. (1997) 'The Psychopharmacological Treatment of Aggression and Violence in the Substance Using Population', *Journal of Psychoactive Drugs*, 29(4): 321–29.

Lawrence, F. (1999) *Punishing Hate: Bias Crime under American Law*, Cambridge MA: Harvard University Press.

Lea, J. and Young, J. (1984) *What Is To Be Done about Law and Order?* Harmondsworth, UK: Penguin.

Le Blanc, M. and Loeber, R. (1998) 'Developmental Criminology Updated', *Crime and Justice* 23: 115–98.

Lemert, E. M. (1951) *Social Pathology: Systematic Approaches to the Study of Sociopathic Behavior*, New York: McGraw-Hill.

——(1971) *Instead of Court: Diversion on Juvenile Justice*, Washington DC: National Institute of Mental Heath, Centre for Studies of Crime and Delinquency.

——(1981) 'Diversion in Juvenile Justice: What Hath been Wrought', *Journal of Research in Crime and Delinquency* 18(1): 34–46.

Levi, M. and Maguire, M. (2002) 'Violent Crime', in M. Maguire, R. Morgan and R. Reiner (eds) *The Oxford Handbook of Criminology*, 3rd edn, Oxford: Oxford University Press.

Liebrich, J. (1993) *Straight to the Point: Angles on Giving Up Crime*, Otago, NZ: University of Otago Press.

Lister, M., Kelly, K., Dovey, J., Giddings, S. and Grant, I. (2003) *New Media: A Critical Introduction*, London: Routledge.

Lister, R. (1996) 'Introduction: In Search of the "Underclass"', in IEA Health and Welfare Unit, *Charles Murray and the Underclass: The Developing Debate* (Choice in Welfare no. 33), London: The IEA Health and Welfare Unit. First published 1990.

Lloyd, A. (1995) *Doubly Deviant, Doubly Damned*, Harmondsworth, UK: Penguin.

Loader, I. and Sparks, R. (2002) 'Contemporary Landscapes of Crime, Order, and Control: Governance, Risk, and Globalization', in M. Maguire, R. Morgan and R. Reiner (eds) *The Oxford Handbook of Criminology*, 3rd edn, Oxford: Oxford University Press.

Lodge, T. S. (1974) 'The Founding of the Home Office Research Unit', in R. Hood (ed.) *Crime, Criminology and Public Policy: Essays in Honour of Sir Leon Radzinowicz*, London: Heinemann.

Lombroso, C. (2006) *Criminal Man*, N. Rafter (ed.), Durham NC: Duke University Press.

Lombroso, C. and Ferrero, W. (1895) *The Female Offender*, London: T. Fisher Unwin.

Lyman, M. D. and Potter, G. W. (2004) *Organized Crime*, New Jersey: Prentice Hall, 3rd edn.

Lynch, M. (1990) 'The Greening of Criminology', *The Critical Criminologist* 2: 11–12.

Lynch, M. and Stretsky, P. B. (2003) 'The Meaning of Green: Contrasting Criminological Perspectives', *Theoretical Criminology* 7(2): 217–38.

Lyng, S. (1998) 'Dangerous Methods: Risk Taking and the Research Process', in J. Ferrell and M. S. Hamm (eds) *Ethnography at the Edge: Crime, Deviance and Field Research*, Boston MA: Northeastern University Press.

Lyon, D. (2004) *The Electronic Eye: The Rise of Surveillance Society*, Cambridge: Polity. First published 1994.

——(2005) 'Synopticon and Scopophilia: Watching and Being Watched', in K. D. Haggerty and R. V. Ericson (eds) *The New Politics of Surveillance and Visibility*, Toronto: University of Toronto Press.

——(2006) 'The Border Is Everywhere: ID Cards, Surveillance and the Other', in E. Zureik and M. B. Salter (eds) *Global Surveillance and Policing: Borders, Security, Identity*, Cullompton, UK: Willan.

Maguire, M. (2002) 'Crime Statistics: The "Data Explosion" and Its Implications', in M. Maguire, R. Morgan and R. Reiner (eds) *The Oxford Handbook of Criminology*, 3rd edn, Oxford: Oxford University Press.

Martin, S. E., Maxwell, C. D., White, H. R. and Zhang, Y. (2004) 'Trends in Alcohol Use, Cocaine Use and Crime, 1989–1998', *Journal of Drug Issues* 34(2): 333–59.

Marx, K. (1954) *Capital, Volume I*, London: Lawrence and Wishart.

——(1964a) *Theories of Surplus Value, Part 1*, trans. E. Burns, London: Lawrence and Wishart.

——(1964b) *Economic and Philosophic Manuscripts of 1844*, New York: International Publishers.

Mason, G. (2005) 'Hate Crime and the Image of the Stranger', *British Journal of Criminology* 45: 837–59.

Mathiesen, T. (2000) *Prison on Trial*, Winchester, UK: Waterside.

Matza, D. (1964) *Delinquency and Drift*, New York: Wiley.

Mawby, R. and Walklate, S. (1994) *Critical Victimology*, London: Sage.

McClintock, A. (1995) *Imperial Leather: Race, Gender and Sexuality in Colonial Contest*, London: Routledge.

McGhee, D. (2005) *Intolerant Britain? Hate, Citizenship and Difference*, Milton Keynes, UK: Open University Press.

McLaughlin, E. (2005) 'From Reel to Ideal: The Blue Lamp and the Popular Cultural Construction of the English "Bobby"', *Crime, Media, Culture* 1 (1): 11–30.

Mednick, S., Gabrielli Jr, W. and Hutchings, B. (1984) 'Genetic Influences in Criminal Convictions: Evidence from an Adoption Cohort', *Science* 224: 891–94.

Mendelsohn, B. (1956) 'Une nouvelle brouche de la science bio-psycho-sociale: victimologie', *Revue internationale de criminologie et de police technique*: 10–31.

Merton, R. (1938) 'Social Structure and Anomie', *American Sociological Review* 3: 672–82.

Messerschmidt, James W. (1993) *Masculinities and Crime: Critique and Reconceptualization of Theory*, Lanham MD: Rowan and Littlefield.

Metropolitan Police (2007) 'Working Together for a Safer London', available at: www.met.police.uk/crimefigures/textonly_month.htm (retrieved 25/08/07).

Milanovic, D. (1997) *Postmodern Criminology*, New York: Garland.

——(2002) *Critical Criminology at the Edge. Postmodern Perspectives, Integration, and Application*, Westport CT: Praeger.

Miles, R. (1992) *The Rites of Man: Love, Sex and Death in the Making of the Man*, London: Paladin.

Miller, C. (1995) 'Environmental Rights: European Fact or English Fiction?', *Journal of Law and Society* 22(3): 374–93.

Moffitt, T. E., Caspi, A., Rutter, M. and Silva, P. A. (2001) *Sex Differences in Anti-Social Behaviour: Conduct Disorder, Delinquency, and Violence in the Dunedin Longitudinal Study*, Cambridge: Cambridge University Press.

Mooney, J. (2000) *Gender, Violence and the Social Order*, London: Macmillan.

Morris, L. (1994) *Dangerous Classes: The Underclass and Social Citizenship*, London: Routledge.

Morris, T. P. (1957) *The Criminal Area: A Study in Social Ecology*, London: Routledge and Kegan Paul.

Moyers, B. (with the Centre for Investigative Reporting) (1990) *Global Dumping Ground: The Internatioonal Traffic in Hazardous Waste*, Washington DC: Seven Locks Press.

Mueller, G. O. W. (1979) 'Offenses Against the Environment and Their Prevention: An International Appraisal', *Annals of the American Academy of Political Science* 444(1): 56–66.

Muncie, J. (2000) 'Decriminalising Criminology', in George Mair and Roger Tarling (eds) *The British Criminology Conference: Selected Proceedings. Volume 3*. Papers from the British Society of Criminology Conference, Liverpool, July 1999. Available at: http://britsoccrim.org/volume3/010.pdf (retrieved 18/04/07).

——(2004) *Youth and Crime: A Critical Introduction*, 2nd edn, London: Sage.

Murray, C. (1996) 'The Emerging British Underclass', in IEA Health and Welfare Unit, *Charles Murray and the Underclass: The Developing Debate* (Choice in Welfare no. 33), London: IEA Health and Welfare Unit. First published 1990.

Mythen, G. and Walklate, S. (2006) 'Criminology and Terrorism: Which Thesis? Risk Society or Governmentality?', *British Journal of Criminology* 46: 379–98.

Naffine, N. (1997) *Feminism and Criminology*, London: Allen and Unwin.

Narcoterror (2002) Available at: www.narcoterror.org/background.htm (retrieved 30/08/07).

Newburn, T. (2002) 'Young People, Crime and Youth Justice', in M. Maguire, R. Morgan and R. Reiner (eds) *The Oxford Handbook of Criminology*, 3rd edn, Oxford: Oxford University Press.

Newburn, T. and Jones, T. (2007) 'Symbolizing Crime Control: Reflections on Zero Tolerance', *Theoretical Criminology* 11(2): 221–43.

Newman, G. and Clarke, R. (2003) *Superhighway Robbery: Preventing E-commerce Crime*, Cullompton, UK: Willan.

Newman, O. (1972) *Defensible Space*, London: Architectural Press.

Norris, C. and Armstrong, G. (1999) *The Maximum Surveillance Society: The Rise of CCTV*, Oxford: Berg.

Nye, F. (1958) *Family Relationships and Delinquent Behavior*, New York: John Wiley.

O'Brien, M. (2005) 'What is Cultural about Cultural Criminology?', *British Journal of Criminology* 45(5): 599–612.

Paradise, P. R. (1999) *Trademark Counterfeiting, Product Piracy, and the Billion Dollar Threat to the U.S. Economy*, Westport CT: Quantam Books.

Park, R. E., Burgess, E. W. and McKenzie, R. D. (eds) (1967) *The City*, Chicago: University of Chicago Press.

Parker, H., Aldridge, J. and Measham, F. (1998) *Illegal Leisure: The Normalisation of Adolescent Recreational Drug Use*, London: Routledge.

Payne, B. K. (2005) *Crime and Elder Abuse: An Integrated Perspective*, Springfield IL: Charles C. Thomas.

Pearce, S. and Tombs, F. (1998) *Toxic Capitalism: Corporate Crime and the Chemical Industry*, Aldershot, UK: Ashgate.

Pearson, G. (1983) *Hooligan: A History of Respectable Fears*, Basingstoke, UK: Palgrave Macmillan.

Pease, K. (1998) 'What Shall We Count when Measuring Zero Tolerance?', in M. Weatheritt (ed.) *Zero Tolerance Policing: What Does It Mean and Is It Right for Policing in Britain?*, London: The Police Foundation.

Penna, S. and Yar, M. (2003) 'From Modern to Postmodern Penality? A Response to Hallsworth', *Theoretical Criminology* 7: 469–82.

Pepinsky, H. E. (1991) 'Peacemaking in Criminology and Criminal Justice', in H. E. Pepinsky and R. Quinney (eds) *Criminology as Peacemaking*, Bloomington: Indiana University Press.

Pepinsky, H. E. and Quinney, R. (eds) (1991) *Criminology as Peacemaking*, Bloomington: Indiana University Press.

Pernanen, K., Cousineau, M.-M., Brochu, S. and Sun, F. (2002) *Proportions of Crimes Associated with Alcohol and Other Drugs in Canada*, Ottawa: Canadian Centre of Substance Abuse.

Pfohl, E. and Henry, S. (1993) *The Deviance Process*, Somerset NJ: Transaction.

Phoenix, J. and Oerton, S. (2005) *Illicit and Illegal: Sex, Regulation and Social Control*, Cullompton, UK: Willan.

Piquero, A. R. (2004) 'Somewhere Between Persistence and Desistance: The Intermittency of Criminal Careers', in S. Maruna and R. Immarigeon (eds) *After Crime and Punishment: Pathways to Offender Reintegration*, Cullompton, UK: Willan.

Piquero, A. R., Farrington, D. P. and Blumstein, A. (2007) *Key Issues in Criminal Career Research: New Analyses of the Cambridge Study in Delinquent Development*, Cambridge Studies in Criminology, Cambridge: Cambridge University Press

Porter, R. (2000) *Enlightenment*, London: Penguin.

Presdee, M. (2000) *Cultural Criminology and the Carnival of Crime*, London: Routledge.

Probation Circular (2005) *Implementation of National Sex Offender Strategy*, Circular 20/2005, London: Home Office.

Procida, R. and Simpson, R. (2003) *Global Perspectives on Social Issues: Pornography*, Lanham MD: Lexington Books.

Pudney, S. (2002) *The Road to Ruin? Sequences of Initiation into Drug Use and Offending by Young People in Britain*, London: Home Office.

Putwain, D. and Sammons, A. (2002) *Psychology and Crime*, London: Routledge.

Quinney, R. (1977) *Class, State and Crime*, New York: Longman.

——(1991) 'The Way of Peace: On Crime, Suffering, and Service', in H. E. Pepinsky and R. Quinney (eds) *Criminology as Peacemaking*, Bloomington: Indiana University Press.

——(2000) 'Socialist Humanism and the Problem of Crime: Thinking About Erich Fromm in the Development of Critical/Peacemaking Criminology', in K. Anderson and R. Quinney (eds) *Erich Fromm and Critical Criminology: Beyond the Punitive Society*, Urbana and Chicago: University of Illinois Press.

Rafter, N. H. (1997) *Creating Born Criminals*, Urbana and Chicago: University of Illinois Press.

——(2000) *Shots in the Mirror: Crime Films and Society*, Oxford: Oxford University Press.

Rastrick, D., Hodgson, R. and Ritson, B. (eds) (1999) *Tackling Alcohol Together: The Evidence Base for a UK Policy*, London: Free Association Books.

Ray, L. and Smith, D. (2002) 'Hate Crimes, Violence and the Culture of Racism', in P. Iganski (ed.) *The Hate Debate: Should Hate Be Punished as a Crime?* London: Profile Books/Institute for Jewish Policy Research.

Reckless, W. (1961) 'A New Theory of Delinquency and Crime', *Federal Probation* 25: 42–46.

Reiman, J. H. (2003) *The Rich Get Richer and the Poor Get Prison: Ideology, Class, and Criminal Justice*, Boston MA: Allyn and Bacon.

Reiner, R. (2002) 'Media Made Criminality', in M. Maguire, R. Morgan and R. Reiner (eds) *The Oxford Handbook of Criminology*, 3rd edn, Oxford: Oxford University Press.

——(2006) 'Beyond Risk: A Lament for Social Democratic Criminology', in T. Newburn and P. Rock (eds) *The Politics of Crime Control: Essays in Honour of David Downes*, Clarendon Studies in Criminology, Oxford: Oxford University Press.

Reiss, A. (1951) 'Delinquency as the Failure of Personal and Social Controls', *American Sociological Review* 16: 196–207.

Rhodes, R. (1997) *Understanding Governance: Policy Networks, Governance, Reflexivity and Accountability*, Buckingham, UK: Open University Press.

Rock, P. (1986) *A View from the Shadows*, Oxford: Clarendon Press.

Rock, P. and Holdaway, S. (eds) (1997) *Thinking About Criminology*, London: UCL Press.

Rodmell, S. (1981) 'Men, Women and Sexuality: A Feminist Critique of the Sociology of Deviance', *Women's Studies International Quarterly* 4(2): 143–55.

Room, G. (1995) 'Poverty and Social Exclusion: The New European Agenda for Policy and Research', in G. Room (ed.) *Beyond the Threshold: The Measurement and Analysis of Social Exclusion*, Bristol, UK: Policy Press.

——(1995) *Beyond the Threshold: The Measurement and Analysis of Social Exclusion*, Bristol, UK: Policy Press.

Rose, N. (2000) 'Government and Control', *British Journal of Criminology* 40 (2): 321–39.

Roshier, B. (1989) *Controlling Crime: The Classical Perspective in Criminology*, Milton Keynes, UK: Open University Press.

Ruggiero, V. (2006) *Understanding Political Violence: A Criminological Analysis*, Maidenhead, UK: Open University Press.

Runciman, W. R. (1990) 'How Many Classes are there in Contemporary British Society?', *Sociology* 24(3): 377–96.

Rusche, G. and Kircheimer, O. (1939) *Punishment and Social Structure*, New York: Columbia University Press.

Sampson, R. J. and Laub, J. H. (2005) *Developmental Criminology and Its Discontents: Trajectories of Crime from Childhood to Old Age*, London: Sage in association with the American Academy of Political Science.

Savitz, L., Turner, S. and Dickman, T. (1977) 'The Origin of Scientific Criminology: Franz Joseph Gall as the First Criminologist', in R. Meier (ed.) *Theory in Criminology: Contemporary Views*, Beverly Hills CA: Sage.

Schmid, A. P. and Johgman, A. J. (1988) *Political Terrorism: A New Guide to Actors, Authors, Concepts, Data Bases, Theories and Literature*, New York: Transaction Books.

Schwendinger, H. and Schwendinger, J. (1970) 'Defenders of Order or Guardians of Human Rights', *Issues in Criminology* 7: 72–81.

See, Letha A. (Lee) and Khashan, N. (2001) 'Violence in the Suites: The Corporate Paradigm', *Journal of Human Behaviour in the Social Environment* 4 (2/3): 61–83.

Shanahan, M. and Trent, S. (2003) 'Chemical Crustaceans: Pesticides and Prawn Farming', *Pesticides News* no. 59 (March 2003): 4–5; www.pan-uk.org/pestnews/pn59/pn59p4.htm (retrieved 11/05/06).

Shapiro, S. (1990) 'Collaring the Crime, not the Criminal: Reconsidering the Concept of White Collar Crime', *American Sociological Review* 55: 364–65.

Sharp, C., Baker, P., Goulden, C. and Ramsay, M. (2001) *Drug Misuse Declared in 2000: Key Results from the British Crime Survey*, Findings 149, London: Home Office.

Shaw, C. R. (1930) *The Jack Roller: A Delinquent Boy's Own Story*, Chicago: University of Chicago Press.

——(1931) *The Natural History of a Delinquent Career*, Chicago: University of Chicago Press.

Shaw, C. R. and McKay, H. D. (1942) *Juvenile Delinquency in Urban Areas*, Chicago: University of Chicago Press.

Shearing, C. (1989) 'Decriminalising Criminology', *Canadian Journal of Criminology* 31(2): 169–78.

Sherman, L. W. (1995) 'The Hotspots of Crime and the Criminal Careers of Places', in J. E. Eck and D. Weisburd (eds) *Crime and Place*, New York: Criminal Justice Press.

Silke, A. (ed.) (2003) *Terrorists, Victims and Society: Psychological Perspectives on Terrorism and Its Consequences*, Chichester, UK: John Wiley.

Silver, E. (1998) 'Actuarial Risk Assessment: Reflections on an Emerging Social-Scientific Tool', *Critical Criminology* 9(1/2): 123–43.

Simon, J. (1988) 'The Ideological Effects of Actuarial Practices', *Law and Society Review* special issue: 'Law and Ideology', 22(4): 771–800.

——(1997) 'Governing through Crime', in G. Fisher and L. Friedman (eds) *The Crime Conundrum: Essays on Criminal Justice*, Boulder CO: Westview Press.

Simon, R. J. (1975) *Women and Crime*, Toronto: Lexington.

Slapper, G. and Tombs, S. (1999) *Corporate Crime*, London: Longman.

Slocum, S. (1975) 'Woman the Gatherer: Male Bias in Anthropology', in R. Reiter (ed.) *Toward an Anthropology of Women*, New York: Monthly Review Press.

Smart, C. (1977) *Women, Crime and Criminology*, London: Routledge and Kegan Paul.

——(1990) 'Feminist Approaches to Criminology', in L. Gelsthorpe and A. Smart (eds) *Feminist Perspectives in Criminology*, Buckingham, UK: Open University Press.

Snider, L. (2000) 'The Sociology of Corporate Crime: An Obituary', *Theoretical Criminology* 4(2): 169–206.

Social Exclusion Unit (2002) *Reducing Re-offending by Ex-Prisoners*, London: Social Exclusion Unit.

Sollund, R. (ed.) (2008) *Ecological Crime and Speciesism*, Oslo: Nova Science Publishers.

Soothill, K., Ackerley, E. and Francis, B. (2004) 'Profiles of Crime Recruitment – Changing Patterns over Time', *British Journal of Criminology* 44(3): 401–18.

South, N. (1998) 'A Green Field for Criminology? A Proposal and a Perspective', *Theoretical Criminology* 2(2): 211–33.

South, N. and Beirne, P. (2006) *Green Criminology*, Aldershot, UK: Ashgate.

Sparks, R. (1992) *Television and the Drama of Crime*, Buckingham, UK: Open University Press.

Squires, P. and Stephen, D. (2005) *Rougher Justice: Anti-social Behaviour and Young People*, Cullompton, UK: Willan.

Stanko, E. (1990) *Everyday Violence*, London: Pandora.

——(2001) 'Reconceptualising the Policing of Hatred: Confessions and Worrying Dilemmas of a Consultant', *Law and Critique* 12: 309–29.

Stedman Jones, G. (1971) *Outcast London*, Oxford: Oxford University Press.

Stevens, A., Trace, M. and Bewley-Taylor, D. (2005) *Reducing Drug Related Crime: An Overview of the Global Evidence*, The Beckley Foundation Drug Policy Programme, Report no. 5, Oxford: Beckley Foundation.

Strinati, D. (1995) *An Introduction to Theories of Popular Culture*, London: Routledge.

Sumner, C. (1994) *The Sociology of Deviance: An Obituary*, Buckingham, UK: Open University Press.

Sutherland, E.H. (1947) *Principles of Criminology*, Philadelphia PA: Lippincott.

——(1949) *White-Collar Crime*, New York: Holt, Rinehart and Winston.

Sykes, G. and Matza, D. (1957) 'Techniques of Neutralization: A Theory of Delinquency', *American Sociological Review* 22: 664–70.

Szasz, A. (1986) 'Corporations, Organised Crime and the Disposal of Hazardous Waste: An Examination of the Making of a Criminogenic Regulatory Structure', *Criminology* 24(1): 1–27.

——(1994) *EcoPopulism, Toxic Waste and the Movement for Environmental Justice*, Minneapolis: University of Minnesota Press.

Tannenbaum, F. (1938) *Crime and the Community*, Boston MA: Ginn and Company.

Tappan, P. (1947) 'Who Is the Criminal?', *American Sociological Review* 12: 96–102.

Taylor, I. (1971) 'Soccer Consciousness and Soccer Hooliganism', in S. Cohen (ed.) *Images of Deviance*, Harmondsworth, UK: Penguin.

Taylor, I. and Walton, P. (1971) 'Industrial Sabotage: Motives and Meanings', in S. Cohen (ed.) *Images of Deviance*, Harmondsworth, UK: Penguin.

Taylor, I., Walton, P. and Young, J. (1973) *The New Criminology: For a Social Theory of Deviance*, London: Routledge and Kegan Paul.

——(eds) (1975) *Critical Criminology*, London: Routledge and Kegan Paul.

Thomas, D. and Loader, B. (2000) 'Introduction: Cybercrime, Law Enforcement, Security and Surveillance in the Information Age', in D. Thomas and B.

Loader (eds) *Cybercrime, Law Enforcement, Security and Surveillance in the Information Age*, London: Routledge.

Thomas, T. (2006) *Sex Crime: Sex Offending and Society*, 2nd edn, Cullompton, UK: Willan.

Thomas, W. I. (1923) *The Unadjusted Girl: With Cases and Standpoint for Behavior Analysis*, Boston MA: Little, Brown.

Thompson, J. B. (1984) *Studies in the Theory of Ideology*, Cambridge: Polity.

——(1995) *Media and Modernity: A Social Theory of the Media*, Cambridge: Polity.

Thornhill, R. and Palmer, C. T. (2000) *A Natural History of Rape: Biological Bases of Sexual Coercion*, Boston MA: MIT Press.

Thorpe, D. H., Smith, D., Green, C. J. and Paley, J. H. (1980) *Out of Care: The Community Support of Juvenile Offenders*, London: Allen and Unwin.

Thrasher, F. (1927) *The Gang*, Chicago: University of Chicago Press.

Tittle, C. (1995) *Control Balance: Towards a General Theory of Deviance*, Boulder CO: Westview Pess.

Tom, G., Garibaldi, B., Zeng, Y. and Pilcher, J. (1999) 'Consumer Demand for Counterfeit Goods', *Psychology and Marketing* 15(5): 405–21.

Trickett, A., Osborn, D. R. and Ellingworth, D. (1995) 'Property Crime Victimisation: The Roles of Individual and Area Influences', *International Review of Victimology* 3(4): 273–95.

Tzanelli, R., Yar, M. and O'Brien, M. (2005) '"Con Me if You Can": Exploring Crime in the American Cinematic Imagination', *Theoretical Criminology* 9(1): 97–117.

United Nations Office on Drugs and Crime (2002) *Results of a Pilot Survey of Forty Selected Organized Criminal Groups in Sixteen Countries*, Geneva: Global Programme Against Transnational Organized Crime.

Van Kesteren, J. N., Mayhew, P. and Nieuwbeerta, P. (2000) *Criminal Victimisation in Seventeen Industrialised Countries: Key Findings from the 2000 International Crime Victims Survey*, The Hague: Ministry of Justice, WODC.

Vithlani, H. (1998) *The Economic Impact of Counterfeiting*, Paris: OECD.

Von Hentig, H. (1948) *The Criminal and His Victim*, New Haven CT: Yale University Press.

Von Lampe, K. (2001) 'Not A Process of Enlightenment: The Conceptual History of Organized Crime in Germany and the United States of America', *Forum on Crime and Society* 1(2): 99–116, United Nations Centre for International Crime Prevention.

Waddington, P. A. J. (1986) 'Mugging as a Moral Panic: A Question of Proportion', *British Journal of Sociology* 46(4): 245–59.

Walby, S. and Allen, J. (2004) *Domestic Violence, Sexual Assault and Stalking: Findings from the British Crime Survey*, Home Office Research Study 276, London: HMSO.

Walker, N. D. (1974) 'Lost Causes in Criminology', in R. Hood (ed.) *Crime, Criminology and Public Policy: Essays in Honour of Sir Leon Radzinowicz*, London: Heinemann.

Walklate, S. (1995) *Gender and Crime: An Introduction*, Hemel Hempstead, UK: Prentice-Hall/Harvester Wheatsheaf.

Wall, D. (2001) 'Cybercrimes and the Internet', in D. Wall (ed.) *Crime and the Internet*, London: Routledge.

Walters, R. (2006) 'Crime, Bio-Agriculture and the Exploitation of Hunger', *British Journal of Criminology* 46(1): 26–45.

Wandall, R. H. (2006) 'Actuarial Risk Assessment. The Loss of Recognition of the Individual Offender', *Law, Probability and Risk* 5(3/4):175–200.

Whitehead, A. (2005) 'Man to Man Violence: How Masculinity May Work as a Dynamic Risk Factor', *The Howard Journal* 44(4): 411–22.

Whyte, D. (2003) 'Lethal Regulation: State-Corporate Crime and the United Kingdom Government's New Mercenaries', *Journal of Law and Society* 30(4): 575–600.

——(2004) 'Regulation and Corporate Crime', in J. Muncie and D. Wilson (eds) *Student Handbook of Criminology and Criminal Justice*, London: Cavendish.

Wikström, P-O. H. (1991) *Urban Crime, Criminals and Victims: The Swedish Experience in Anglo-American Comparative Perspective*, New York: Springer-Verlag.

Wikström, P-O. H., Clarke, R.V. and McCord, J. (eds) (1995) *Integrating Crime Prevention Strategies: Propensity and Opportunity*, Stockholm: National Council for Crime Prevention.

Wilkins, L. T. (1964) *Social Deviance*, London: Tavistock.

Wilson, J. Q. (1983) *Thinking About Crime*, 2nd edn, New York: Basic Books.

——(1985) *Thinking About Crime*, New York: Random House. First published 1975.

Wilson, J. Q. and Herrnstein, R. (1985) *Crime and Human Nature*, New York: Simon and Schuster.

Wilson, J. Q. and Kelling, G. (1982) 'Broken Windows: The Police and Community Safety', *Atlantic Monthly*, March: 29–38.

Winlow, S. and Hall, S. (2006) *Violent Night: Urban Leisure and Contemporary Culture*, Oxford: Berg.

Worrall, A. (1997) *Punishment in the Community*, London: Addison-Wesley.

Wright, A. (2006) *Organised Crime*, Cullompton, UK: Willan.

Wright, E. O. (2005) *Approaches to Class Analysis*, Cambridge: Cambridge University Press.

Wright, M. (1991) *Justice for Victims and Offenders*, Milton Keynes, UK: Open University Press.

Wykes, M. and Welsh, K. (2007) *Violence, Gender and Justice*, London: Sage.

Yar, M. (2004) 'The Quest for Objectivity in the Social Sciences', in K. Kemf-Leonard (ed.) *Encyclopedia of Social Measurement*, San Diego CA: Academic Press.

——(2005) 'The Global "Epidemic" of Movie "Piracy": Crime-Wave or Social Construction?', *Media, Culture and Society* 27(5): 677–96.

——(2006) *Cybercrime and Society*, London: Sage.

Young, J. (1971) *The Drugtakers: The Social Meaning of Drug Use*, London: Paladin.

——(1975) 'Working Class Criminology', in I. Taylor, P. Walton and J. Young (eds) *Critical Criminology*, London: Routledge and Kegan Paul.

——(1986a) 'Ten Points of Realism', in R. Matthews and J. Young (eds) *Issues in Realist Criminology*, London: Sage.

——(1986b) 'The Failure of Criminology: The Need for a Radical Realism', in R. Matthews and J. Young (eds) *Confronting Crime*, London: Sage.

——(1992) 'Ten Points of Realism', in J. Young and R. Matthews (eds) *Rethinking Criminology*, London: Sage.

——(1999) *The Exclusive Society*, London: Sage.

——(2003) 'Merton with energy, Katz with Structure: The Sociology of Vindictiveness and the Criminology of Transgression', *Theoretical Criminology* 7(3): 389–414.

——(2004) 'Voodoo Criminology and the Numbers Game', in J. Ferrell, K. Hayward, W. Morrison and M. Presdee (eds) *Cultural Criminology Unleashed*, London: Glasshouse Press.

——(2007) *The Vertigo of Late Modernity*, London: Sage.

Zedner, L. (2004) *Criminal Justice*, Oxford: Clarendon Press.

Zehr, H. (1990) *Changing Lenses: A New Focus for Crime and Justice*, Scottsdale PA: Herald Press.

——(1995) 'Justice Paradigm Shift? Values and Visions in the Reform Process', *Mediation Quarterly* 12(3): 207–16.

INDEX